D1171990

Comparative Ethnic Relations

CONSULTING EDITOR

•

Peter I. Rose
SMITH COLLEGE

T
21
323

Comparative
Ethnic
Relations

A Framework for
Theory and Research

•

R. A. SCHERMERHORN

Case Western Reserve University

RANDOM HOUSE • NEW YORK

212754

Copyright © *1970 by Random House, Inc.*
All rights reserved under International and Pan-American Copyright Con-
ventions. Published in the United States by Random House, Inc., New York,
and simultaneously in Canada by Random House of Canada Limited, Toronto.

Library of Congress Catalog Card Number: 69–20299

Grateful acknowledgment is made to the following for permission
to quote from their published works:

H. M. Blalock, Jr., *Toward a Theory of Minority-Group Relations*,
New York, John Wiley & Sons, Inc., 1967, pp. 204–206.

Gino Germani, "Social Change and Intergroup Conflicts," in Irving L.
Horowitz, ed., *The New Sociology*, New York, Oxford University Press,
1964, pp. 394, 399.

Robin M. Williams, Jr., *The Reduction of Intergroup Tensions*, New York,
Social Science Research Council, 1947, pp. 54–61 *passim*.

Hans L. Zetterberg, *On Theory and Verification in Sociology*, rev. ed.,
New York, The Bedminster Press, 1963, pp. 33–34.

Manufactured in the United States of America
by The Haddon Craftsmen, Inc., Scranton, Pa.

Typography by Leon Bolognese

*To the memory of my parents
whose world view and concern were contagious.*

Foreword

The study of racial and ethnic relations has undergone several marked shifts in emphasis since the beginning of the twentieth century. Briefly stated, a concentration on differences gave way to an interest in uniformities; a focus on traits was replaced by an examination of relationships; a sense of detachment, almost of noblesse oblige, was supplanted by involvement.

As a Sumnerian view of intergroup relations was superseded by a Parkian one, subordinates began to attract far more attention than elites. Indeed, there was a decided swing in the sociological pendulum toward "victimology" and the effects of discrimination.

The first signs of these changes occurred during the halcyon days in the Department of Sociology at the University of Chicago, where Robert E. Park and his colleagues offered the first regular courses in the comparative study of "Races and Nationalities" and on "American Minorities." Despite a significant theoretical foundation for the comparative course, including Park's own "race relations cycle," the latter subject proved far more popular. It centered attention on the plight of minorities in this society and on the causes of prejudice. In time, research was undertaken on minority communities and on the attitudes of members of the dominant groups. The findings tended to corroborate the views that "racism" was pervasive and that discrimination was damaging to those marked by oppression.

Concentration on such matters resulted in a tendency toward a cultural myopia about race and ethnic relations. However, despite the fact that preoccupation with endemic problems had decided theoretical (if not practical) limitations, some sociologists began to assemble propositional inventories that summarized the findings of various researchers and offered some scaffolding for subsequent theory building. Robin M. Williams' bulletin, *The Reduction of Intergroup Tensions* (1947), published by the Social Science Research Council, is the best example of that approach. Still, being primarily concerned with American society, it was of limited value for comparative study.

In recent years a few sociologists have begun to venture—literally and figuratively—beyond America's borders to study racial and ethnic relations comparatively. They join a somewhat larger group of Europeans who have been doing so for some time. According to Richard A. Schermerhorn, their work has tended to fall roughly into one of five categories: descriptive, interpretive, classificatory, paradigmatic, or abstractly theoretical.

The writings of such scholars as Guy Hunter, Harry Hoetink, Brewton Berry, Pierre van den Berghe, and H. M. Blalock may be placed in each of these categories, respectively. Schermerhorn's own work, as shall be apparent to all who read this book, tends to touch all bases. It is at once descriptive, interpretive, classificatory, paradigmatic, and theoretical. In fact, it may best be described as a series of interlocked working papers in the field of comparative ethnic relations. As such, this book offers the student an exciting example of the application of sociological theory to issues of great significance as well as a good deal of insight into the relations between peoples.

For many years Professor Schermerhorn, the author of *These Our People* (1949) and *Society and Power* (1961) has been concerned with the strains extant in plural societies and the relative position of members. An early proclivity for a "conflict approach" gave way to a more dialectical view. In a paper entitled "Polarity in the Approach to Comparative Research in Ethnic Relations" published in 1967, Schermerhorn asserted that "the task of intergroup research is to account for modes of integration-conflict (as dependent variables) in the relationships between dominant groups and subordinate ethnic groups in different societies." As for independent variables, he suggests two that are "most promising": (1) the degree of enclosure in the subordinate ethnic group as measured by such indices as endogamy, ecological concentration, institutional duplication, associational clustering, and the like; and (2) the control of scarce values by dominant groups. In addition, the direction of "movement" toward or away from one another by those who hold power and those lacking it is suggested as a critical intervening factor to be taken into account.

What is important in this latest work, *Comparative Ethnic Relations,* is Schermerhorn's emphasis on both systemic and relational matters, i.e., the whole-to-part "functionalist" orientation and the part-to-whole "conflict" orientation, at least when considering *intergroup* relations at a macrosociological level. The shift to a dialectical approach in which there is a constant interplay between the two dominant perspectives is evident throughout the volume. For example, in a chapter on "Some Unexplored Types of Integration," he considers the problems of legitimation, cultural congruence, and goal-definitions from the points of view of both those holding power and attempting to maintain a particular system and subordinates (minorities as well as mass subjects).

Schermerhorn's treatise includes many other matters; "typologies of problem relevance," classification schemes that divide societies in "multi-national sectors" and/or along a continuum according to the dominance of either the polity or the economy (as "Pol-Ec Societies or "Ec-Pol Societies"), discussions of cross-sectional research on plural societies in which he illustrates attempts at *rapprochement* between diachronic and synchronic approaches. The later chapters are richly illustrated with data drawn from a wide variety of empirical reports on ethnic relations in various parts of the world.

Ultimately, Schermerhorn offers his own paradigm for comparative study. The model pulls together many disparate issues. It is offered as a tentative guide for future research and study.

I am certain that *Comparative Ethnic Relations* will be used as the author intended. It is one of those rare books that is at once easy to read and difficult to take in. More treatise than text, Schermerhorn's volume merits careful study and gradual digestion. It is a major contribution to the literature of sociological theory and to the comparative study of ethnic relations.

Northampton, Massachusetts   PETER I. ROSE
April 1969

Preface

It seems like ancient history since the slogan, "One World," captivated the minds of men. Today the tide runs in the opposite direction as separatism makes its conquests. On the international scene NATO is pulling apart, Warsaw Pact countries are defying their Russian leader, and the Common Market is losing its *élan*. Within supposedly sovereign nations, internal fragmenting becomes so common that it has lost any element of surprise. In Southeast Asia, a revolutionary regionalism is already threatening the unity of Burma, Thailand, and India. On the African continent the Congo is hanging together by a thread, while Nigeria fights a civil war in which Biafra is trying desperately to secede. In the Western Hemisphere, Guatemala moves toward a seemingly inevitable explosion that threatens to pit its peasant Indians against the Ladinos, while Guyana's conflict between African Creoles and East Indians alternates between an uneasy peace and open hostilities. In the United States where it has long been taken for granted that Negroes demand integration first, last, and foremost, an increasing number of their leaders are swinging toward a black nationalism that calls for autonomy notably like apartheid, except that it is self-chosen rather than imposed. As a perceptive reporter declared recently, "This crowded world is cracking asunder. Togetherness is out. It is now a dirty twelve letter word. The 'in' thing is to split, separate, get sore and quit." (Todd Simon, "World on a Fission Trip," *Cleveland Plain Dealer*, September 8, 1967). Reflection on this modern divisiveness often leads one to think of Toynbee's "time of troubles" that he identified with the decline of civilizations.

The present volume does not, in any way, explore such metahistorical theories to account for this state of affairs on a world scale, but it is born out of the contemporary *Zeitgeist* nevertheless. It is an effort to explore the internal divisions of societies in determinate ethnic and racial dimensions, and to put under scrutiny the forms of social organization that foster integration or conflict in nations differing widely from each other.

The assumptions underlying this work are that (1) basic research in macrosociology should have priority in the understanding of ethnic and racial pluralities; (2) such research should be
comparative on a world-wide scale; (3) new tools of analysis
need development if such research is to achieve maximal fertility;
(4) these new schemes or frameworks must be geared to the
state of scientific knowledge at its present state of development;
and (5) value-commitments, while to some extent unavoidable,
must be flexible rather than rigid. In other words, regarding the
last assumption, there is no inherent reason why an observer
should regard all ethnic group ventures toward separatism as
deplorable (as Todd Simon seems to do), or allow preferences
for "national unity" to ride roughshod over group self-respect.
These are questions that can only be answered in situational contexts. But at the broad, cross-cultural level prevailing in these
pages, normative decisions must remain tentative.

While each of these five assumptions is the basis for considerable discussion throughout the book, the third is really the center
and crux of the entire exposition. On the whole this is a set of
working papers in which I offer my colleagues a series of conceptual tools for scientific exploration that will, hopefully, facilitate more productive results in the future. In related fashion,
the fourth assumption implies that comparative ethnic relations
as a discipline of world-wide scope is still in a rudimentary stage
of development; it therefore demands a conceptual apparatus
much more loosely organized and at a lower level of generality
than microstudies insist upon. There will undoubtedly be some
uneasiness among the methodological purists at what seems to be
a proliferation of typologies and paradigms presented here, and
some will doubtless make the accusation that the whole venture
reeks of Ptolemaic complexity. There is some truth in this charge,
but not enough to do permanent damage. Since sociology admittedly has failed to find its Copernicus or its Newton, it might
be argued that a Ptolemaic order could still be an advance on
what we have cross-culturally. On this basis one could still await
the consummation of unified knowledge, although this kind of
unified theory has not really appeared in post-Einsteinian physical
science, and it may well be fallacious to look for it in sociology
where the chance of attaining it in the foreseeable future is far less.

But the book must speak for itself. If it proves to be a catalytic agent for comparative research, I shall be amply satisfied.

There remains the pleasant duty of offering thanks and appreciation to those who have contributed much to whatever cogency and plausibility the present volume may have. At the outset I owe a special debt to Leo Despres for convincing me that the first draft of my work was faulty and inconclusive so that I was forced to make a fresh start. His sensible though devastating criticism of the early formulations made it necessary to rethink my position and reexamine the argument as a whole. In addition I would like to thank Raymond Mack for reading the manuscript and encouraging me to pursue publication.

To Marisa Zavalloni, Associate Director of the Centre International d'Etudes des Relations entre Groupes Ethniques, go many thanks for reading the manuscript and for sending valuable comments and criticisms on each chapter. I also extend sincere appreciation to Robin Williams, Jr., for his closely detailed critique of the text and suggestions for improvement of both content and style at many points. Then for an especially painstaking, searching analysis of the second draft, and for judicious counsel on nearly every major component in the entire book, extraordinary thanks are due to Pierre van den Berghe. Not only were his comments on theory and method of great value, but by his numerous corrections, he disposed of a number of substantive errors as well. My debt to him is greater than I can express.

I hasten to add that the readers just mentioned must be absolved of any final responsibility for what appears here, for I have not always followed their cautionary advice.

The same remark applies to the editor of this series, Peter Rose, whose constant revisions and redactions have smoothed over many a rough spot in the text, and modified quite a number of shaky interpretations. He is the type of editor it is a joy to work with —patient, prompt, probing, and a perfectionist in the best sense.

To Mrs. Leonore Hauck, Miss Leona Huberman, and the other members of the editorial staff at Random House, I give a salute for their meticulous care that has transformed the manuscript into a finished product. Also to Marcia Hanna for bibliographical and other aides, as well as to Dianne Ferris, Alice Schubach, and Car-

olyn Durway go many thanks for proficient and cheerful typing
service, often under extreme pressure.

Finally, to my wife, Helen, a salaam for her patient endurance of
the self-imposed isolation perpetrated by her bemused husband
during the writing of this book.

Cleveland, Ohio   R. A. SCHERMERHORN
July 1968

Contents

Figures

Tables

Comparative Ethnic Relations

Introduction:
Directions
in Ethnic Research

.

There is little doubt that the social ferment of the mid-twentieth century has stimulated renewed interest in race and ethnic relations on a global scale. The end of World War II ushered in a new epoch of world history—one whose full significance looms larger with every passing year. Probably more than any other single factor, decolonization has provided the basic source for decisive change as more than fifty new sovereign states have emerged from colonial status to gain complete independence since 1945. This massive legion of new nations has forced political and economic leaders of the West to rethink their programs and commitments. What of academia?

A Sociology of Intergroup Relations

Decolonization and the emergence of new nations have also given new impetus to the professional interests of economists, political scientists, anthropologists, and sociologists. America was unprepared for the sudden assumption of world leadership thrust upon her in the aftermath of World War II and, similarly, American social scientists were unequipped to fulfill torrential demands of the postwar era to furnish comparative research needed by new nations in their haste to "modernize." Or equally plausible might be an alternative explanation that the social scientists at that time had very little to offer in the way of cross-cultural research, so the demands *appeared* to be distressingly torrential. In either case the result was the same—an awakened interest in comparative research. In the future, no doubt, someone concerned with the sociology of knowledge will trace the growth of cross-cultural studies to the postcolonial stimulus rather than to the pressure of theoretical interests per se.

Whatever the explanation, this new wave of interest affected economics first (in research on "development"), spread to demographic studies, to political science (aided by anthropology with a renewed interest in government), to social psychology (studying national character and national images), and eventually reached sociology with an initial impact on the study of comparative family systems. The ruling *Zeitgeist* seemed to favor questioning of formerly accepted truths, and this was a good climate in which to begin a whole series of new assessments in social science. Likewise, once the leaven of curiosity about multiple cultures began to work, it permeated inquiry at every point, awakening investigators to the realization that in pursuing what appeared new to them, they were returning to the main task of social science: the discovery of generalizations that transcend the boundaries of single societies.

Specialists in ethnic and race relations were, of course, affected by these wider concerns, but for a good many years this had not led to a new assessment. Perhaps the chief reason for this is that these sociologists had already made extensive use of data from foreign countries, beginning with the writings of Robert E. Park in the 1920s and extending to those of Lind, Berry, Shibutani, and Kwan in the 1950s and 1960s. Most investigators were satisfied to draw on the work of these men supplemented by a few authorities in anthropology—all used primarily for pedagogical and illustrative purposes. However, after World War II, as fresh reports from abroad continued to pour in from economists, demographers, and political scientists, it became quite evident to the sociological fraternity in general, and to race and ethnic group specialists in particular, that they could no longer draw on the limited capital of past studies but would have to organize new forays of empirical research abroad in order to advance the cause of social science in the future. The number of American students in race and ethnic relations doing field work abroad by the 1960s, however, could almost be counted on the fingers of two hands. The upshot has been that most of our specialists in intergroup relations have lacked first hand contacts with population groups in the developing nations and because of this, have missed the stark contrasts that exist between ethnic enclaves in the new states and those in more industrialized societies.

These contrasts tend to focus on political realities just because the most visible changes in developing nations seem to appear in the governmental sphere. As one political scientist has reviewed the situation in a succinct but penetrating analysis:

> Of the eighty-four countries considered in this study, forty have been victims of successful coups or serious attempts to over-throw the established governments. Fourteen former colonies achieved independence in the period 1945–55; in eleven of these, the governments have been either attacked or overthrown by extralegal forces. In Afro-Asia alone, twenty-three states have experienced extraconstitutional governments. (Von der Mehden, 1964, 1)

The role of ethnic groups, either as activators or passive recipients of such outbreaks is being neglected in research and—what is more important from the standpoint of social science as a whole —is not conceived in a common framework with other ethnic relations so that some general propositions can result from a multi-national comparison.

As in so many other scientific endeavors, early workers in the field of ethnic and race relations set in motion what eventually became familiar intellectual habits; as these have crystallized into patterns they are repeated and worn smooth by a generation of users who perpetuate rather than question them. In the postwar world, many of these familiar but rigid patterns appear anachronistic under close scrutiny, but full awareness of this fact has been delayed by scarcity of field research and general ignorance of related cross-cultural studies made by social scientists in other disciplines. I should like to single out three of these thought patterns that appear in the writings of American specialists in ethnic relations—scientists who have restricted their work within limits that seem to inhibit the search for more comprehensive principles. The "thought patterns" are: (1) preoccupation with problems of prejudice and discrimination; (2) the depiction of minorities or ethnic groups solely in the role of victims; and (3) interpreting progress in ethnic research as primarily a problem of "updating." How do these well-worn ideas obstruct a wider view?

Prejudice and Discrimination as Major Concerns

If we begin with the matter of prejudice, any approach to the field from this viewpoint has a subtle tendency to psychologize group relations by seeing them as personality processes writ large. This trend seems to have started in 1932 when the first important textbook in the field, Donald Young's *American Minority Peoples* (Harper & Row, 1932), began its pages with a disquisition on racial prejudices. This set the pattern for a number of texts to follow, right up into the 1960s when both Simpson and Yinger (1965) and Vander Zanden (1966) continued to follow suit.

It is not only that the theme of prejudice served to introduce readers to the field, but that it too often monopolized attention to the neglect of societal and structural conditions. To illustrate: in Westie's review of the entire area of "Race and Ethnic Relations" in 1964, he focused most of his discussion on the topic of prejudice and devoted half or more of his bibliography to its study. An exposition of this character tends to start at the individual level and to project the attitudes of single persons into large-scale social effects. Even though some of the textbook writers eventually get around to more comprehensive views, their readers are subject to the impression that prejudice, which receives so much initial attention, is somehow a prime mover in ethnic or minority problems. This is to put the cart before the horse. If research has confirmed anything in this area, it is that prejudice is a product of *situations*, historical situations, economic situations, political situations; it is not a little demon that emerges in people simply because they are depraved. This is not to deny that the subject of prejudice has a genuine importance, but only that it is not central to the explanation of ethnic and race relations. We gain the clearest view of prejudice when we see it as a dependent or intervening variable. Leading authorities now stress this point in many different ways unnecessary to repeat here (Raab and Lipset, 1959; Allport, 1954, Chap. 13).

A somewhat different judgment must be made about the far-reaching use of "discrimination" as a term correlative with "prejudice" for the study of intergroup relations. There is no question that an increasing emphasis on "discrimination" as the key factor in ethnic and race relations has brought a salutory shift from attitudes to behavior, and from subjective to objective elements. This focus on overt action not only leads the researcher to seek for more observable and hence more verifiable data, but it furnishes a more identifiable target for action programs in the reduction of intergroup conflict. These are clear gains. Yet they are matched by other serious disadvantages as well. For "discrimination," as employed by writers in intergroup relations, is an invidious, moralistic term; it fastens a value judgment on the persons engaging in the designated acts. It implies that the people performing such acts are violating a widespread social norm and that, really, they shouldn't (Cf. Simpson and Yinger, 1965, 13–14). One can only applaud such humanitarian sentiments while remaining puzzled over their explanatory value. Are not such morally reprehensible acts something to be explained, just as the social scientist tries to explain the acts of the criminal? In the long run, "discrimination," no less than its subjective counterpart "prejudice," is a dependent variable.

How unrevealing "discrimination" may be in comparative research (even as a dependent variable) is shown by Arnold Rose's tentative probe in this direction. He supervised a pilot study of intergroup conflict in different historical societies researched by his students with the major aim to determine the relative "harshness" of discrimination applied to minorities as correlated with types of social structure (feudal societies, slave societies, societies where religion is closely integrated with government, societies where the dominant group feels strong nationalism, societies where the subordinate group is perceived as an economic or political threat, societies with greater or lesser respect for legal authority, societies with well-defined class systems). The correlation of such social structures, however arbitrary they may seem, with a measure of "harshness" produces indifferent or nonsignificant results as shown by his tables. Rose acknowledged the limitations of this admittedly preliminary study, and it may be that more satisfactory results could have been obtained with a different selection of social structures. Yet the reader is left unsatisfied with both the ambiguous character of "harshness" of discrimination (according to twentieth-century standards, or those of some other century in the country being examined?) and with its vagueness arising from its judgmental character (Rose, 1960).

Victimology

Another shortcoming of previous studies is that a great many American sociologists, immured in their own society, have developed a sort of pathos of minorities as "victims" conceptualizing the relations between subordinate and dominant groups in such a way that the former are invariably oppressed and exploited. By disregarding the experience of numerous other societies, they have totally ignored cases in which ethnic groups have posed a threat to the very existence of states. For example, Wallerstein, commenting on the new nations of Africa, declares, "every African nation, large or small, federal or unitary, has its Katanga. Once the logic of secession is admitted, there is no end except in anarchy. And so every African government knows that its first problem is how to hold the country together when it is threatened by wide disintegration" (Wallerstein, 1961, 88). Had he been writing in 1967 or 1968 he could easily have substituted Biafra for Katanga.

Looking back from our present perspective, it is easy to see today that American students of ethnic relations were alerted over twenty years ago to the wider range of issues by Louis Wirth in his typology of assimilationist, pluralist, secessionist, and militant minorities (Wirth, 1945, 354–63). However, American sociologists, constricted by their own national boundaries, busied themselves with the analysis of the first two types only, since they were the ones most clearly exemplified in the United States, and referred to the others only in passing—partly in deference, it seemed, to Wirth's own prestigious authority. Only today, in the international climate of the postcolonial world, is it becoming painfully clear that such cavalier omissions are no longer defensible.

Updating—Its Insufficiency

A third deficiency in the prevalent treatment of intergroup relations in recent years has been to depend more on updating the results of scientific studies in the field than on rethinking them. The grounds for this assertion are admittedly less persuasive than what has been offered for the two preceding judgments so someone is bound to cry "foul!" Yet any consideration of the literature for the last twenty years will reveal not only the preoccupation with prejudice, discrimination, and victimization in textbooks that are frequently revised, but the same trends appear in the research topics. Between 1947 and 1964 there have been three major reviews of intergroup research. In the first of these, compiled and organized by Robin Williams (1947), 73 per cent of the research titles concerned issues like prejudice, attitude scales, or social distance measurements—in a word, psychological issues. The next compilation by the same author (1957) shows a rapid decrease in psychological themes to 36 per cent of the total; it is impossible to judge from titles alone how many were devoted to discrimination. However, only seven years later, another summary by Frank Westie (1964) shows that psychological studies regain a good deal of ground, rising to approximately 50 per cent of the titles listed.

If we examine the same three summaries for evidences of local (U.S.) as opposed to foreign studies, the evidence is far more compelling—and more consistent. The results are:

Compilation: Year Published	*Per cent of Researches Listed Done in the U.S. Alone*
1947	99
1957	84
1964	89

This is an index of provincialism, in a way, but it also gives evidence that updating has not led to rethinking, particularly in the matter of cross-cultural analysis.

The whole purpose of the present volume is to open up ways of rethinking intergroup relations in a world perspective. It is not in any sense a substantive contribution and hence can be easily misunderstood. To put it in the simplest terms, this is a *prospective* rather than a *retrospective* presentation. It presents the *prospects* for ethnic research on a global scale and tries to show how this demands reorganization of both conceptual and methodological frameworks. In all I have written here I have tried to keep attention directed to the *maximal areas of payoff for future research*. All previous writings in the field, so far as I am aware, have been retrospective, i.e., they have reviewed the findings of *previous* research. My aim is quite different; since it is *prospective*, I am chiefly interested in systematic assessement of the most promising leads for investigators in the years to come, in the conviction that their explorations will necessarily be increasingly comparative.

This does not mean that previous works will be wholly neglected. In actual fact the selected few that have dealt with cross-cultural studies have followed one or more of the following paths:

1. Gathering new data with minimal attention to theory
2. Gathering new data and interpreting them theoretically
3. Ordering vast quantities of already collected data by taxonomic means
4. Organizing vast quantities of already collected data by means of a single, unified theory or a specially constructed theory
5. Organizing a limited series of comparative case studies dealing with particular societies and utilizing the same theoretical framework for each

The first alternative is the characteristic mode of the Institute of Race Relations in London; the second approach appears in Robert E. Park's posthumous work *Race and Culture* (1949) and the volume by Everett C. Hughes and Helen MacGill Hughes, *Where Peoples Meet* (1952); in the third case a number of textbook writers furnish the most prominent examples, i.e., Paul A. F. Walter, Jr., *Race and Culture Relations* (1952), Alain Locke and Bernhard J. Stern (eds.), *When Peoples Meet* (1942), and Brewton Berry, *Race and Ethnic Relations* (1958); the fourth, trend is exemplified by Tamotsu Shibutani and K. M. Kwan's *Ethnic Stratification* (1965) or Hubert M. Blalock's *Toward a Theory of Minority-Group Relations* (1967); finally there are two examples of the fifth alternative, one being Charles Wagley and Marvin Harris' *Minorities in the New World* (1958) and the other Pierre L. van den Berghe's *Race and Racism* (1967).[1]

The cross-cultural trend in ethnic studies parallels and, to a considerable degree, reflects the wider concerns of sociology as a whole. As Edward Shils has pointed out, the ways of comparing societies and their organization has not only changed in the last generation or two, but is actually still in midpassage. He comments:

> . . . we are in the middle phase of the development of the comparative method . . . from the enumeration and correlation of isolated items, in the style of Hobhouse, Wheeler and Ginsberg, or of the Human Relations Area Files, to the universal propositions, which are formed from the orderly scrutiny of the full range of societies, historical and contemporary, and utilized in the analysis and explanation of particular instances. Comparative analysis in its present state functions primarily as a standpoint for the case study of particular societies. (Shils, 1963, 19)

If I understand him correctly, Shils is saying that case studies, though they advance our knowledge further than "enumeration and correlation of isolated items," are still not sufficient for comparative analysis. For the latter we must press on to macrosociological viewpoints and generalizations. In the same vein, I submit that the cross-cultural study of ethnic relations is in transition from the five previous patterns discussed above to what Marsh calls "a systematic specification of which theories and propositions hold for all societies, which for only certain types of societies, and which for only individual societies" (Marsh, 1967, vii). To fulfill this purpose I am offering the framework of analysis outlined in the present volume, labeling it, for want of a better name, "inductive typology." The significance of this seemingly innocuous title will appear in due course, with the fullest exposition reserved for later chapters. None of the elements of inductive typology are in any sense new, though I trust that their arrangement and patterning actually are. However, by introducing them, I am in no way suggesting the abandonment of all, or indeed any, of the five procedures just outlined above; each of them can still be pursued with profit. The purpose of introducing inductive typology is not to replace or supersede the earlier approaches but to show how they may be redirected for greater productiveness, and how a repatterning of future research efforts will increase scientific fertility. In sum, we want this book to be a catalyst.

A Preview

In the rest of this brief introduction I should like to present a panoramic view of what is to follow, in the conviction that a capsulated version of the larger whole, if presented at the outset, will give the reader a sense of authentic interconnections in advance of the details. The latter can then fall into place naturally as patterned elements rather than as isolated components. First of all let me explain how a few key terms will be used throughout this analysis.

Each society in the modern world contains subsections or subsystems more or less distinct from the rest of the population. The most fitting generic term to designate this fraction of the whole is "ethnic group." An ethnic group is defined here as a collectivity within a larger society having real or putative common ancestry, memories of a shared historical past, and a cultural focus on one or more symbolic elements defined as the epitome of their peoplehood. Examples of such symbolic elements are: kinship patterns, physical contiguity (as in localism or sectionalism), religious affiliation, language or dialect forms, tribal affiliation, nationality, phenotypical features, or any combination of these. A necessary accompaniment is some consciousness of kind among members of the group. This would place it in Bierstedt's category of "societal group" (Bierstedt, 1963, 295ff).

A second term requiring definition is the expression, "dominant group." As used throughout this discussion, dominant group signifies that collectivity within a society which has preeminent authority to function both as guardians and sustainers of the controlling value system, and as prime allocators of rewards in the society. It may be a group of greater or lesser extensity, i.e., a restricted elite, incumbents of a governmental apparatus, an ethnic group, a temporary or permanent coalition of interest groups, or a majority.

In the third place, it is imperative to circumscribe the meaning of the term "minority group." In order to do this, however, we must look at the two dimensions of size and power as characteristics of groups in a larger society. This gives us the following paradigm:

FIGURE 1.

Dominant Groups

	Size	Power	
Group A	+	+	Majority Group
Group B	−	+	Elite

Subordinate Groups

Group C	+	−	Mass subjects
Group D	−	−	Minority Group

AD and BC = typical intergroup configurations[2]

It is quite possible, of course, to employ the term "minority" for group B, though it would then be necessary to add the adjective "dominant." In order to avoid confusion, the constant use of qualifiers, and continual departure from common usage, I prefer to restrict the term "minority" to groups of the D type rather than the B type, and the term "majority" to the A type rather than the C type. The designation "mass subjects" is a bit awkward, but clear in terms of the table.

As for ethnic groups, they may be either dominant or subordinate; in strict terms they run the whole gamut from A to D in the figure. However, since each society can, by our definition, have only one dominant group but a plurality of subordinate groups, it follows that an overwhelming preponderance of ethnic groups are in subordinate rather than dominant positions; it therefore seems justifiable to drop the adjective "subordinate" as pragmatically unnecessary instead of adding it over and over again. There are times, of course, when the use of the adjective is necessary for purposes of clarity in a given context. But on the whole I will employ the term "ethnic" without a qualifier for those in C and D groupings and add the word "dominant" in those cases where it does apply.

Combining the characteristics of size, power, and ethnicity, we then use "minority group" to signify any ethnic group in category D; this implies that it forms less than half the population of a given society, but is an appreciable subsystem with limited access to roles and activities central to the economic and political institutions of the society. When ethnics form an actual majority of the population but are in a status of subordination (Group C) they will be designated as mass ethnics.

Finally, a word about the term "society." For the purposes at hand, I am deliberately excluding the broader, generic meaning for a more limited one. Instead of orienting the choice to the whole evolutionary panorama of societies, the meaning is narrowed here to a much more limited sphere. In terms of Parsons' three-fold typology of societies as primitive, intermediate, and modern (Parsons, 1966, 3), attention is centered wholly on his third category, and the definition that follows denotes that type alone. Thus in the modern world, it seems most appropriate to define a society as a nation-state, i.e., a social unit territorially distinguished from other such units, having a set of governmental institutions of a central character preeminent over local political controls, and empowered to act for the entire unit in external relations (Modified from M. G. Smith, 1957, 766).

So much for preliminary definitions. We now ask: What is the central question to which comparative research in ethnic relations seeks an answer? Briefly, it is this: *What are the conditions that foster or prevent the integration of ethnic groups into their environing societies?* How this question is answered will depend, of course, on the meaning we give to "integration." And at the outset, the fact that I am speaking of integration in a generic sense much broader than the familiar meaning attributed to goals for the Negro in the United States must be underscored.[3] As presented here, integration is not an end-state but a *process* whereby units or elements of a society are brought into an active and coordinated compliance with the ongoing activities and objectives of the dominant group in that society.

If this formulation leads us in the right direction, it is then proper to infer that the task of intergroup research is to account for the modes of integration (and conflict) as dependent variables in the relations between dominant groups and subordinate ethnic groups in different societies. It implies a search for the significant independent and intervening variables, and for invariant relations between independent and dependent variables under specified conditions. This is an exploration in macrosociology, and may well be more revealing of the nature of societies as wholes than any comparative studies now in process.

Before going into detail on the schematic design for research that will occupy our attention in later chapters, a skeleton outline of the main themes to follow is hereby offered to alert the reader to central issues immediately: we begin with the proposition that when the territory of a contemporary nation-state is occupied by peoples of diverse cultures and origins, the integration of such plural groups into each environing society will be a composite function of three independent and three intervening variables. The independent variables posited here are: (1) repeatable sequences of interaction between subordinate ethnics and dominant groups, such as annexation, migration, colonization; (2) the degree of enclosure (institutional separation or segmentation) of the subordinate group or groups from the society-wide network of institutions and associations; and (3) the degree of control exercised by dominant groups over access to scarce resources by subordinate groups in a given society.

The intervening or contextual variables that modify the effects of independent variables are: (1) agreement or disagreement between dominant and subordinate groups on collective goals for the latter, such as assimilation, pluralism; (2) membership of a society under scrutiny in a class or category of societies sharing overall common cultural and structural features, such as Near East societies, Sub-Saharan African societies; (3) membership of a society under scrutiny in a more limited category of societies distinguished by forms of institutional dominance, i.e., polity dominating economy or vice versa.

Finally, the dependent variables to be explained are the interweaving patterns of integration and conflict[4] either in the relations between subordinates and superordinates on the one hand, or between subordinates and the total society on the other. Of the three dependent variables advanced here, the first two deal with the former relationship (between subordinates and dominant groups) and are correlative with each other; the third variable operationalizes the latter relation (between subordinates and the society as a whole). The three dependent variables therefore are: (1) differential participation rates of subordinates in institutional and associational life (including rates of vertical mobility) as compared with rates for the dominant group; (2) the extent of satisfaction or dissatisfaction of both subordinate and dominant group members with the differential patterns of participation as they see them, together with accompanying ideologies and cultural values; and (3) overt or covert behavior patterns of subordinates and dominants indicative of conflict and/or harmonious relations; assessment in terms of continued integration.

However, it is unsatisfactory to leave this formulation at what might appear to be an ad hoc level. The scheme of analysis to be developed here has, like any other, a number of assumptions rooted in broader theory. A central purpose of any general sociological theory is, *inter alia*, to postulate the essential nature of social interaction. For example, the "structural-functionalist" might regard this basic nature as system maintenance and therefore governed by norms and regularities that transcend any and all particular situations; the "symbolic interactionist" might speak of a tentative process of reciprocal role-taking in immediate experience as the fundamental nature; the "conflict theorist," however, might refer to the constraints and inequalities of all interactions as engendering incessant and stressful change in the relations between individuals and groups. In conventional scientific procedure, it has been customary to derive special theories from such general theories by some carefully articulated process of inference. Thus any particular special theory such as one pertaining to the family, the community, or to ethnic relations, is related to the wider general theory by logical connections that issue in a set of propositions specially applicable to a limited and unique set of data. As distinguished from the general theory, the task of the special theory is to explain the relationships between specified variables applied to a carefully bounded field of investigation.

The movement of thought between the whole and the part is therefore alternate and reciprocal. Not only is the subfield dependent logically on a general theory that postulates the essential characteristics of all interactive relations but, conversely, a central aim of every subfield is to make a substantial contribution to the total domain of knowledge encompassing it. How does this apply to our task here? To be explicit, the following treatise is an appeal to view intergroup relations as a special case of societal relations in their broadest and most generic sense, rather than as a separate and unrelated field of inquiry. To see it in this fullest and most comprehensive sense, the exposition that follows will begin at the greatest or highest level of generality before unfolding the many particulars. The way we plan to do this is by first reviewing the leading features of two general theories that appear to contradict each other, and then reflect on the meaning of their opposition when we come to explain intergroup relations. We deliberately choose this seemingly cumbersome and roundabout method of approaching comparative ethnic relations, in spite of its drawbacks, for a special reason: this procedure will relate everything that follows to perennial historical concerns of sociology, and thus preserve a fruitful continuity with our classical past. The next chapter will set the pace for this exploration.

· NOTES ·

1. The interested reader will find a trenchant discussion of these works and a series of textbooks in a recent volume by Peter I. Rose entitled *The Subject is Race*, 1968.
2. I am indebted to Irving Rosow for suggestions in the development of this paradigm.
3. A fairly common meaning tacitly or openly approved in civil rights movements is stated as follows: integration is "a condition in which individuals of each racial or ethnic group are randomly distributed through the society so that every realm of activity contains a representative cross section of the population. In that sense, the object is the attainment, in every occupational, educational, and residential distribution, of a balance among the constituent elements in the society" (Oscar Handlin, 1966, 661).
4. Such a formulation rests on the conviction that integration and conflict are social processes sometimes antithetical, sometimes complementary.

This is only one of the many implications of the dialectical position discussed later on.

· REFERENCES ·

Allport, Gordon W., *The Nature of Prejudice.* Cambridge, Mass.: Addison-Wesley, 1954.

Berry, Brewton, *Race and Ethnic Relations.* 2nd ed. Boston: Houghton Mifflin, 1958.

Bierstedt, Robert, *The Social Order.* New York: McGraw-Hill, 1963.

Blalock, Hubert M., Jr., *Toward a Theory of Minority-Group Relations.* New York: Wiley, 1967.

Handlin, Oscar, "The Goal of Integration," in Talcott Parsons and Kenneth B. Clark (eds.), *The Negro American.* Boston: Houghton Mifflin, 1966.

Hughes, Everett C., and Helen MacGill Hughes, *Where Peoples Meet: Racial and Ethnic Frontiers.* Glencoe, Ill.: Free Press, 1952.

Locke, Alain, and B. J. Stern (eds.), *When Peoples Meet.* New York: Progressive Education Association, 1942.

Marsh, Robert M., *Comparative Sociology.* New York: Harcourt, Brace & World, 1967.

Park, Robert E., *Race and Culture.* Glencoe, Ill.: Free Press, 1949.

Parsons, Talcott, *Societies, Evolutionary and Comparative Perspectives.* Englewood Cliffs, N. J.: Prentice-Hall, 1966.

Raab, Earl, and Seymour M. Lipset, *Prejudice and Society.* New York: Anti-Defamation League of B'nai B'rith, 1959.

Rose, Arnold, "The Comparative Study of Intergroup Conflict," *Sociological Quarterly,* 1 (January 1960), 57–66.

Rose, Peter I., *The Subject is Race.* New York: Oxford University Press, 1968.

Shibutani, Tamotsu, and K. M. Kwan, *Ethnic Stratification.* New York: Macmillan, 1965.

Simpson, George E., and J. M. Yinger, *Racial and Cultural Minorities.* 3rd ed. New York: Harper & Row, 1965.

Smith, M. G., "Social and Cultural Pluralism," *Annals of the New York Academy of Science,* 83, Art. 5 (January 20, 1957), 763–77.

van den Berghe, Pierre L., *Race and Racism.* New York: Wiley, 1967.

Vander Zanden, James W., *American Minority Relations.* 2nd ed. New York: Ronald Press, 1966.

Von der Mehden, Fred R., *Politics of the Developing Nations.* Englewood Cliffs, N. J.: Prentice-Hall, 1964.

Wagley, Charles, and Marvin Harris, *Minorities in the New World.* New York: Columbia University Press, 1958.

Wallerstein, Immanuel, *Africa, The Politics of Independence.* New York: Vintage Books, 1961.

Walter, Paul A. F., Jr., *Race and Culture Relations.* New York: McGraw-Hill, 1952.

Westie, Frank R., "Race and Ethnic Relations," in R. E. L. Faris (ed.), *Handbook of Modern Sociology.* Chicago: Rand McNally, 1964.

Williams, Robin M., Jr., *The Reduction of Intergroup Tensions.* New York: Social Science Research Council, 1947.

——, "Racial and Cultural Relations," in Joseph B. Gittler (ed.), *Review of Sociology*. New York: Wiley, 1957.

Wirth, Louis, "The Problem of Minority Groups," in Ralph Linton (ed.), *The Science of Man in the World Crisis*. New York: Columbia University Press, 1945.

1

❦

Dual Perspectives
on Society
and Ethnic Relations

The two macroscopic theories of society that have the greatest relevance for ethnic relations are variously labeled. John Horton calls them order and conflict theories (1966); van den Berghe prefers the terms functionalism and dialectic (1963); Dahrendorf speaks of integration and coercion (1959, 161–62). For reasons that will appear later, we prefer to employ the terms "system theory" and power-conflict *theory*.

In approaching these two viewpoints it is well to begin with a common-sense model of a subordinate ethnic group confronting a dominant group in a situation where discord and contention are pronounced. What features are likely to strike the observer? If he reflects at all on the place of the subordinate ethnic group in this kind of a situation, he will probably notice that there are limits or restrictions on the behavior of such ethnic group members and that these limits go beyond those regulated by the standards of the group itself but are imposed from the outside by those who appear to have self-interested reasons. However, these outsiders not only have the power to enforce their decisions but they are in some way authoritative figures who are part of the Establishment; in the wider society *they* are the insiders[1] and, in more ways than one, constitute a dominant group. In simplest terms, the relation between the upper and lower group has become polarized, and thus is likely to involve a clash of interests over scarce values like economic goods, prestige, and power, or over incompatible views regarding each other's values. From such relationships flow the estrangement and antagonism that arise in their encounter with each other.

Such reflections give rise to further inferences: what, for example, are the usual perspectives of the upper group or the lower group in their mutual confrontation? Do we not naturally assume that those in the dominant position will regard their authority as legitimate rather than to deny it or have doubts about it? Whatever policy they adopt, the uppers tend to have an attitude of self-justification. They may obliterate, suppress, segregate, manipulate, tolerate, transform, or convert the lower group—in one sense it does not matter what, since the superordinates have the power to decide and carry out their decision with conviction of its right and warrant. This is the perspective of the upper position growing out of the privilege inherent in that place. The very nature of the situation often makes the uppers prone to make unilateral decisions, thus transforming the lowers into instruments or tools.

The subordinates' point of view causes them to seek escape from this unilateral constraint and make the arena truly bilateral. To do this, they must challenge the dominance of the upper group *in some respect or other*, and convert the situation into something truly interactive. The occupants of a lower position may make their challenge in a straightforward or devious manner, with limited means or by massive efforts. Their unprivileged and deprived condition forces them to face up to the dilemma of action vs. inaction, the movement toward change (not *any* change, but change that alters the relative position of upper and lower groups) vs. acceptance of the status quo. On a rational basis, i.e., where the distinction of ends and means is reasonably clear, decisions to challenge the uppers will be accompanied by manifest awareness of what they will gain or lose in the venture. Even more frequently, their decision is likely to be nonrational so that their challenge encompasses a melange of motives: masculine assertions, desires for revenge, escapes from deprivation, status longings, enthusiasm for a leader—the possibilities are endless. Impulses like these, just because they are so diffuse, can often rise to such intensity that they blot out any sense of danger in the venture, or make it puerile to count the cost.

The only other alternative for those in lower positions is simply inaction or immobility. At times this is nothing but habit. But it has other meanings too: dull acquiescence in a condition the reversal of which seems inconceivable, feelings of security connected with a familiar round of activities, cowed subservience in the face of threat, or at times a vague, impelling sense of danger at the thought of abandoning zones of safety promising survival, not to speak of the strong inhibitions of sacred beliefs. When reason awakes, inaction can also signify biding one's time as a shrewd tactic preparatory for an assault.

Moving Away from a Conflict Model

The perspectives of upper and lower groups conceived in this way reveal the outlines of a crude "conflict model." There is no question of the immense advantages of this model, the chief of which is that it is composed of clear and distinct ideas. This is also, paradoxically enough, one of its chief drawbacks. Those who recall their history of philosophy may be reminded of Descartes whose insistence on clarity and definiteness precipitated a cleavage of thought that has taken literally centuries to bridge. A. N. Whitehead, in one of his inimitable lectures, once commented on Descartes: "There is only one difficulty with clear and distinct ideas. When we finally achieve them, we can be sure that something has been left out."[2] A similar, though Hobbesian rather than Cartesian, clarity illumines us here. Following the metaphor, it seems that the spotlight of distinctness, like all spotlights, casts a vivid glare over its narrow circle that prevents us from seeing beyond it into the penumbra where other realities remain to be observed. So it is with a gross conflict model when it monopolizes attention. What happens when we explore its periphery?

To continue the metaphor, we notice that the spotlight does not follow us. Once we are out of the spotlight, we enter a darker region and accustom our eyes to shaded variations of the scene that only now appear, nuances of perception with more delicate outlines, here and there blending and merging with each other. Further observation reveals that we have left a zone of agitation and movement for one of quiet and relative calm. Eventually, as we familiarize ourselves with the new medium, our vision gains a new dimension, enabling it to extend its reach to wider and wider ranges of apprehension. In sociological terms, we have entered the portals of the social system.

Alerted to new possibilities by this somewhat cryptic image, let us drop our metaphor for a moment and return to the intergroup arena. Looking again at our simple model of superordinates and subordinates in a mutual encounter, we find that we can carry the analysis further if we do not confine ourselves to a single strand of experience by relentless exclusion of other strands in the concrete situation. Shifting attention to them and enlarging the perspective soon bring to light elements of system.

Some of these neglected elements are suggested by one of the definitions given above. For example, we have defined the dominant group as "that collectivity within a society which has preeminent authority to function as guardians and sustainers of the controlling value system, and as prime allocators of rewards in the society." (See p. 12–13). If we take this definition seriously, it means that the task of the superordinates goes beyond a simple exertion of their power, as a simplified conflict model would have it. The demands of their upper position are not single but dual: privilege *and* responsibility. It is quite true that when they grasp the first horn of this dilemma, they are pressured toward inclinations to exploit their subordinates while buttressing and enlarging their own power; such tendencies are often strong enough to override all other considerations. Yet they cannot press their advantage too far without raising serious opposition, trouble, and disorder from those in lower echelons. Even in order to exploit them, the privileged must see to it that those in subordinate positions not only subsist, but are motivated to continue playing their roles in a system to which both upper and lower groups contribute, though in functionally different ways. Whether they like it or not, the elite need their subordinates, even to exploit them. And for the sake of smooth functioning in the system (stability, order, predictability, or other correlative terms to suit) the upper stratum finds itself driven to accept responsibility for satisfying minimal requirements of those in lower status positions and motivating them to continue their necessary activities.

This correlative demand for upper-level personnel has been dubbed "tension management," (W. E. Moore, 1963, 10) and it requires more effort, puzzlement, and uncertainty than the gratifying and self-pampering impulses of aggrandizement. Few men are attracted to tension management and often only the direst emergency will drive them to it. All, however, acknowledge its necessity, and this is a tacit recognition of larger system demands. Except in the most decadent aristocracies, there is enough awareness of tension management's importance so that some members of the upper echelons will bring pressure on their fellows with leadership potential to carry out this role, however thankless the task. And of course there may be a few volunteers who undertake it for personal, family, and even sacred reasons.

Ideologically, too, the system wins. When it comes to public doctrines or popular oratory, it is appeals couched in terms of the whole that take first place. It is hardly possible to broadcast views supporting open exploitation or the interests of the specially privileged, for reasons too obvious to mention. But discourses on teamwork, cooperation, everyone pulling together, "England expects every man to do his duty" and the like, take precedence over all other forms of public utterance, reaching their mark even more unerringly when given the aura of sacred principle to which all give allegiance. Such ideological pronouncements reinforce system needs and help to keep the whole society functioning. They are definitely integrative, emphasizing the very real fact that upper and lower groups belong to a totality greater than either, that mutual dependencies require reciprocal contributions on the part of all, regardless of position. This is true even when the dilemma remains for the superordinates, and even at times when the tug of privilege overpowers the faint stirrings of responsibility and principled interests.[3]

Subordinates, too, are pressured toward system interests. Being in a lower position, they suffer from lack of "inside" knowledge and the expertise of those who manage. Underlings, also, face a double alternative; for them it is the choice between opposition and subservience. Neither is a sure thing. Opposition could bring additional gains but it could also inflict a withholding of benefits. Subservience may bring peace yet could equally well encourage an additional turn of the screw. Over and above these more limited alternatives is the desire for order and stability which subordinates share with dominant groups. In a way, the need for order weighs even more heavily upon those in lower positions than upon superordinates, because any disturbance of enduring relations will find subordinates more vulnerable, less able to adapt, and with far less room to maneuver than the more fortunate. Added to the inertia of dull habit is fear of disturbing that habit. The greeting of the Mexican peasant, "Go with God, and may nothing new happen to you," well expresses the widespread conservatism of the lowly, a conservatism that has been the despair of revolutionaries in many lands, in many eras. One is tempted to believe that this conservatism of lower status groups contributes more to the stability of social systems than all the combined planning or "tension management" of all the elites in history. It is certainly an important factor that sensitizes lower groups to appeals for cooperation and fulfilling of duties when urged by the pronouncements of superior authorities.

The Bonds of Conflict and Constraint

Forms of mutuality appear even when conflicts are deep. In the case of South Africa, the cleavage between whites and blacks seems like a yawning chasm and yet there are connecting links that prevent complete rupture. Max Gluckman invokes what he calls "the bonds in the colour bar" to account for the viability of a total social system in that country. As he presents the picture, it is the divisions of interest among blacks and among whites which often establishes alliances across the color line. For instance, the incursion of white missionaries into Zulu territory led to many conversions to Christianity. This divided the Zulu into Christian and non-Christian groups who not only opposed each other on religious issues but also on the imitation of "Western" innovations. Christians tended to adopt such practices in the face of non-Christian resistance, even joining forces with whites to hasten the acceptance of new customs among their fellow Zulu. Another internal division was composed of the blacks who worked for the (white) government as police, technical assistants, or magistracy clerks, highly dependent as they were on political administration for their livelihood. Here was another link uniting whites and blacks of the governmental apparatus with common interests for implementing official policies. In addition there were countless other blacks who entered the larger economic system in domestic or industrial labor as employees of whites, forging new ties of dependence on both sides as symbiotic links between employer and employee were gradually strengthened. At least in the earlier stages some of the blacks established important links across the color line but still among other workers—like those with white labor leaders or national congress leaders.

All of these bonds, limited though they were, set up relations of cohesion in the wider society, holding it together (Gluckman, 1955, 137–65). Under such conditions norms of reciprocity cannot help but build up. As one Afrikaans clergyman bluntly put it, "we need them and they need us" (quoted in Van der Horst, 1965, 139). Naturally, it has been the aim of apartheid policy to abolish as many links as possible in these reciprocal chains. Government policy has eventually excluded black Africans from trade unions where they participate with other workers (Van der Horst, *op. cit.*, 119–20), stopped government subsidies to mission schools for non-whites, discouraged most biracial religious gatherings, prohibited practically all other interracial meetings, set up Group Areas laws that require the most stringent residential separation, and fashioned a net of surveillance over all get-togethers of more than three people to make sure that the policies will be obeyed (E. J. Kahn, Jr., 1968). This rigid consistency of almost total separation has so polarized relations between the races that conflict seems irresolvable were it not for the inability of the dominant whites to follow logic to its final conclusion and exclude black workmen from the economy altogether. This, however, is the sticking point. To do this would destroy the very foundation of South African prosperity that now surpasses the standard of living in all African countries. Gluckman states quite candidly that it is *money* that keeps Africans working, whatever may have been the original inducements, for it is money that builds up reciprocal interests between whites and blacks, holding them together in an economic system in spite of the competitive features built into it (Gluckman, *op. cit.*, 140). Van den Berghe makes the point even more vividly when he declares that "The utter dependence (at a starvation or near starvation level) of the African masses on the 'white' economy in South Africa has been one of the main inhibiting factors to such mass protest actions or general strikes" (van den Berghe, 1965, 82).[4] Thus societies experiencing massive but suppressed conflict may be held together by systems of instrumental interest where other integrative bonds are lacking. Psychologically it may well be that the low level of commitment to such jobs without a future makes for stability in itself. As Van der Horst comments, "there appears to be relatively little personal involvement with a job or firm. This lack of involvement has probably contributed to the remarkably peaceful industrial relations which have prevailed in South Africa" (Van der Horst, *op. cit.*, 130).

No doubt South Africa is an extreme case where the linkages between conflicting elements are not as numerous as they are in many other societies. It is the merit of the system analysts[5] to call attention to the often hidden features of intermeshing organizations, as well as to the norms and values that underlie the more conspicuous elements of total societies.

Capsule Version of System Analysis

A brief review of system analysis will give some idea of its relevance to the comparison of societies. The first thing to notice is the panoramic perspective, i.e., system analysis begins with the notion of a whole having predominance over its parts. From this standpoint the question follows: how are societies as wholes maintained by their constituent elements? To this question there is an answer in generic terms and then by specification of the generic principles. Generically, societies as wholes can survive as "going concerns" only if fundamental needs are met. These needs, usually called functional imperatives or functional requisites, listed somewhat differently by individual writers, include such items as provisions for physiological functioning and survival, reproduction and replacement, shared goals and perspectives, socialization,

communication, organization of roles, control and regulation of
deviance, and general regularization of activities in patterned
forms.[6]

If these needs are to be met reliably and predictably, they must
be supported by structures, i.e., by uniformities of action that
recur when called for by the situation. At this point the generic
principles become specified in determinate patterns, organizations,
or institutions like the family, the economy, government, education, religion, and the like. These are the structural forms organized around basic needs, providing for their fulfillment and
maintenance in such a way that the satisfaction of one does not
interfere with the satisfaction of another. As settings and contexts
change, the requisites and structures may change too, at least in
emphasis and accentuation (Levy, 1952, 40). In simpler societies the structures are more fused, multifunctional and informal in operation, while in more complex societies the structures
become more differentiated, unifunctional, and formal. In either
case, however, the needs of society as a whole demand that the
structures form a system of interrelated activities that are mutually
supportive if the society is to remain stable.

Thus a system consists of a complete set of reciprocal interdependencies that can only be conceived, not perceived. Such
systems are at depth levels far below the vision of nonscientific
observers, and their intricacy is such that, even with the more
sophisticated instruments of knowledge, it is difficult to make
full practical use of our information. "Such highly complicated,
highly interdependent systems of action are well beyond our
present capacities for explicit planning on a rational basis" (Levy,
1966, 777). At the same time it seems to be an implicit, if not
explicit, belief of the system analysts that the true essence of
societies is to be found in their systematic character. Thus:
"Force is a sanction but never the essence of a society. A society
based solely on force would be a contradiction in terms" (Levy,
1952, 139). The unstated inference seems to be that the essence
is rather to be found in the web of mutual interdependencies
holding each society together. Without this network of interweaving structures, a population is a collection, a heap, or an
aggregation, not a society.

The ramifications of this view are so extended and far-reaching
that they have filled many volumes and cannot be pursued further

here. What is important is to insist on the cogency of this view which deals with the deepest and most profound issue of social science. The system analysts by their holistic approach have forced the recognition of realities that appear in no other perspective. They have made it quite clear that interrelationship of structures is presupposed in every analysis undertaken by the social scientist. Each of the related structures has its function to perform for the system as a whole, whether it be adaptive in economic subsystems, goal-attaining in political subsystems, pattern-maintenance in education and training, or integration in religious or other value systems (Parsons, Bales, and Shils, 1953, Chap. 4). The subsystems mesh together in a total system whose overall function is to maintain the identity of the society as a whole, and, in its singular organization from one setting to another, mark off each society as a determinate entity. Societies are therefore distinguishable, in scientific terms, by their social systems, i.e., by their different arrangements of structures, not by surface phenomena available to common sense observation. The latter must give way to long-term patient analysis that eventually reveals interrelated patterned characteristics.

One way to put the essential truth of system analysis would be (in negative terms) the following statement: whenever the interdependence of a society's social system is violated, and to the extent that it is violated, the society loses its viability for self-maintenance at least to the same degree. It is interesting to note that this sort of argument is advanced, not only by present-day functionalists who stem chiefly from the Durkheim tradition, but by Marx himself who is often quoted as an opponent of such views (Lockwood, 1964, 244–57).

Before leaving the subject, I want to direct attention to two main characteristics of social systems as they are often represented, one explicit and the other implicit. The first, which is quite unequivocal, is the principle of functional hierarchy as an inherent feature of systems. The second is only intimated but seems to pervade the discursive account of systems like an atmosphere rather than a doctrine. Let us call it the preference for symmetry. These two characteristics which might, on the face of it, appear contradictory, are both united in system analysis and deserve further consideration.

Hierarchy, the first principle, is regarded as a generic feature of total societies, manifesting itself in all subsystems too by a kind of inherent necessity. From the standpoint of the whole, it is an expression of total needs that can only be satisfied when functions are differentiated; naturally the roles which serve these functions are inevitably of unequal importance. It follows that in such a societal system the more important roles are fewer in number than the less important ones, since their requirements are so high that there will be a relative scarcity of qualified personnel to fill them. Ergo: "Social inequality is thus the unconsciously evolved device by which societies insure that the most important positions are conscientiously filled by the most qualified persons" (Davis, 1949, 367). Management, governance, or direction of the many by the few of greater capabilities, competence, and proficiency is a hierarchical principle recognized in all social systems. There is nothing startling in this and certainly nothing new. It is only a recognition of the wisdom of the ages.

Likewise hierarchical organization is so ubiquitous that it is verified by continual observation.

> The overwhelming proportion of all relationships in all societies contain hierarchical elements both ideally and actually. In fact it is difficult for most individuals to give examples, apart from friendship, of relationships that are ideally and/or actually egalitarian. Family relationships certainly aren't; bureaucratic relationships aren't; relationships within the government rarely are; universities aren't; business firms aren't, etc. (Levy, 1966, 151)

But from a strictly theoretical standpoint, it is not observability that makes hierarchy important per se; it is rather its functional character, its efficacy in maintaining any complex system.

The second element, that of symmetry, is more difficult to pin down. Some passages in the works of system analysts can even be quoted to the contrary. For example, Talcott Parsons recognizes that "no social system can be completely integrated; there will, for many reasons, always be some discrepancies between role expectations and performance of roles" (Parsons and Shils, 1962, 204). His admission, like many others referring to strains, dislocations, or deviations, could well be made, however, as a compensatory statement, or from the realization that the whole tenor of the analysis runs in the other direction toward complementarity, boundary-maintenance, mutuality of role-expectations, pattern consistency of cultural norms, and other symmetrical arrangements. The very idea of a generalized system stems from biology, and Parsons contends that it was "most fully developed" by the physiologist Cannon "on a relatively complete and explicit level" (Parsons, 1954, 218). As the image that not only influenced its development but the one that strongly impresses itself on the mind of the reader, the organic type of system forms a kind of prototype. Though presented as strictly an analytic model not identified with any specific society, the preoccupation with its due proportions, the frequent reference to its balance and regularity, or the methodical care given to consistencies and compatibilities leave no doubt that these are the characteristics of social systems that really merit attention, and all are derivable in one way or another from analysis of organic systems.[7] They focus unmistakably on symmetrical features. Since society, too, is a boundary-maintaining system where the parts have no meaning apart from the whole, the parts, too, have the dual aspects of being system-determined and system-maintaining simultaneously as is true in the organism. It is the whole that pervades and orders the parts, as "first the universal imperatives, the conditions which must be met by any social system of a stable and durable character, and second, the imperatives of compatibility, those which limit the range of coexistence of structural elements in the same society . . ." (Parsons, 1951, 167).

The emphasis here on what *must be* underlines what are clearly symmetrical requirements, even though it may be argued that they are minimal requirements. The notion of balance coupled with stability has a corresponding ring. Thus while societies *may* deviate from such balanced conditions or even develop radical imbalances, "nevertheless, insofar as social systems are stable over any extended period of time they are not in fact characterized by considerable imbalances of this sort and certainly not by imbalance of this sort on the level of generality on which the system is being studied" (Levy, 1966, 691). While this avoids the crass *definition* of social systems as symmetrically organized relationships, it nevertheless points to these relations as the ones most truly deserving investigation, leaving others as residual factors to be explored for the sake of completeness, yet with noticeably diminished zeal and thoroughness.[8] The total impression left by

Parsons' discussion of these issues is shrewdly assessed by Robin Williams when he remarks, "Even with all its careful disclaimers and qualifications, the scheme does have the net effect, for many readers, of emphasizing stability, and, by omission, understating the problem of radical discontinuities and rapid, massive, and violent conflicts and changes in social systems and sub-systems" (Williams, 1961, 94).[9]

Another source of evidence for the importance of balance and symmetry comes from propositions about the functional contributions of structures to societal systems as a whole. For a system analyst influenced by Merton's distinctions of function and dysfunction, as Levy definitely is, he presents eufunctions (sustaining the whole) and dysfunctions (making for lack of persistence of the whole) in such fashion that the former must outweigh the latter and thus preserve the balance necessary for system viability (Levy, 1952, 177–8).

System Analysis under Scrutiny

A brief critique of system analysis can well begin at this very point where objections arise to challenge the penchant for symmetry. Stating two of these in the form of questions we then ask: (1) Is it possible that some functional requirements may actually contradict others? (2) Is it possible that a single structure may have contradictory functional requirements that contradict each other? Gideon Sjoberg raises the first question and gives it an affirmative answer. He argues persuasively that all social systems are "plagued by contradictory functional requirements (or imperatives) and that these are associated with the formation of mutually antagonistic structural arrangements that function to meet those requirements. Implied in this is the notion that some of these mutually contradictory structures may actually be essential to the 'operation' or 'maintenance' of the system" (Sjoberg, 1960, 199). Perhaps the simplest case (though not actually mentioned by Sjoberg) would be the requirements for family structure, i.e., reproduction and socialization, which come into conflict with societal requirements for economic structures, i.e., contribution to sustenance and survival of the entire com-

munity. Though admittedly the requirements are less at odds
with each other in some societies than in others, there is probably
no social order in which this dual combination of requirements
does not create dilemmas of choice for those fulfilling both sets
of demands; yet the very contradiction itself is in a way necessary
for the preservation of the society. It is more than a dilemma of
roles for the individual—it exists for *sets* of individuals. Thus in
this sense it is a built-in structural dilemma inseparable from the
operation of the society as a whole. Both structures are eufunctional—there is no choice here between eufunctional and dysfunc-
tional structures. It is not a matter of the former "outweighing"
the latter.

The second question—Is it possible that a single structure may
have contradictory functional requirements?—must, I believe,
receive an affirmative answer also. A hierarchical structure furnishes a good example. Inherent in the position of the leader or
authority at the apex of the structure is the contradiction between
opposing (correcting) and at the same time leading the followers;
on their side is the corresponding contradiction of compliance or
resistance (particularly to harmful demands). It would seem that
functional requirements are therefore *both* complementary and
contradictory. Each side of the contradiction has functions for
the relationship, even though the functions may be incompatible
with each other. In short, the structure is dialectical, not univocal.
Sjoberg's analysis of hierarchy makes a similar point, though he
puts it in diachronic terms by pointing out that leaders, in order
to reinforce their authority, evoke emulation from their followers,
but the more successful their venture is, the more likely will the
time come when some of the followers challenge the superiority
of the leaders. In such cases as economic development, there is
another kind of hierarchy—that of givers and receivers. Here the
giving of foreign aid may have the long-time effect of raising the
status and expectations of recipients to levels approaching those
of the donors, so the former become more aggressive and chal-
lenging (Sjoberg, *op. cit.*, 204). Reflections like these raise questions about the appropriateness of symmetry for all analyses of
social systems.

However, I would not be misunderstood. This does *not*, as
some conflict theorists seem to imply, entitle us to dispense with

the concept of system altogether, and cast ourselves adrift on a sea of ceaseless flux with only the waves to guide us. It only means that any use of system analysis must become more flexible, relativistic, and circumspect, alert at the same time to inductive and categorical difficulties.

One way of doing this is to begin by starting to correct what appears to be an excessive dependence on cultural factors to carry the explanatory load in system analysis. At the outset, of course, it is necessary to insist on the analytic distinctions between cultural factors and structural factors, each of which implies the other without becoming wholly engulfed by it. Parenthetically, it is just such distinctions that Louis Wirth had in mind when he observed "the fact that territory, political authority, people and culture rarely coincide" (Wirth, 1945, 365). The Parsonian analysis has the merit—and the drawback—of uniting cultural and structural factors firmly together but accenting the former more than the latter. The norms of the social system (which are cultural items on any reckoning) play a major role in social structure since it is the norms that define the regularity and patterning of interaction among actors; not only are they the constitutive elements of social institutions but they are also transmitted, through the process of socialization, to actors who internalize them so that they become dependable motives for maintaining the system.

> It is only by internalization of institutionalized values that a genuine motivational integration of behavior in the social structure takes place, that the 'deeper' layers of motivation become harnessed to the fulfillment of role expectations. This integration of a set of common value-patterns with the internalized need-disposition structure of the constituent personalities is the core phenomenon of the dynamics of social systems. (Parsons, 1951, 42)

These value patterns, of which norms are important components, are simultaneously cultural items, structure-defining constituents, and motivational guides. On this reading, disruption of the system must therefore be sought either in imperfect socialization of the younger members, or in motivations toward nonconformity by mature members, the latter given a strongly psychological interpretation (Parsons, 1951, 251–67). However, there are no systematic pressures accounting for the latter, but only contingent factors that must be discovered by empirical observation in each individual case as a supplement to psychological variables.

The one-sidedness of this scheme draws sharp criticism from Lockwood who argues that Parsons has weighted the scales so heavily in favor of the normative elements that he has omitted the more realistic features. In a word, Lockwood accuses Parsons of singling out ends to the exclusion of means in social processes, arguing that it is the scarcity of means in any society that *also* structures human interests in predictable ways; it is actually the scarcity of means that accounts for the relationships of power and social conflict systematically—features of the social system to which Parsons gives scant attention. What Parsons explains as a deviation from societal ends or values (on a psychological basis), Lockwood insists can be more adequately explained as a pressure of interests engendered by scarce means (on a sociological basis). Lockwood's term for these realistic elements of the social system is the *substratum*, defined as "the factual disposition of means in the situation of action which structures differential *Lebenschancen* and produces interests of a non-normative kind, that is, interests other than those which actors have in conforming with the normative definition of the situation" (Lockwood, 1956, 136). To a large degree, this substratum may be identified with Marx's materialism expressed in the economic means of production, although it has wider application also in Weber's work which Gerth and Mills call "an attempt to 'round out' Marx's economic materialism by a political and military materialism" (H. H. Gerth and C. Wright Mills, 1946, 47). The important fact to emphasize is that the interests engendered by scarce means whether economic, political, or military, produce social structures whose dimensions are not quite definable in terms of Parsons' norms.

Lockwood's analysis makes it clear why such a gulf exists between the two views of system, why Parsons leans so heavily on "socialization" as a primary process (Marx neglecting it) and why Marx puts his accent on "exploitation" (which Parsons ignores completely). It explains, too, why Parsons distinguishes different stratification systems by relating them to the dominant value patterns of various societies, while Marx describes them as types of ownership and control of means. "Here are two notions of "social structure," both characterized by "exteriority" and "constraint," the one *de jure* and the other *de facto*. Marx's own analysis tended to focus on the latter meaning" (Lockwood, *op. cit.*, 138).[10] The point is, however, that Marx, too, envisaged a system of interlocking structures which, when properly organized, would actually produce a well-integrated society. We conclude that *if we are to take system analysis seriously, it must encompass the structures of both ends and means.*

A retrospective evaluation of system analysis in the structural-functional tradition is now in order. Several dominant themes stand out. In the first place, by adopting a kind of organic analogy, the scheme begins by taking the viewpoint of societies as wholes which can only persist as total system needs are satisfied. These needs engender structures or regularities that make the maintenance of the system stable and predictable. The touchstone of their operation is function (eufunction) for the whole, not whether it is "good" or "bad" in terms of individual preferences or partial group standards, but in terms that an objective observer with sufficient knowledge would judge as compatible fulfillment of system needs.

In the second place, this is a view "behind the scenes" and not available to immediate inspection. The actors who perform their roles in the system may have little or no awareness of the functions of their action in promoting integration or the lack of it. As the quotation from Kingsley Davis intimated, each structure, like that of inequality which he specifically mentioned, is "an unconsciously evolved device by which societies ensure" the performance of necessary functions. This has interesting analogies with the Freudian "cunning of the unconscious" and attributes some sort of hidden rationality to the subterranean processes taking place in society. This is compatible with a kind of holistic optimism which, of course, can be denied for the operation of any specific society, while inspiring confidence that societal balances tend to correct imbalances as an inherent feature of *all* societies.

A third major theme is one of great significance, i.e., the constant preoccupation with consequences of structures for the system as a whole. If the major scientific task is to trace out such objective consequences, this soon becomes a program for determining the pattern of structures in interrelation, a task so intricate that in the end, one seems driven more and more to a Gestalt where consequences are absorbed in the Major Consequence in a synoptic view of all together. This simultaneity of perspective may well be, in the long run, a philosophical culmination of what began as scientific analysis, but even in its programmatic outline, by singling out consequences rather than causes, it can become one-sided—a premature synthesis that shuts out causal analysis with unintended finality. In order to have causal assessment we must descend from the dizzying heights of simultaneity to the more prosaic realm of temporality, to the tracing of contingent connections under specified conditions that we hope against hope are not contingent—giving us clues to the reasons why structures are thus and so and not otherwise. As Meyer Fortes has put it, "There is no way of establishing an order of priority where all institutions are interdependent, except by criteria that cannot be used in a synchronic study; and synchronic study is the *sine qua non* of functional research" (Fortes, 1953, 20).[11] In short, the study of causality demands a *diachronic* approach. It is one thing to assert that the two are complementary and equally necessary for different purposes. It is quite a different thing to employ one to the exclusion of the other. This is to accept the half as the whole and avoid the aspect so central to science—concern for establishing priorities among variables in concrete situations.

Fourthly, the preference of system analysts for symmetrical relationships has led to selective emphasis on congruence, mutuality, complementarity, and a kind of organic balance.[12] The influence of the biological model with its implied symmetry of the organism is a pervasive feature of the structural-functional approach, even though it is more implicit than explicit. The "imperatives of compatibility" subtly underscore the same point. Likewise, stability in the system is supported by a balance of reciprocally, interlocking structures, and this balance is one of symmetry. Finally, the balance needed for system maintenance is one in which eufunctions must outweigh dysfunctions. In a different, but related, way, this again accentuates symmetrical relationships. It has become apparent, however, that such considerations are one-sided because they neglect the dialectical contradictions within and between the functional characteristics of structures. Not only may some functional requirements contradict others, but even a single structure may have contradictory functional requirements. Some of these contradictory functional requirements can engender antagonistic processes that actually uphold the system. As Simmel said so long ago, "Contradiction and conflict not only precede unity but are operative in it at every moment of its existence" (Simmel, 1955, 13). It is this insight that has led Lewis Coser to his more elaborate analysis of the multiple forms of conflict that are functional for social systems in different ways (Coser, 1956). The notion of social system, then, must incorporate more explicitly than the functionalists have indicated, equally necessary but contradictory requirements for its very maintenance, requirements that call for conflict as integral rather than residual features of system. If this dialectical dimension is added to the more symmetrical schemes of Parsons or Levy, a more flexible and tractable view of systems becomes possible. An attempt to incorporate this broader view has been made by van den Berghe (1963) and given empirical application independently by Williams in his analysis of American society. For instance Williams, in the following passage, shows the relevance of a dialectic interpretation quite explicitly, viz., "without these relatively fluid, criss-crossing allegiances it seems highly probable that conflict would be increased, assuming that class differentiation would not diminish. American society is simply riddled with cleavages. The remarkable phenomenon is the extent to which the various differences 'cancel out'—are non-cumulative in their incidence" (Williams, 1951, 531).

However, recognition of the dialectic and its importance must not be misinterpreted. Two important errors can arise from hasty inference and they must be disposed of. One mistake is to assume that since it is possible to find *some* contradictory requirements in a dialectical relation, that *all* must be so. As Sjoberg points out, it would be pressing the issue too far to conclude that all social systems are wracked by contradictions. What we apparently have here is a principle of limited relevance. If and when it is applied, it should be demonstrated. As he concludes, some structures are undoubtedly complementary rather than contradictory,

(Sjoberg, *op. cit.*, 205) though, following out his logic, these too should be demonstrated. However, to see the dialectic every- where is to engage in what Gurvitch calls "dialectical fetichism" (Gurvitch, 1962, 207). A second and related error, though one less likely to appear, is to assume that because some conflicts are functional, all must be so. It is hardly necessary to point out that certain forms of conflict, especially those arising from deep structural cleavages in the social system, may eventually disrupt and destroy the whole. Thus there are conflicts which are not functional in any sense of the word. The chief value of the dialectic is to make us dissatisfied with an easy answer to this problem. We shall return to an appraisal of the dialectical ap- proach at the end of the next section where the power-conflict theory will occupy the center of attention.

Perspective on People: Power-Conflict Theory

In sociological analysis a crucial distinction must be made between the realm of ends and the realm of means; the latter constitutes the realistic features of society that Lockwood has designated as the substratum. The curious fact encountered here is that those who begin with the realistic approach often abandon system analy- sis entirely. Apart from Marx who is exceptional in this regard, we find practically every other representative of this viewpoint either avoiding or postponing all considerations of system in- definitely. It is worth exploring the reason for this state of affairs in order to see the main outline of our major problem of investi- gation throughout these pages, i.e., the integration of ethnic groups into societies as a whole. In the previous chapter we tacitly accepted the realistic approach at a common-sense level and found that it led us to consider the nature of systems. Now we must follow out in more detail the implications of a power-conflict analysis to see where it leads. In doing so, we come upon an essen- tial difference that distinguishes each view from the other.

Those who direct their attention to the analysis of scarce means in society begin with individuals and groups rather than with society as a whole. The entire tenor of investigation is from part to whole rather than from whole to part. Don Martindale speaks of this as the "atomistic" rather than the "holistic" approach, though "atomistic" has overtones of isolated entities that seem a bit extreme (Martindale, 1964, xv). Gerhard Lenski uses a suggestive metaphor to denote the difference, viz., "where functionalists see human societies as social systems, conflict theorists see them as stages on which struggles for power and privilege take place" (Lenski, 1966, 17). To put it another way, the approach through the "substratum" postpones all consideration of system during the earlier stages of analysis (often in later stages as well) to center on individuals, groups, and associations confronting each other in temporal encounters. Societies as wholes emerge as by-products from these interactions, reflecting the crosscurrents of impulses, desires, and interests that precipitate the multiple encounters discovered empirically. Plurality is the starting point, and sometimes it is the last word. For purposes of the present discussion we shall refer to this form of analysis as power-conflict theory as distinguished from system analysis.

Power-conflict theory begins with an initial advantage over system analysis since it appeals to the facts of familiar, everyday observation, tracing out their relations by gradual and easy stages, often avoiding the baffling complications encountered in the contrasting view. Beginning with the immediate experience of limited social encounters, the power-conflict theory stresses the obvious fact of inequality in most interactions, i.e., that what one has, the other wants, or what one wants, the other has. Confrontations like these are unavoidable, and each of the two parties will focus on these items because they are either crucial to survival or the self-esteem of either one. What divides the two contenders is the inherent scarcity of means. The attempt to control these means leads directly to open or concealed conflict in which the exertion of power[13] is needed to attain the goal. Such encounters occur at all levels of society and between all sorts of concrete groupings like nations, political parties, regional associations, ethnic groups, labor vs. management, rural vs. urban sectors, and the like. These many centers of interest are constantly clashing and thereby engendering new structures that contain and regularize such conflicts without actually eliminating them. Authority structures are, however, of quite variable duration, and while some endure longer than others, all are marked by instability as the incessant pounding of human interaction inevitably changes relationships: subordinates weaken or strengthen their position, while conversely superordinates superimpose their might and alternately withdraw it. So all structures have the "seeds of their own decay" and the total process is, in Gurvitch's words, "the structuration and destructuration of types" (Gurvitch, 1955, 37). This, in a word, is the nature of social change. Structure becomes a way station, a temporary halt between opposing forces of modally unequal power.

Since power-conflict theory is many-sided and has taken many forms in the views of its exponents, we limit this brief review to but a few salient features. Four issues stand out and we now turn to them without in any way dismissing the importance of others: (1) notions of human nature; (2) views of egalitarianism; (3) relations of structures to incipient systems; and (4) the dialectic. In summary of these issues, we shall lean heavily on Gerhard Lenski's exposition.[14]

Since the French Enlightenment power-conflict theory has until quite recently taken an optimistic view of man. Political radicals who have espoused such views have held that man was fundamentally good but was corrupted by human institutions, particularly the state. A strong anarchic strain in this radicalism revealed itself in Marx's utopian view of the future when the state would wither away and the classless society would release man's full potentialities which could then be freely actualized. In recent times, however, Lenski's version of the power-conflict theory has not only denied that the optimistic view has any inherent connection with an emphasis on power and conflict, but has insisted that it is incompatible with the scientific evidence. In a long and cogent discussion, Lenski tries to show that the view of human nature forced upon us by modern psychology and derivative notions highlights man's egoism and the overwhelming weight of his self-interests in social interaction. Not only is the human infant self-centered to an extreme degree, but in later life the individual accepts social pressures to conform or cooperate only insofar as these serve to satisfy or maximize his own desires and interests.[15]

Lenski acknowledges that traces of altruism are also present from time to time but that they appear most clearly at inter-personal levels of greatest involvement like primary groups. However, as social circles widen more and more, this other-regarding motive becomes weaker and weaker, often merging with "partisan self-sacrifice" or "partisan group interests" replacing individual egoism with group egoism at intermediate and societal levels. This is summed up in his second postulate about human nature, i.e., "when men are confronted with important decisions where they are obliged to choose between their own, or their group's interests and the interests of others, they nearly always choose the former" (Lenski, 1966, Chap. 2, esp. 30). Not only does Lenski insist that this notion of human nature is strongly grounded empirically, but he implicitly suggests that it is far more consonant with conflict theory than the optimistic view that stemmed from the Enlightenment. He is therefore reinforcing pre-Enlightenment' views like those of Machiavelli and Hobbes. In fact his second postulate is only one step removed from Hobbes' "war of all against all" and seems to agree with it in basic essentials.

As another and somewhat different supporting argument for this view of human nature, Lenski urges us to consider that the highest priority among man's interests is that of survival itself. Exceptions to this are minor (martyrdom, etc.) just as altruistic actions are a minor fraction of the total behavior of men. And if survival is truly the primary interest of man in all seasons and climes, "then it follows that the ability to take life is the most effective form of power . . . Hence force stands in the same relationship to other forms of power as trumps to the other suits in the game of bridge, and those who can exercise the greatest force are like those who can control trumps" (*Ibid.*, 37, 50). From such a view of human nature it then becomes possible to make inferences about the way that human motives operate, since it gives a clear notion of priorities. It is only fair to add that there are other forms of power, less extreme and yet often highly effective; these Lenski also recognizes. To follow out the figure, one does not always require trumps in order to win a game, and it is not unknown to win on some other basis. However, it is important for Lenski's theory that, at the widest social level, involving total societies, force is always a major component, not only "the foundation of political sovereignty, it is also the foundation of the distributive system in every society where there is a surplus to be divided" (*Ibid.*, 51).

A second issue is the relationship of egalitarianism to power-conflict analysis. It is interesting to observe a certain convergence at this point in the views of the power-conflict exponents and the system analysts. As already noted in the previous chapter, one of the latter theorists, Marion Levy, insists on the ubiquitous character of hierarchy in every aspect of the social system. In this respect the power-conflict theorists are in full accord; it follows from their central principles that social structures are the product of social constraint, i.e., are authority structures with upper and lower echelons.[16] The major difference in the two schemes is not so much in their empirical observations since both envisage the same phenomena, but in the way such hierarchies are interpreted. For the system analysts hierarchies are necessary because they are functional to the preservation of the system which could not be maintained without clearly superior management and coordination by those qualified to carry out these responsibilities. On the other hand, the power-conflict theorists are more likely to stress compulsion or fraud as endemic among upper authorities, and the way the latter impose their will on the lower echelons who then are regarded as victims, for one reason or another unable to defend themselves from the encroachments of the powerful.[17]

Thus the logical tendencies of system theory, at least among functionalists like Parsons and Levy, appear to support conservatism, while those of power-conflict theory seem to gravitate toward radicalism. I say "seem to" because, in the present historical era, conflict theorists from Marx to Mills have taken radical positions that overtly or covertly criticize the legitimacy of authority as it actually exists. However, there is reason to believe that this perspective is a historical artifact and not an inherent feature of conflict theory. Ideologically the latter can ally itself either with those in command or those in subjection, as the example of social Darwinists who favored the former demonstrates. It is only when mixed with the explosive potential of egalitarianism that conflict theory becomes ideologically wedded to the fate of the masses, and since this is a contingent factor, not in any way demanded by the theory, it is a good subject for study by the sociology of knowledge.

We cannot pursue this fascinating by-path here except to say that again the difference seems traceable to the Enlightenment whose egalitarian notions were seized upon by some writers and definitely rejected by others.[18] In any case, as Lenski points out, "If the major egalitarian movements of the eighteenth century were directed at the destruction of *legal* inequality, those of the nineteenth and twentieth centuries have been aimed at eradication of *economic* inequality" (Lenski, *op. cit.*, 11). But further digressions are unnecessary. The main point to emphasize is that the tenets of system analysis often lead to conservatism since the superior qualifications of those in command positions deserve to be recognized[19] but in the case of power-conflict theory, a choice for superordinates is no more required than one for subordinates. Only when merged with egalitarianism is the latter alternative preferred.

A third issue of importance is the relationship of structures to systems. Again if we take Lenski as our prime example, we find him saying that "both structure and dynamics are abstractions from the same reality" as a general principle; yet his whole thesis stresses the primacy of change powered by the drives of egoistic individuals and groups that clash in the encounter of divergent interests. Ultimately, he declares, it is "processes which give rise to structures" (*Ibid.*, 43, 73, 35ff). There is, however, a complicating factor. Oriented as Lenski is to the critical importance of surplus economic goods, he maintains that societies without an economic surplus are pressured toward forms of equal distribution that reflect their condition; consequently, societies with the simplest technologies and little or no surplus will distribute their economic goods on the basis of need (*Ibid.*, 46). This is, of course, a concession to the functionalists whose emphasis on the primacy of needs for total social systems is a strong one, even though they may discard the term itself for a more suitable one like "necessary conditions of existence" (Radcliffe-Brown, 1952, 178). Yet the concession is minor in view of Lenski's main interest which is to explain the forms of distribution in more advanced societies; for them, he contends that distribution is increasingly a function of power rather than need (Lenski, *op. cit.*, 46). It is when he turns his attention to such advanced societies that he gives his main account of structural elements. Among societies

above the subsistence level there are more clearly outlined structures, notably that of class which he defines broadly as "an aggregation of persons in a society who stand in a similar position
with respect to some form of power, privilege, or prestige" (*Ibid.*,
304, 309). In all such complex societies, however, the lower
classes provide surplus goods and services for those with greater
power and privilege in the upper classes, so here Lenski drops the
use of "need" as an explanatory principle, thus parting company
with the functionalists. Nevertheless he admits—even insists—that
in the long run it has only been because of the exploitation and ex-
propriation of the surplus by upper classes that the arts and in-
ventions making for the amenities of life have been secured (*Ibid.*,
64n–65).

If power is the main basis of human organization in most societies, the question then arises: what is the relationship of power
structures to a total society or total system? Lenski replies that
the concept of system employed by the functionalists has been
an effective tool chiefly as a criticism of individualism or psychological reductionism, but that in a positive sense it is less
satisfactory because it employs categories on an all-or-none basis
rather than as variables. When we actually examine societies
empirically, we find that:

> systems vary greatly in the degree of the interdependence and
> integration of their parts. The constituent parts of human so-
> cieties enjoy a measure of independence and autonomy which
> far exceeds that of the parts of most biological organisms or
> mechanical systems . . . Second, there is no such thing as a per-
> fect human social system in which the actions of the parts are
> completely subordinated to the needs of the whole. (*Ibid.*, 34)

Lenski concludes that social scientists would do better to postulate
the existence of all human organizations as *imperfect systems* and
explore the nature of their variations empirically without an
a priori model of perfect interdependence, either as a starting
point, or as a limit to their investigations. (*Ibid.*)

From this point on Lenski drops the term system from his
vocabulary except as a heuristic device for describing two structural forms: the class system and the distributive system. Class, as
already defined, is a smaller structural unit but since it may rest
on variable or multiple forms of power, each of these forms may

define its appropriate class system. So "a class system may be said to be a hierarchy of classes ranked in terms of some simple criterion . . . each class system in a society contains within it all the members of that society. Thus every member of American society holds simultaneous membership in some class within the occupational, property, racial-ethnic, educational, age, and sexual class system" (*Ibid.*, 70–80). The distributive system is then the totality of class systems in any given society and resembles a pattern of "wheels within wheels" (*Ibid.*, 84). Throughout the entire discussion, Lenski gives explicit attention to the interrelations of these systems in their singular interlocking but without much attempt at generalization beyond saying that the complexities of these systems are a function of the level of technology (*Ibid.*, 84). Societies as wholes are not analyzed as systems, though each society has a single distributive system.

This brings us finally to our fourth issue: the employment of the dialectic in power-conflict theory. In his analysis, Lenski recognizes at the outset that it is necessary to give a definite place to each of the opposing principles of need and power to account for the characteristics of distributive systems in societies as wholes (*Ibid.*, 44), but as already noted, he slights the concept of need except for primitive societies without a surplus, focusing his main attention on the operation of power and privilege in advanced societies where he no longer feels the necessity of appealing to need. Indeed he makes it quite clear that for him, the concept of need is rather commonplace, and quite unworthy of extended analysis. Thus he comments, "Of the two principles which govern the distributive process, need and power, the first is relatively simple and poses few problems of great importance or difficulty" (*Ibid.*, 50). This is in marked contrast with a functionalist like Malinowski whose elaborate analysis of basic needs, derived needs, and their relation to cultural systems requires several chapters to render it intelligible (Malinowski, 1944, 85–131). It would therefore be fair to say that the basic dialectic of need and power receives nothing more than formal recognition by Lenski; in actual practice he ignores the principle of need after his opening chapters.

Only at one other point does Lenski make explicit, if minor use of a dialectical interpretation. In this case he declares:

If one is fond of paradox and irony, one might go further and argue that cooperation itself is one of the basic sources of conflict in human life. If men were a solitary species, with each individual living apart from all the rest except for mating, as is the case with certain animals, there would be far less conflict among men. If each produced only for himself and there were no division of labor and exchange of goods, one of the major sources of human strife would be eliminated. By contrast, when men join forces in a cooperative enterprise, whether it be a family or a total society, both the opportunity and the motivation for conflict are greatly increased. This is an aspect of the human scene which most conservative theorists have neglected" (*Ibid.*, 28).

This statement, whatever its more general importance, has chiefly a polemical value; it enables Lenski to "turn the tables" on the functionalists by showing that on the latter's own principles, it is necessary to give conflict a more prominent place than they have accorded it. But Lenski does not go beyond this, and in his later exposition he disregards dialectical analysis. In fact, an examination of the conflict theorists as a whole (with the exception again, of Marx) shows little if any attention to the dialectic. This is especially noticeable in Ralf Dahrendorf who generally ignores it in his major work, *Class and Conflict in Industrial Society;* he only adds it as a kind of afterthought in a later lecture where he speaks fleetingly of the "dialectics of power and resistance" without further specification (Dahrendorf, 1966, 31). Is it significant that Marx[20] is the one prominent conflict theorist who gives the dialectic major attention and at the same time stresses systemic characteristics (the interlocking structures of productive relations and property relations)? If it is true, as Lenski himself affirms, that conflict theory is modally antisystemic (*Ibid.*, 33) and it is also true, as noted above, that it usually plays down the dialectic, and if Marx is an exception to both rules, his example could either be interpreted as unrepresentative and mistaken, or a sign that there is more than a chance connection between systemic theory and dialectical thought. The latter is surely an intriguing hint. While neither Parsons nor Levy leans toward dialectical analysis, their present prominence as leading functionalists obscures the quite explicit use of the dialectic by another system analyst of major importance, namely, Sorokin.[21] The position that we shall take is that dialectical analysis has no essential incompatibility with either power-conflict theory or system theory since it crosscuts both in its own unique fashion. It is time now to examine this issue more closely.

The Dialectic—Its Limited Meaning

What is the central meaning of the dialectic, and what is its value for the social scientist (excluding at the moment its use in philosophy or the natural sciences)? The common elements in the sociological notion of dialectic are well stated by Gurvitch (1962, 24–26) and may be put briefly as follows, with some modifications:

1. The dialectic is a way of observing social wholes in movement or change, involving both the recognition and representation of wholes in movement and constituent parts in movement. This point of view refuses to dissolve unities into multiplicities or multiplicities into unities, insisting on the contribution of both to the ongoing process or movement (though not necessarily to the same degree).
2. The dialectic, preoccupied as it is with movement and change, also focuses attention on interpenetrations. For this reason it is not wholly satisfied with the categories of formal logic which would make interpenetration impossible. (For example, Freud's notion of ambivalence juxtaposes two logical entities that belong apart rather than together. Numerous other examples of the same kind occur in concrete social life.)
3. The dialectic viewpoint regards all forms of stability or structure in social life as problematic and not fixed.
4. The dialectic perspective involves the recognition, and attempts to portray, many types of duality that appear in continually changing social wholes, from complementarity and mutual implication to ambiguity, ambivalence, and polarization. Thus some types of duality involve oppositions and conflicts while others do not. As change continues, some types of duality are transformed into others under special conditions. One of the

tasks of social research is to seek out these conditions and specify them in particular cases.

Turning to the second part of our question, we again ask: What is the value of the dialectic for the social scientist? The reply is that there are a number of values which reinforce each other. A dialectical viewpoint keeps the observer constantly face to face with the concreteness of social situations with their fluid complexities, and at the same time corrects the one-sidedness of narrow explanations. Recognizing the indefinite (if not infinite) multiplicity of social phenomena in the process of change, the dialectic also keeps in focus the amplitude of perspectives taken by social actors, and the thresholds of awareness imposed both by these perspectives and the circles of ignorance due to their limited knowledge or awareness. In this primordial state which is the "human condition," it would be surprising if the inherent demands for decision, cognitive or practical (both separate and conjoined) did not set up singular chains of consequences whose outcome (relative again) did not have *both* predictable and unforeseen elements. The dialectic is a way of taking these basic conditions into account—perpetually rather than spasmodically. The dialectic is therefore a *way* of knowing suitable to continual social change, although in itself it explains nothing. It only leads us up to the door of explanation, and after we have entered the portals by way of causal explanation (however provisional), the dialectic lingers long enough to raise new questions that lead to further doors *ad infinitum*. As viewed here the dialectic is not used ideologically to bolster any particular position; in fact it is a weapon that can be used against all ideologies, an empirical sort of probing that asks whether unsuspected dualities are lurking in our answers—sometimes leading to affirmative, sometimes to negative replies.

Thus the dialectic is not *a priori* in the sense that it enables us to know the answers in advance—too many of these distortions of its meaning are strewn through the history of philosophy, particularly in accompaniment of mysticism or absolutism in such figures as Plotinus, Dionysus the Areopagite, Augustine, Pascal, Fichte, Hegel, and others (Gurvitch, *op. cit.*, 31–95). The dialectic about which we are speaking asks questions but does not give answers, opposing its solvent to the freezing of systems; at the same time it retains flexibility in the recognition of provisional systems, and then presses on with renewed questions about their implications, both singular and general. In the social sciences, the dialectic combats dogmatism on the one hand and skepticism on the other. In observing social wholes, the dialectic sensitizes the investigator to the twin potentialities of beneficent and dangerous tendencies of rigidity on the one hand, and fluidity or spontaneity on the other. It raises questions about the supposed harmony of primary groups, for example, and alerts the observer to the perpetual schisms that are so common there. In the analysis of temporal changes, the dialectic probes into the fluctuations of intensity that occur, directing attention to cumulative effects that at times culminate in abysmal cleavages and violent conflicts. There are countless other features of this protean orientation but perhaps these are sufficient to establish its value. Suffice it to say that the major sociologists in the classic tradition have made use of the dialectical orientation in one form or another, wittingly or unwittingly.

System Analysis and Power-Conflict Theory as Dialectically Related Perspectives on Ethnic Relations

By this time the attentive reader is doubtless beginning to wonder what the relevance of these theoretical issues is to the study of ethnic group relations. While no easy answer to this question can be given, it is imperative to make the attempt. At this stage of the discussion I can suggest only the barest outline of the resolution this query can receive and leave it to the rest of the volume to round out the story.

In the first place a comparative study requires a view of ethnic groups in a macrosociological perspective, i.e., in their relation to total societies. In observing these relations it is fruitful to become aware of the two major theoretical interpretations of total societies given by the system analysts and the power-conflict theorists. In this all-too-brief review of the two perspectives

I have tried to present them in ways that would be useful for the purposes of comparative study. Parsons and Levy are singled out as the most significant contemporary representatives of system analysis, and Lenski is designated as the chief exponent of power-conflict theory with Dahrendorf as a subordinate figure. Applying system analysis to comparative ethnic relations actually centers attention on the functions the ethnic group performs for the entire system, viewing the ethnic group itself as a subsystem gradually fitted into the entire society by a series of adaptive adjustments regulated by the norms and values of its institutions that eventually become internalized by members of the ethnic groups involved. On the other hand, from the standpoint of power-conflict theory one can view each ethnic group as being in an embattled position, fighting for its life, its identity, or its prestige, subject to perpetual constraints that threaten its survival, its freedom, or its life chances in a precarious world. All of the discussion so far has suggested that I am not fully committed to either view. Actually, neither perspective can exclude the other without unwarranted dogmatism. This holds true both at the global level of total societies as well as in the more limited spheres of ethnic groups and their interactions with dominant groups. In the broader perspective Robin Williams' proposition states explicitly what most sociologists would now accept with very little argument, i.e., "all interacting human populations show both coerced and voluntary conformity" (Williams, 1966, 718). In like manner another functionalist concludes that "opposition, i.e., organised and regulated antagonism, is, of course, an essential feature of every social system" (Radcliffe-Brown, 1952, 181n).

But the problem is also an empirical one. It is important to search out, by inductive inquiry, observation and analysis, the meanings of such propositions as Williams and Radcliffe-Brown have advanced, then to apprehend their meaning by seeing the specific properties of the facts to which our two different theories apply. And perhaps no field of inquiry is better fitted to exemplify the dual relevance of such ostensibly clashing theories than the sphere of ethnic relations.

To illustrate: the expansion of European peoples to other parts of the globe from the fifteenth to the nineteenth centuries was a succession of conquests overpowering innumerable "native" peoples by coercion. To a number of Western Hemisphere countries with such a historical past came millions of immigrants in the nineteenth and twentieth centuries; yet in this latter invasion, strife and violence were exceptional rather than the rule. To anticipate later discussion in the present volume: here are two contrasting social situations, conquest and migration, where quite opposite forms of social interaction ensue. Stanley Lieberson refers to the former as "migrant superordination" and the latter as "migrant subordination," asserting that warfare is common in the first case, while the absence of long-term conflict characterizes the second (Lieberson, 1961).

A simple way of resolving these situational differences is to divide and rule, i.e., apply the power-conflict theory in those instances where it is pertinent, and do the same for system analysis in another set of situations amenable to *its* form of explanation. This mode of operation may be called *mechanical allocation*. It has the general support in Dahrendorf's suggestion that the uprising of East German workers in 1953 has a suitable explanation in "coercion theory," while the addition of a personnel manager's role to bureaucratic organization in modern industry is better interpreted by "integration theory" (Dahrendorf, 1959, 161–2). Theoreticians may smile at the apparent simple-mindedness of this approach and yet mechanical allocation is definitely a step forward. By allocating disparate theories to alternate sectors of the research field, it is certainly preferable to a theoretical monopoly on one side or the other. Monopoly in this case would bring with it either one or the other of two fateful consequences: (1) procrustean dogmatism stretching a theory beyond its clearly relevant application by rigid retention of categories regardless of their fitness; or (2) selective attention to problems and situations that the theory explains quite creditably, and ignoring all others. It is reassuring to reflect that social scientists in the main have opted for the second error rather than the first; at least the second alternative leaves the way open to fill in the areas left incomplete, while the first will accept any distortion so long as it supports the *a priori* assumptions. Thus the lapse of *omission* is less damaging than the positive offense of *commission;* though Dahrendorf formally recognizes mechanical allocation as an advance on selective attention—criticizing Parsons for the latter—his own elaborate exposition of conflict theory eventually turns out to be fully as one-sided in its way as the Parsonian is in the opposite way.

The field of ethnic relations lends itself so readily to power-conflict analysis that it runs the same risk of selective attention. On the face of it, as already noted, the relationship between subordinate ethnic groups and dominant groups in any society is a power relationship that gives the superordinates the chance to use sanctions on those below them with little fear of successful retaliation. It is possible to set up a macrosociological theory which makes the sole independent variable a set of power relations; these can then be assumed to have explanatory validity in accounting for the modes of action on the part of subordinates and superordinates vis-à-vis each other. I have already amplified and enlarged such a view in an earlier article where the implications of this type of theory are developed in some detail (Schermerhorn, 1964). Only after repeated unsuccessful attempts to apply this interpretation universally to ethnic relations throughout the world have I been driven to the conclusion that the framework is insufficient. It would require another volume to spell out all the reasons for this in detail—a task for another quite different and separate analysis—but at least it is possible to indicate briefly here and now the central reason for shifting to a more dialectical view in which system analysis assumes correlative importance.

As much as any one influence, the writings of Max Gluckman on conflict have been crucially important. What comes through clearly from his analysis is that conflict interactions between groups of unequal power *engender* integrative bonds that have system characteristics. They are not something superadded but an inherent feature of the process of change. Gluckman's portrayal of colonial conquest in South Africa, for example, has so many overtones reminiscent of parallel movements throughout the world, that it furnishes a kind of paradigm for them. He shows quite clearly that mutuality even appears at times when social conflict would seem to destroy it. In initial stages, the encounter as he pictures it, is highly ambiguous with numerous attempts (and successes) at finding reciprocal interests.

For example, when the British penetrated South Africa at first, they found Shaka, a Zulu king, who had established an empire of conquest over many adjacent tribes. As British traders opened up commerce with the Zulus, some traders became regular visitors to Shaka's court and soon were favored personages there. As a mark of royal favor, Shaka made them his "chiefs" at Port Natal and incorporated them into his political system. Soon the Boers entered from the west, and when Shaka's brothers fought over the succession, one brother formed a coalition with the Dutch to oust the other. Later the British and Dutch came into opposition, but when Zulu tribes massacred the Boer trekkers, the British formed an alliance with the Dutch against the Zulu. Then as the British continued to extend their domains by force, many tribes, formerly conquered by Shaka, rallied to the British and, quite unsought, claimed protection from the latter. Eventually the Swazi called upon the British to stop Zulu attacks on the former, and another coalition came into existence. Thus a historical period that was, from one point of view, a series of intermittent conflicts, was also, from the opposite point of view, a period in which mutual interests found frequent, if temporary, stable points of reference. Alliances and coalitions changed rapidly, each of them constituting a temporary social system bringing order with it for the time being; when that order was threatened, a new order was quickly formed to prevent utter chaos and anarchy.

Gluckman then states the significance of these processes in the shape of a principle: "when the members of two societies come into relationship with one another, they quickly establish regularized relations, and the form of these relations may be shaped by internal conflicts in either society" (Gluckman, 1955, 143).[22] It is also true that the vicissitudes of these shifting temporary systems in South Africa proved unsatisfactory and partial, so they were finally superseded by the *pax Britannica*. While this was obviously established by the superior force of British arms, it was also facilitated by the fact that it "seemed a blessing to many Zulu" and "while that rule put an end to certain things which the Zulu valued, it satisfied other Zulu interests, both general and particular" (*Ibid.*, 145). The fluctuations of such temporary alliances were also a feature of British colonials in their relations with American Indians at an earlier date, complicated by the presence of the French in North America, as it was by the Dutch in South Africa (McLeod, 1928).

Such forms of order also appear after the intermittent hostilities of initial conquest. System unities bind men together in functional bonds even when the more permanent rule is harsh and oppressive. With the passage of time, institutional links then bring a web of interdependencies that even the most unprivileged hesitate to break. We have already noted such relationships in the money economy of South Africa and its accompanying industrial organization. Such institutional bonds contain conflicts in ways not fully explained by the constraints of police or military personnel.

Thailand offers another and quite different example of the way that conflict and system linkages go hand in hand. There the Chinese community is only about ten per cent of the total population; intermittent conflict between Thai and Chinese is endemic. Much of this stems from the fact that the Chinese are outsiders, on the one hand (immigrants or of immigrant descent), or that they have captured the lion's share of commerce in Thailand's economy, on the other hand. As political regimes change, varieties of legislation are introduced with the Chinese as targets—now restricting immigration, now sharply limiting the privileges of citizenship, now putting differential regulations on the granting of licenses to Chinese for commercial purposes. The intense rivalry for shares of the market that exists among entrepreneurs in both communities, exacerbated by the special privileges that Thai legislation grants to members of its own group, has eventually precipitated a mechanism to regulate the discord and keep it within bounds. This regulatory mechanism is covert, clandestine, and noninstitutional. It embraces ties of mutual advantage between economic leaders of the Chinese group and political figures of upper or lower status among the Thais. In the top echelons, the more wealthy Chinese not only have close connections with Thai rulers and the nobility, but often bring the latter into business partnership. In this way the Thai upper classes could win financial gain without expending much effort while the Chinese managers win protection. In the lower echelons the initiative often comes from Thai police or minor government officials who offer "protection" to Chinese for a fee whenever taxes are collected, licenses granted, or discriminatory regulations are to be enforced. This amounts to a kind of surplus tax on Chinese commerce with a faint touch of blackmail (G. W. Skinner, 1958).

The upshot of these arrangements is that instrumental ties linking members of both ethnic groups together at many status levels are informal bonds that hold an over-arching system together by exploiting the very conflict that would otherwise be highly explosive. "To a very considerable extent Chinese blood and Chinese money are now so deeply embedded in the metabolism of leadership, bureaucracy and industry in Bangkok that the city could scarcely survive without it" (Hunter, 1966, 47).

FIGURE 2.   RARE LINKAGE OF INTEGRATION AND CONFLICT

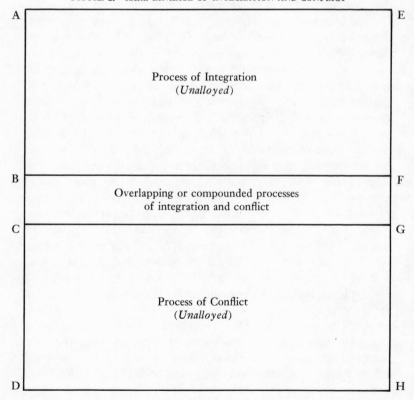

A ... E

Process of Integration
(*Unalloyed*)

B ... F

Overlapping or compounded processes
of integration and conflict

C ... G

Process of Conflict
(*Unalloyed*)

D ... H

Three tentative conclusions result from observations like these: (1) system analysis obtrudes itself even at points where conflict theory is genuinely pertinent; (2) certain types of ethnic relations draw on sets of assumptions from *both* theories as heuristic guidelines for interpretive purposes; (3) "mechanical allocation" as described above is insufficient; it is a definitely limited principle that must be superseded by positing some kind of dialectical relationship even though the latter has *differential theoretical relevance* in one society as compared with another.

In the area of ethnic relations it is possible to bring out this duality by denying that integration is inevitably harmonious, or conflict necessarily disruptive. *There are times when integration can only occur in and through conflict, and conversely, other*

FIGURE 3.　MODAL LINKAGE OF INTEGRATION AND CONFLICT

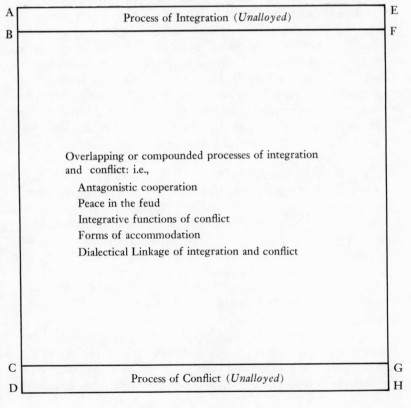

A

Process of Integration (*Unalloyed*)

E

B

F

Overlapping or compounded processes of integration and conflict: i.e.,

    Antagonistic cooperation

    Peace in the feud

    Integrative functions of conflict

    Forms of accommodation

    Dialectical Linkage of integration and conflict

C

Process of Conflict (*Unalloyed*)

G

D

H

*times when conflict is necessary to reach a new order of integra-
tion.* Whether relationships like these are modal or whether they
are exceptional is a matter to be determined empirically; the
probability surely is that on a comparative basis there will be
widespread societal differentials on these parameters. It may
turn out that the usual common-sense assumption is correct, i.e.,
modally, integration stands for a set of harmonious relations
while conflict represents destructive ones—and the exceptions
will be negligible. This conclusion is symbolized by Figure 2.
However, the result could be quite the opposite with integration
usually compounded with conflict and likewise conflict displaying
integrative features. This possibility is shown in Figure 3. For
purposes of the figure, integration will be regarded as a process whereby units or elements of a society are brought into a
more active and coordinated compliance with the ongoing activities and objectives of the total society at any given period of
time. On the other hand, conflict will be thought of as a process
whereby units or elements of a society develop incompatible
differences of objective, either with parallel units, authoritative
units, or both, resulting in social clashes, disputes, tensions, or
competitions at any given period of time. The two variables of
integration and conflict are linked in ways to be determined by
empirical observation; in general these ways are intermediate between the extremes portrayed in figures 2 and 3. Figure 2 and
Figure 3 are constructs of two hypothesized extremes in the relations between integration and conflict. Sections ABFE and
CDHG in both figures represent what are termed the unalloyed
operations of integration or conflict as opposites in pure form. In
this pure form they are hypothesized to stand in inverse relation
to each other, such that the increase of either process necessarily
entails a decrease of the other. BCGF in both figures represents
a condition governed by an opposite hypothesis, i.e., one in
which the two processes of integration and conflict no longer
negate each other but combine in different ways and proportions.

Thus each figure has two types of sectors, each governed by
an opposite assumption. If the first assumption (the common-
sense belief that conflict and integration are pure opposites with
a negative relation to each other)—if this assumption governed

all social phenomena we would have to redraw the figures and leave out the area BCGF, substituting a movable line in place of the area. This line could move upward as far as AE or downward as far as DH on the naive view that a society may be totally integrated and harmonious, or so ridden with conflict that it is wholly self-destructive. If the second assumption governs all social phenomena, conflict and integration are *always* processes of combination, never found separately; thus the area BCGF would expand until it was coextensive with ADHE. In general this was the view of C. H. Cooley who once remarked, "The more one thinks of it, the more he will see that conflict and cooperation are not separable things, but phases of one process which always involves something of both" (Cooley, 1918, 19).

It seems more realistic to keep both of these assumptions but deny each of them unlimited relevance. This is precisely the function of a dialectical probe which regards an absolute dichotomy between integration and conflict as naivete, and a complete linkage at every point as hopelessly speculative in addition to being unprovable without perfect induction. The position accepted here is that both the common sense assumption and the assumption of *linked paired variables* have limited or circumscribed validity. And while we have labeled sector BCGF as dialectical linkage, this does not imply a synthesis in the manner of vulgar Hegelianism or vulgar Marxism—a synthesis that would cancel out the differences in an overriding unity, for sector BCGF represents an area in perpetual movement, either upward toward integration or downward toward conflict. Synthesis too often symbolizes permanent resolutions of opposing forces. It is this permanence which the social scientist must deny.

· NOTES ·

1. Cf. Ruth Glass, "Insiders-Outsiders, The Position of Minorities," 1964 (see *References* for full citation).
2. From author's student notes in Whitehead's Harvard course, "Cosmologies, Ancient and Modern," 1930–31.
3. This gross distinction between exploitative interests and principled interests is suggested by Lasswell and Kaplan's somewhat different, but parallel distinction between expediency interests and principled interests

which they apply to groups without explicit attention to hierarchical relations as is done here (Lasswell and Kaplan, 1950, 42–45).

4. Van den Berghe also emphasizes *structural* conflicts as factors underlying *group* conflicts by showing that the political system with its apartheid, and the economic system with its interdependence, are pulling in opposite directions.

5. This reference is to those structural-functionalists who give system models a definite priority. It therefore includes Talcott Parsons (together with his followers) and Marion J. Levy, but it excludes Robert K. Merton.

6. For an example of a complete list cf. Levy, 1952, 151.

7. An anthropologist like Radcliffe-Brown recognized this clearly when he commented, "The concept of function applied to human societies is based on an analogy between social life and organic life" (Radcliffe-Brown, 1952, 178).

8. This statement is more applicable to Parsons than to Levy whose relatively foreboding outlook on the "modernizing societies" displays a lively sense of their persistent imbalance (Cf. Levy, 1966, Part I, Chap. 2; Part III, Chaps. 2–4).

9. Williams' further comments also deserve attention, i.e., "A particularly agonizing question here, as in most other portions of the conceptual scheme, is whether the Parsonian scheme can generate real predictions or is restricted to *post facto* classifications and interpretations . . . And further, if predictions can be derived, whether the data required are too massive and fugitive to justify the effort required, i.e., would we have to know 'too much' in advance in order to make predictions?" (Williams, 1961, 95)

10. In later writings, Parsons modifies his position somewhat. For example, after introducing his four modes of action, i.e., the adaptive, goal-attainment, pattern-maintenance, and integration, he declares that "The concrete structure of systems of action cannot be derived from this functional paradigm alone. For each unit is subjected to exigencies other than those defined by its primary goal interest. These exigencies, as traced through hierarchies of system-subsystem relationships, will 'deflect' the structural patterning of the system in certain respects from the 'pure type' of a functionally differentiated system" (Parsons, 1959, 642). Here he definitely points to elements over and beyond cultural norms. Yet the reference is almost fugitive for the implications are passed over. In like vein he tells us in the same article that he is introducing the term *potency* to mean "relative capacity to influence the outcome of a process" and that "The rank order of units with respect to this capacity is, so far as it is legitimized by values, the *stratification* of the system" (*Ibid.*, 639). This statement, on its face, is a tentative move toward convergence with power and conflict theories in contrast with his earlier more exclusively normative emphasis (Parsons, 1953, 92–128). The change, however, is piecemeal and fragmentary, an isolated element that departs from the main tenor of his works.

I regard these clues, however, as an encouraging sign of Parsons' movement toward an intermediate position and away from what appears to be a premature closure in his earlier theoretical stance.

11. Lemert directs a parallel criticism against Cooley's organicism when applied to social disorganization. "Central to the Cooley formulation is the notion of social life as an organic process involving the mutual interaction of society and the individual . . . Cooley was averse to assigning to any particular factors a fixed causative value in so far as social phenomena were concerned. Thus, in his scheme of thinking, economic factors held no more importance than political, religious, or any other factors. Rather it was the way in which various factors worked together mutually influencing one another, which impressed Cooley . . . The concept that the factors of human behavior have no fixed value but instead derive their value solely from dynamic interplay is an extreme of thinking which creates serious methodological problems. It sets us off on what amounts to a directionless inquiry into sociocultural phenomena, ending in a morass of dog-in-the-manger variables, none of which have priority" (Lemert, 1951, 9, 11).

12. We have not, however, attributed "equilibrium" notions to system analysts, since Parsons avoids the use of this terminology almost entirely, while Levy quite explicitly distrusts it (Cf. Levy, 1966, 222).

13. We have defined power elsewhere as "the processural relation between two parties modally characterized by (1) asymmetrical influence, in which a perceptible probability of decision rests in one of the two parties, even over the resistance of the other party; and (2) the predominance of negative sanctions (threatened or actual) as a feature of behavior in the dominant party" (R. A. Schermerhorn, 1961, 12).

14. We select Lenski as the best representative of power-conflict theory in its modern form partly because of his greater emphasis on induction in theory construction, partly because of his definite, though sometimes wavering orientation to societies as wholes, a feature much less evident in Dahrendorf. Classifying Lenski as a power-conflict theorist may seem unwarranted in view of his specific assertion that he is attempting a new synthesis of opposing theories. However, what he actually gives is an attempted synthesis of *radical* and *conservative* views but not of functionalism and power-conflict theory. Thus, while he recognizes that both *need* and *power* are the two complementary principles accounting for the distribution of goods, *need* has no explanatory value for his analysis except in primitive societies, and his own view is that *need* is a simple idea hardly worth analyzing (Lenski, *op. cit.*, 44, 46, 47, 50). Another straw in the wind is his rejection of Coser as a true conflict theorist because his view of Coser's work is: "its basic purpose is to show how conflict serves society as a whole. In short, the underlying theoretical orientation is functionalist" (*Ibid.*, 16n, 23). Ergo Lenski appears to reject it.

15. The corresponding principle for functionalism would appear in a residual category like "inadequate" or "imperfect" socialization.

16. Full working out of these principles appears in greatest detail throughout Dahrendorf's major work (1959).

17. It is worth noting that at least one system analyst we have not mentioned has combined these two views by merging superior power with superior intelligence and sagacity (Pareto, 1935). However, such a combination has not been made by later functionalists, much less enlarged or elaborated. This in spite of the fact that a system analyst like Parsons explicitly acknowledges indebtedness to Pareto (Parsons, 1951, vii).

18. There are interesting hints for exploring this subject in Lenski's work where he finds roots of the egalitarian ideal in the early Judaic-Christian tradition and the Buddhist-Jainist attempts to reform Hinduism. However, in his account, both trends become submerged in later epochs reappearing in later Christianity but with no mention of its renascence in Asian religion (Lenski, 1966, 3–5, 7–10). Lenski then summarizes briefly the secularization of this ideal in the West from Locke and Rousseau to Marx (*Ibid.*, 10–11).

19. This does not mean, of course, that system analysts cannot be attracted to egalitarianism or even espouse it, but only that in doing so they seem to be violating their own principles. It is otherwise with the power-conflict theorists who have more "freedom of maneuver" within their own scheme.

20. Historically, Marx's penchant for system is sometimes traced to Hegelian influence, though this is in part conjecture. However, it is worth noting that his dialectical scheme was based on a vulgar simplification of Hegelian philosophy that he imbibed in his youth, a version which took the progression of thesis-antithesis-synthesis too literally since Hegel himself seldom employed this pattern of thought. For an account of this and other over-simplifications of Hegel and how they became common currency in the intellectual market of ideas, cf. Gustav Mueller, (1958). I am indebted to Martha Sachs for calling attention to this important source.

21. Cf. the interchange between Louis Schneider and P. A. Sorokin in Zollschan and Hirsch (1964). On the other hand, Levy speaks of the dialectic with a certain dignified irritation and says that it is "usually presented with a tone of authority as an undefined argument quencher" (Levy, 1966, 215n).

22. As van den Berghe succinctly puts it, "the whole complex history of Boer-British-African conflict in South Africa can . . . be reduced to a few simplifying generalizations such as that, when the Africans constituted a threat, the Boer and the British stopped fighting each other and ganged up on the Africans. Conversely, when the Africans were subjugated, Boer-British conflicts became reactivated. The situation is one of "two-tiered" conflict (white-non-white and Boer-British) in which two levels of conflict stand in rough inverse relation to each other" (Personal communication). One must add, in view of our main point here, that conflicts at one level or tier precipitated coalitions and reciprocal bonds at the other level.

· REFERENCES ·

Cooley, C. H., *Social Process*. New York: Scribners, 1918.

Coser, Lewis, *The Functions of Social Conflict*. New York: Free Press, 1956.

Dahrendorf, Rolf, *Class and Class Conflict in Industrial Society*. Stanford: Stanford University Press, 1959.

———, *In Praise of Thrasymachus*. The Henry Failing Distinguished Lecture, University of Oregon, Eugene, Oregon, April 25, 1966.

Davis, Kingsley, *Human Society*. New York: Macmillan, 1949.

Fortes, Meyer, "The Structure of Unilineal Descent Groups," *American Anthropologist*, 55 (1953), 17–41.

Gerth, H. H., and C. Wright Mills, "Introduction," in H. H. Gerth and C. Wright Mills, (eds.) *From Max Weber, Essays in Sociology*. New York: Oxford University Press, 1946.

Glass, Ruth, "Insiders-Outsiders, The Position of Minorities," in *Transactions of the Fifth World Congress of Sociology, 1962*. International Sociological Association, 111, 1964, 141–55.

Gluckman, Max, *Custom and Conflict in Africa*. Oxford: Basil Blackwell, 1955.

Gurvitch, Georges, *Dialectique et Sociologie*. Paris: Flammarion, 1962.

Horton, John, "Commentary and Debate. Order and Conflict Theories of Social Problems and Competing Ideologies," *American Journal of Sociology*, 71 (1966), 701–13.

Hunter, Guy, *South-East Asia, Race, Culture and Nation*. New York and London: Oxford University Press, 1966.

Kahn, E. J., Jr., "A Reporter at Large. South Africa. III. The Peace of the Grave," *The New Yorker*, Feb. 10, 1968, pp. 36ff.

Lasswell, Harold D. and Abraham Kaplan, *Power and Society: A Framework for Political Inquiry*. New Haven: Yale University Press, 1950.

Lemert, E. M., *Social Pathology*. New York: McGraw Hill, 1951.

Lenski, Gerhard, *Power and Privilege. A Theory of Social Stratification*. New York: McGraw-Hill, 1966.

Levy, Marion J., *The Structure of Society*. Princeton: Princeton University Press, 1952.

———, *Modernization and the Structure of Societies*. 2 vols. Princeton: Princeton University Press, 1966.

Lieberson, Stanley, "A Societal Theory of Race and Ethnic Relations," *American Sociological Review*, 26 (1961), 902–10.

Lockwood, David, "Some Remarks on the Social System," *British Journal of Sociology*, 7 (1956), 134–46.

———, "Social Integration and System Integration," in George K. Zollschan and W. Hirsch (eds.), *Explorations in Social Change*. Boston: Houghton Mifflin, 1964.

Malinowski, Bronislaw, *A Scientific Theory of Culture and Other Essays*. Chapel Hill: University of North Carolina Press, 1944.

Martindale, Don, "Introduction," in George K. Zollschan and W. Hirsch (eds.), *Explorations in Social Change*. Boston: Houghton Mifflin, 1964.

McLeod, W. C., *The American Indian Frontier*. New York: Knopf, 1928.

Moore, W. E., *Social Change*. Englewood Cliffs, N. J.: Prentice-Hall, 1963.

Mueller, Gustav, "The Hegel Legend of Thesis-Antithesis-Synthesis," *Journal of the History of Ideas*, XIX (1958), 411–14.

Pareto, Vilfredo, *The Mind and Society*. Andrew Bongiorno and Arthur Livingston (trans.). New York: Harcourt, Brace, 1935.

Parsons, Talcott, *The Social System*. Glencoe, Ill.: Free Press, 1951.

——, "An Approach to Psychological Theory in Terms of the Theory of Action," in Sigmund Koch (ed.), *Psychology: A Study of a Science* III. New York: McGraw-Hill, 1959, 612–711.

——, *Essays in Sociological Theory*. Rev. ed. New York: Free Press, 1954.

——, Robert F. Bales, and Edward A. Shils, *Working Papers in the Theory of Action*. Glencoe, Ill.: Free Press, 1953.

Parsons, Talcott, and E. A. Shils, *Toward a General Theory of Action*. New York: Harper Torchbooks, 1962 (orig. ed., 1951).

Radcliffe-Brown, A. R., *Structure and Function in Primitive Society*. Glencoe, Ill.: Free Press, 1952.

Schermerhorn, R. A.: "Toward a General Theory of Minority Groups," *Phylon*, 25 (1965), 238–46.

Simmel, Georg, *Conflict*, Kurt Wolff (trans.). New York: Free Press, 1955.

Sjoberg, Gideon, "Contradictory Functional Requirements and Social Systems," *Journal of Conflict Resolution*, 4 (1960), 198–208.

Skinner, G. W., *Leadership and Power in the Chinese Community of Thailand*. Ithaca, N.Y.: Cornell University Press, 1958.

van den Berghe, Pierre L., "Dialectic and Functionalism: Toward a Theoretical Synthesis," *American Sociological Review*, 28 (1963), 695–705.

Van der Horst, Sheila, T. L., "The Effects of Industrialisation on Race Relations in South Africa," in Guy Hunter (ed.), *Industrialisation and Race Relations*. London and New York: Oxford University Press, 1965.

Williams, Robin M., Jr., "Some Further Comments on Chronic Controversies," *American Journal of Sociology*, 71 (1966), 717–21.

Wirth, Louis, "The Problem of Minority Groups," in Ralph Linton (ed.), *The Science of Man in the World Crisis*. New York: Columbia University Press, 1945.

Zollschan, George K., and Walter Hirsch (eds.), *Explorations in Social Change*. Boston: Houghton Mifflin, 1964.

2

❦

Some
Unexplored Types
of Integration

If the purpose of studying comparative ethnic relations is to discover the conditions that foster or prevent the integration of ethnic groups into their environing societies (see p. 14), then the effort to explore the import of ethnic integration deserves priority on the agenda. The present chapter briefly examines this issue.

The theoretical overview in the preceding chapter suggests a few preliminary comments. For one thing, the acceptance of system analysis as a set of guidelines does not in any way commit the social scientist to the view that social systems in the real world are wholly self-regulative mechanisms guided by an "invisible hand," or that they involve what Horowitz calls "institutional omnipotence and omniscience." I am inclined to agree with his view (taken, as he asserts, out of early sociological thought from Marx to Simmel) that "society is best understood as a selective and collective response to the needs of social interaction in a nonequilibriated world," (Horowitz, 1962, 178) *provided* that this lack of equilibration is not regarded as absolute but as a relative condition *always present* no matter what system characteristics prevail at the time. This is only to assert with Lenski that all empirical social systems are imperfect systems. A dialectical view of the matter will also add that "all interacting human populations that remain in interaction over a period of time develop normative regularities" (Robin Williams, 1966, 718) *and* system interdependencies. These, too, are not absolute but relative; they are quite as surely present in large-scale interactive relations as in those of lesser scope. Empirically speaking, social systems seem to come into being, develop, intermingle, and become transformed over time (Tiryakian, 1967, 74 ff.).

Integration as a process must be seen in the context of societal systems of a mixed character with their special blend of the fluid with the inexorable. The outlines of societal patterns as wholes will occupy attention in Chapter 5 and subsequent discussion. For the moment, attention is focussed on the definition of integration that has already been set forth in the introduction, i.e., *a process whereby units or elements of a society are brought into an active and coordinated compliance with the ongoing activities and objectives of the dominant group.* There are doubtless more inclusive meanings that could be singled out, but it seems best here to present the lowest common denominator. At this manifest level we strip the problem down to its essentials by focussing attention on authority as the core relation of integration.

Such a definition implies, first of all, that we are dealing with a whole range of continuum of possibilities running the gamut from pure coercion to perfectly legitimated authority. At one end of the continuum the appeal to values is unavailing, so it is replaced by naked force imposing order by terror. At the other end is a fusion of authority with the compliance of total consent. This beneficent extreme (considerably idealized) is described by two prominent authorities in these words:

> To the extent that there is consensus concerning the "places" of the various ethnic groups the system remains stable and cooperation occurs smoothly. Differences in rank are taken for granted: in many cases the dominant group shows neither snobbery nor exclusiveness nor does the minority group show sullenness. Differences in status are accepted quietly and do not prevent cooperation and friendliness among those who must work together . . . People just assume that there are different

kinds of human beings and that it is natural for some to rule
and for others to obey . . . The prevailing orientation is conservative: the traditional ways are believed to be just and de-
cent. As long as all the participants conform to the accepted
norms—doing the things that each person regards as proper—
the system of unequal rewards is perpetuated. A well-established system of stratification, then, is a moral order. (Shibutani
and Kwan, 1965, 261)

Both extremes of this continuum, order by consensus and order
by ruthless coercion are really limiting cases or pure types only
approximated in reality. It is clear that ethnic relations in the
empirical world always involve a mixture or composite of the
two variables—as with other opposites too. As W. E. Moore
says of another case, "such distinctions as ascription-achievement
or consanguine-conjugal, although usually depicted as mutually
exclusive alternatives useful for characterizing differences between
societies or groups, are more accurately viewed as conflicting
principles always present" (Moore, 1963, 67). Likewise, in the
real world of ethnic relations there is a perennial interplay of
reciprocal influences.

Let us return once again to the definition. We have spoken
of integration within an intergroup context as "a process whereby
units or elements of a society are brought into an active and coordinated compliance with the ongoing activities and objectives
of the dominant group." Now we must call attention to the
words, "brought into" and "process." These terms are deliberately
chosen to make it clear that integration is not so much a permanent state as a condition to be constantly rewon. It follows
that we conceive integration as a continuing process rather than
a state of being, relative rather than absolute, situational rather
than all-embracing, corrective rather than self-subsistent, a matter of degree rather than an all-or-none phenomenon, and correlative with conflict rather than a displacement of conflict.

To confirm this relative view of integration, we shall devote
the rest of the present chapter to three major issues that require
analysis before the subject is clarified: (1) integration as a problem of legitimation; (2) integration as a problem of cultural
congruence; and (3) integration as a problem of common or
discrepant goal-definitions for subordinate ethnic groups.[1]

Integration as Legitimation

Beginning with the problem of legitimation, the probability is overwhelming that when two groups with different cultural histories establish contacts that are regular rather than occasional or intermittent, one of the two groups will typically assume dominance over the other. This is based on the assumption that complete equality of power is the least probable condition—a kind of limiting case. Something approaching this limit does take place in the simpler societies. Miss Lindgren gives one illustration in which the nomadic Tungus live adjacent to the Cossack agriculturalists. The Tungus exchange their furs for Cossack food but the two do not compete for land or natural resources, and it does not appear that either attempts to dominate the other. Both economies complement each other and conflict is minimal or absent (E. J. Lindgren, 1938). Likewise in some desert areas of the Near East, Bedouins get their livelihood from the milk and meat of camels; in the dry season they barter camels for articles of food, utensils, weapons, clothing, and tents with oasis dwellers. The symbiotic relationship between the Bedouin and the sedentary peoples causes Kroeber to describe the former as having a "half-culture" (Kroeber, 1948, 276–8).[2] Such exceptional cases, however, do not invalidate the premise that inequality of power is typical, especially for more advanced nation-states which occupy our attention here. In the interchange between the two groups, sooner or later the relation between them takes the form of authority, becoming what Max Weber calls "imperatively coordinated" (Weber, 1947, 153).[3] This authoritative relationship immediately raises the question: How is this authority viewed by the members on both sides? Legitimacy is a variable, not a constant. "Power, especially in diversified or complex societies, may range from legitimate to illegitimate forms" (Schermerhorn, 1961, 36). Questions about conflict or integration are intimately connected with the *degree of legitimacy*. Lewis Coser's comment is especially relevant to this issue when he declares that "Legitimacy is a crucial intervening variable without which it is impossible to predict whether feelings of hostility arising out of an unequal distribution of privileges and rights actually lead to conflict" (Coser, 1956, 37).

As an aid to our analysis let us postulate three positions on the continuum of legitimacy. The power relation may be: (1) legitimate, L; (2) illegitimate, I; or (3) partly legitimate, PL. Applying these three views first to superordinates, then to subordinates, we arrive at a nine-fold table of possibilities like the following (Figure 4). Each cell of the table is designated by two letters: the first letter denotes the view the dominant group takes of the legitimacy of its own power; the second letter represents the subordinates' view of the legitimacy of the dominant's power. Thus in cell 1, the letters LL indicate that both parties to the power relationship view it as legitimate; in cell 6, the dominant group regards the power differential as partly legitimate while the subordinates view it as illegitimate—PL–I. Other cells have appropriate notations in like manner and from here on will be referred to by number for quick comparison.

Even a cursory glance at Figure 4 will make it evident that although it encompasses the *logical* possibilities, it nevertheless contains a number of cells so unlikely that empirical examples are impossible to find. On the face of it, cells 7, 8, and 9 appear to be "empty cells" of this character because it is difficult to imagine cases where a dominant group is convinced that its rule is completely illegitimate. Some writers appear to think that the last stages of British colonial rule preceding the independence of her colonies could be viewed in this way, but Churchill's famous dictum that he did not assume office to preside at the liquidation of the British Empire clearly expressed the views of many compatriots; it seems more likely that relinquishment of power to former colonies like India or Nigeria is better characterized by cell 6 than by cell 9. We may then eliminate cells 7 to 9 as literally empty; and cell 4 is doubtful just because subordinates assign *more* legitimacy to the relation than superordinates—a most improbable if not impossible case. Excluding 4, then, we are left with five clearly viable cells: 1, 2, 3, 5, and 6.

Returning to our theme of integration, cell 1, of course, represents a highly stable form since it is based on consensus of views. In this respect it resembles the ideal type of superordination quoted earlier from Shibutani and Kwan (see pp. 66–67). As indicated

FIGURE 4. PARADIGM OF SOCIAL DOMINATION AND LEGITIMACY PERSPECTIVES

L—L(1)

1. Dominant group regards its power as legitimate.
2. Subordinate group regards power of dominant group as legitimate.

L—PL(2)

1. Dominant group regards its power as legitimate.
2. Subordinate group regards power of dominant group as only partly legitimate.

L—I(3)

1. Dominant group regards its power as legitimate.
2. Subordinate group regards power of dominant group as illegitimate.

PL—L(4)

1. Dominant group regards its power as partly legitimate.
2. Subordinate group regards power of dominant group as legitimate.

PL—PL(5)

1. Dominant group regards its power as partly legitimate.
2. Subordinate group regards power of dominant group as only partly legitimate.

PL—I(6)

1. Dominant group regards its power as partly legitimate.
2. Subordinate group regards power of dominant group as illegitimate.

I—L(7)

1. Dominant group regards its power as illegitimate.
2. Subordinate group regards power of dominant group as legitimate.

I—PL(8)

1. Dominant group regards its power as illegitimate.
2. Subordinate group regards power of dominant group as only partly legitimate.

I—I(9)

1. Dominant group regards its power as illegitimate.
2. Subordinate group regards power of dominant group as illegitimate.

L = Definition of superordination as legitimate
PL = Definition of superordination as partially legitimate
I = Definition of superordination as illegitimate
First letter = self-definition of superordinate

there, however, it is more of a limiting case than an actuality. Perhaps it has been approached in the classical Indian caste system, though that departs considerably from our two-group model advanced above. It is also the conviction of many Southerners in the United States that pervasive consensus was the historic condition of race relations during slavery; but the occasional incidence of slave revolts makes this unlikely even with a few possible approximations to that condition. If we do not eliminate cell 1 entirely it is only because there are cultural rather than structural similarities to it, as will be noted below. Of the other four viable cells, 2, 3, 5, and 6, the only agreement of views between superordinates and subordinates appears in cell 5 which furnishes the next or second most likely form of integration in living societies. In this case, the seeds of compromise appear on both sides, making some form of accommodation possible (perhaps likely?). At any rate, this excursus shows that by using legitimacy as the sole variable, the most likely form of integration is an imperfect type based on reciprocal compromise. However, there is also another case of imperfect integration that is found in cell 2; empirically, this applies with greatest force to Lieberson's migrant subordination; in such cases where the immigrants accept the goal of assimilation, the nisus is toward cell 1 where both parties resemble each other in their views of legitimation. There is a contingency factor here, for if the immigrants resist assimilation, several alternatives open up: cell 5, cell 6, or even cell 3. We shall return to this case in another context below.

While the cells of Figure 4 represent cross sectional situations at a given moment of time, it is possible to portray a longitudinal progression by placing the cells in sequence. Here it is worth noting that in the colonial areas of Africa and Asia later gaining their independence, the sequence is 3–2–6 until dominance is broken. Likewise, race relations between Negro and white in the United States show an overall pattern of 3–5–6 for the nation as a whole, complicated by a subpattern within the Southern states of 3–2–3. In the case of Lieberson's migrant superordination, the common progression is 3–2–5, though at times with a strain toward 6. Conversely, for migrant subordination, the sequence begins with 2 (some strain toward 1 at the outset), moving toward 5 and frequent trends toward 1 again.

Integration as Cultural Congruence

We turn now to the second issue of this chapter, namely, integration as a problem of cultural congruence. Here our assumption is that when the ethos of the subordinates has values common to those in the ethos of the superordinates, integration (coordination of objectives) will be facilitated; when the values are contrasting or contradictory, integration will be obstructed. Thus, as we have pointed out elsewhere, similarities in the ethos of the Czechs and of middle-class Americans led to more rapid integration of the former into American communities than was the case for some other immigrant groups whose ethos diverged more sharply from the American pattern (Schermerhorn, 1949, 316 ff.). Integration, then, has another dimension which it is convenient to call cultural or value congruence. However, in making even gross comparisons on this dimension, we must somehow equate the contexts in terms of the power differentials involved. When we do so, we find that our new paradigm incorporates the patterns already found in Figure 4 but now with a greater range of variations.

In Figure 5 sector A is exemplified by migrant superordination and by slavery, both being characterized by large power differentials and notable cultural incongruity. (In slave groups, cultural differences are admittedly short-lived, but their initial impact is profound.) Internal sequences for A are typically 3–2 or 3–2–3. Migrant subordination fits sector B (large power differentials and relative cultural congruity) with a typical progression of 2–5. If we look for examples of sector C, the status of Chinese in Southeast Asian states is relevant. As noted below, this involves a somewhat different type of migration from the two types singled out by Lieberson. In Malaya and Indonesia we might note an internal sequence of 2–3–2–3. Sector D in which there are small power differentials and cultural congruity is somewhat more difficult to pin-point, but the example of Iraq with dominant urban Sunnis and subordinate rural Shiites appears to fit the case. Here too there appears to be a fluctuating sequence of 2–3–2–3. Sector B has more marked integrative trends, while conflict reaches the extreme of open warfare in A, especially in relatively early stages of contact. It is significant that in both C and D where power differentials are not so pronounced, conflict is endemic and oscillatory, no matter how great or how small the cultural differences.

Racism—A Related Theme

Figure 5 gives rise to an important serendipitous discovery. If we examine it closely, we see that the great bulk of ethnic phenomena traditionally labelled "race relations" occur in sector A, with minor and less important cases in sector C. As Blumer has noted, "With few exceptions, present-day instances of race relations have emerged from a background of ordered association of racial groups within some form of preindustrial society. This is to be noted clearly in the case of colonial societies, agricultural societies operating under slavery, and plantation economies employing imported contract labor" (Blumer, 1965, 226). In nearly all of these examples since the European expansion of the fifteenth and sixteenth centuries, the superordinates were Caucasians of lighter complexion, while subordinates were Africans or Asians of darker hue. In the ideological parsimony that followed, dominants fastened on color as a symbol of both status and cultural difference.This formed the kernel of racism, a complex of ideas that eventually had a luxuriant growth.

In its *minimal* form, racism defined darker peoples as backward or less evolved, different in degree but not in kind from their masters, therefore capable, with training and education, to rise individually from their lowly position to a status of equality with the ruling group. The great mass of the lower races, in this view, remained at an inferior level through no fault of their own but because of the accidents of history which made some men rulers and others slaves or servants. In this minimal form of racism, exogamy was tolerated and for the most part the patina of paternalism softened the harsh realities of power. This tended to be the form of racism among Catholic dominants, as in Latin America, or in the French, Spanish, or Portuguese colonies of Africa.

However, racism takes a *maximal* form where the distinctions between superordinates and subordinates assume an absolute rather than a relative character, one of kind and not of degree. This is a cognitive effort to perpetuate the social realities of command. It becomes a highly reassuring ideology because it convinces dominant members that their ascendancy is no accident of history but is part of the natural (even cosmic) order. The key notion in maximal racism becomes the inherent superiority of peoples with lighter color, together with its obverse, the inherent inferiority of the darker colored. In this view, the rule of the former over the latter is therefore inevitable, not arbitrary. It is but the natural working out of vaguely conceived biological forces that bestow intelligence and moral qualities unevenly on different racial aggregations. The inequalities of social dominion are therefore only an expression of the inequalities of endowment, and from these, there is no appeal. For humanitarian reasons, superior racial members may train or educate the members of inferior races, but, in the view of maximal racists, this can never be wholly successful because members of the darker colored races are believed to have inherent limitations that prevent them from attaining intellectual equality with their masters. As the racists of the dominant group see it, such training may actually be harmful if it leads to illusions of equality or to unbearable conceit that infects others, provoking insubordination and disorder. Needless to say, such notions of unbridgeable gulfs between men of different color spawned an aversion to exogamy which came to be viewed as a kind of biological Gresham's law with bad seed driving out good. In its more extreme forms, maximal racism became the basis for an imposed regime of complete separation and avoidance of personal contact—forms of segregation crystallized in custom or institutionalized in law. This was more frequently the view in predominantly Protestant areas.[4]

Sector C is the context of a special form of racism growing out of *migrant intermediation*, a type of migration neglected by Lieberson (see p. 52). Relevant examples occur in Southeast Asia and the Philippines where Chinese have established themselves as entrepreneurs neither high nor low in the stratification scale, but in intermediate positions (Wiens, 1954). In Africa the intermediates have been Arabs, Syrians, Lebanese, and Indians. Confrontations like these have resulted, not in the vertical racism of unilateral superiority that characterized colonialism or slavery but a *racism of interposition*. Reciprocal separatism is frequent, as is selective dominance where the indigenous typically have political power and traditional prestige while the migrants have marked economic power. Both elites and lower groups display strong prejudice toward intermediates who are politically impotent and subject to many legal restrictions. In times of economic or political crisis, intermediates become scapegoats and not in-

FIGURE 5. PARADIGM REPRESENTING LEGITIMACY DEFINITIONS OF
UNEQUAL POWER DISTRIBUTIONS WHERE CULTURAL VARIATIONS OCCUR

A — Large Power Differentials (Cultural Incongruity):

L–L(1)	L–PL(2)	L–I(3)
PL–L(4)	PL–PL(5)	PL–I(6)
I–L(7)	I–PL(8)	I–I(9)

B — Large Power Differentials (Cultural Congruity):

L–L(1)	L–PL(2)	L–I(3)
PL–L(4)	PL–PL(5)	PL–I(6)
I–L(7)	I–PL(8)	I–I(9)

C — Small Power Differentials (Cultural Incongruity):

L–L(1)	L–PL(2)	L–I(3)
PL–L(4)	PL–PL(5)	PL–I(6)
I–L(7)	I–PL(8)	I–I(9)

D — Small Power Differentials (Cultural Congruity):

L–L(1)	L–PL(2)	L–I(3)
PL–L(4)	PL–PL(5)	PL–I(6)
I–L(7)	I–PL(8)	I–I(9)

frequently the objects of mob attacks. Endogamy is typical on both sides but lacks the unilateral compulsive enforcement found in vertical racism.

What have come to be known as "race relations" therefore seem to be instances of sectors A and C in which easily identifiable physiological features become the symbol of separate status. Such relations form only a part, though a significant part, of ethnic relations as a whole. It is important to insist on this for two reasons. First, the indiscriminate use of the term "race relations" to designate all ethnic relations tends to blur distinctions and somehow give the impression that generalizations about the former apply without modification to the latter, which is like arguing that what is true of the part must be true of the whole. In the second place, even careful narrowing of subject matter to intergroup relations defined by racist attitudes, while it may be theoretically and methodologically justifiable, can (and we would argue, does) become myopic, losing the chance to see race relations as a special case of wider, more inclusive multigroup relations. If our premises are correct, structural and dynamic analysis should discover commonalities in ethnic relations that outweigh the singular features of a special subclass like "race relations."

There is still a residuum of "race" unaccounted for, and in Figure 5 it hovers somewhere between A and B, with cultural congruity more a variable than a constant. We refer to the racial ideology of the Hitler period which was not based primarily on the symbol of physical difference (though scattered attempts were made in this direction). Physical differentiation proved unavailing so compulsory emblems like the wearing of a yellow star furnished identification, or family trees were carefully scrutinized to highlight biological separateness between the *Herrenvolk* and the Jewish minority. In this case the dominant group defined the minority "race" less in terms of inferiority than of taint. The definition spoke of "Jewish blood" that manifested itself in trickery, in craftiness, in machinations of power behind the scenes, in conspiracies. Thus Jews as tricksters could perform quite contradictory feats like gaining control of corporate empires on the one hand, or control of revolutionary movements on the other. In Nazi belief, the hereditary Jewish taint corrupted whatever it touched. Not only did it weaken social solidarity, patriotism and loyalty to the Reich, but in the process of intermarriage with the master race, it produced hybrids who were parasitic creatures of cunning rather than the healthy, virile Aryans whose warlike virtues were regarded as the salvation of Germany.

To call this a case of "race relations" is to accept, however hypothetically, the mythical definition of "race" that in its own unique way informed the whole Nazi ideology. But if we do so, we must also recognize the important differences between that ideology and the more standard forms discussed above. The Hitlerian view of race fastened on psychosocial rather than physiological hereditary features; thus it was eccentric, almost a pseudoracism. Nevertheless it had its roots in a literary-academic tradition whose intellectual history shows a steady movement from Boulainvillers to Gobineau to Houston Stewart Chamberlain[5] and the doctrinal "spinoffs" became vestigal remains in European literature where glib references to the Anglo-Saxon race, the French race, or the Italian race became a part of the common vocabulary.

The Nazi version of race is something of a mutant, easily distinguishable from vertical and interposed forms, even when occasionally confused with them. Hence on a comparative basis we regard it as justifiable to classify it as "residual." This should not prevent the recognition that it proved to be the most deadly form of all, culminating in mass murders without precedent in human history. A final factor of prime significance: only when mixed with supernationalism did residual racism become lethal. In the postwar world, this form of racism has receded to more covert patterns without traceable effects on social action. Hence we shall disregard it from now on as a type of race relations to be reckoned with in our discussion, yet always with the proviso that it has the potential for reappearance under the guise of chauvinism.

Integration and Reciprocal Goal Definition

We turn now to our third crucial (though related) issue, namely, integration as a problem of common or discrepant goal definitions for subordinate ethnic groups. The more we reflect on problems of integration, the more obvious it becomes that reciprocal beliefs about the final goals of their relationship are key factors to be considered in assessing relations between superordinate and subordinate groups. Let us approach this issue first from the viewpoint of the subordinates. As early as 1945, Louis Wirth presented a typology of the different policies adopted by minority groups in response to their clearly unprivileged position. These policies he called assimilationist, pluralist, secessionist, and militant. Briefly, the assimilationist policy seeks to merge the minority members into the wider society by abandoning their own cultural distinctiveness and adopting the superordinates' values and style of life. The pluralist strategy solicits tolerance from the dominant group that will allow the subordinates to retain much of their cultural distinctiveness. The secessionist minority aims to separate or detach itself from the superordinates so as to pursue an independent existence. Finally, the militants, in Wirth's quite limited definition of the term, intend to gain control over the dominants who currently have the ascendancy (Wirth, 1945, 354–63). This four-fold typology is a brilliant analysis of the diverse aims that arise among subordinate ethnic groups in response to varying circumstances, and its implications are still relatively unexplored after an interval of more than twenty years. The discussion that follows is based on the conviction that following out the logic of Wirth's insights, and relating them systematically to each other, will throw additional light on problems of integration and conflict in ethnic relations.

It is first necessary, however, to see the limitations of Wirth's formulations. As is already clear, he limits his observations to the reactions of minority groups while neglecting those of the superordinates. If we are to do justice to the problem, we must give equal attention to the latter as well. As our two preceding paradigms have shown, it is the *interaction* between upper and lower groups that is the object of our investigation and what has to be accounted for. If we limit our attention, as Wirth does, to only one part of the transaction, we cut ourselves off from the other and miss the situation as a whole. So, in addition to what Wirth tells us, we must also know *what dominant groups prefer the subordinates to attain.* Do the superordinates believe that minority groups should assimilate or that they should retain their cultural distinctiveness? Does the view of the dominants agree with or does it contradict the aims of the subordinates in the same society? It seems logical to assume that when these views are congruent, the process of integration is well under way, and when they are incongruent, conflict of an overt or covert variety will appear.

There is another limitation in Wirth's discussion, one which he imposes on himself by asserting: "We are less concerned, however, in this analysis, with racial minorities, than with ethnic minorities . . ." (*op. cit.*, 351). At this point, Wirth's lexicon differs semantically from the one adopted here since he uses "ethnic" as a *differentiating* term, while I employ it as a *generic* term. Wirth's "ethnic" vs. "racial" minorities is, in the language of the present book, "nonracial ethnics" vs. "racial ethnics" (or "racially defined ethnics").[6] But, leaving semantic distinctions behind, Wirth's exposition as a whole was, as he saw it, deliberately restricted to nonracial groups or situations, and in that context, his typology has a "goodness of fit" that can hardly be denied.

To put it bluntly, Wirth was really concerned with problems of acculturation, with borrowing of cultural items, or with appropriating styles of life, in short with broad value differences. At least this is the implication of his first two types: assimilation and pluralism. However, suppose that we apply these two categories to a situation defined by vertical racism—one deliberately excluded from Wirth's own focus; here the superordinates are not so much concerned with the life style of the subordinates, but rather with keeping the latter at a well-defined social distance. In such a case the dominants do not seek either assimilation or pluralism for the subordinates but a form of segregation. When we turn to the subordinates and inquire what their goals may be, the glib answer may be "assimilation"; but not only is this term used in a kind of Pickwickian sense, it is inadequate because it misses a central concern of the subordinates. They desire more than to borrow the life style of the dominants; what they want even more is *access* to the groups, associations, and institutional privileges held by the superordinates, something that goes far beyond "cultural borrowing." The same difficulty arises in applying the term "pluralism" to the orientation of the dominant group as the goal they seek for the subordinates. In its original meaning, and the one employed by Wirth, pluralism denotes tolerance for difference. In a racial encounter, however, the term pluralism in this sense seems out of place.[7] In such a case the orientation of the superordinates is neither tolerant nor permissive; it is rather a rejection and repulsion of subordinates with accompanying denial or exclusion of the lower group from specific areas of social participation. It would make more sense to call this interdiction rather than pluralism.

To clarify this problem it is well to insist on the analytic distinction between *culture* and *social structure*. Culture signifies the ways of action learned through socialization, based on norms and values that serve as guides or standards for that behavior. Social structure, on the other hand, refers to "the set of crystallized social relationships which its (the society's) members have with each other which places them in groups, large or small, permanent or temporary, formally organized or unorganized, and which relates them to the major institutional activities of the society, such as economic and occupational life, religion, marriage and the family, education, government, and recreation" (Gordon, 1964, 30–31). Culture has to do with standards or "designs for living" while social structure refers to the clustering of men in patterned ways which may or may not be regulated by the overarching norms and values. Of course this is not a complete dichotomy but a dialectical relation in which each aspect of the social whole interacts with the other. Values and norms often define the human groupings and institutions that circumscribe man's conduct, while on the other hand, man's actions give rise to new or changed values and standards. Yet it is well at this stage to keep the analytic distinction clear between the two categories in order to see the implications of Wirth's typology. When we examine it more closely, we note a difference between the first two and the last two types quite unremarked by Wirth himself; nevertheless it stands out in bold relief when we keep in mind the distinction between culture and social structure. In his first two types, assimilation and pluralism, the accent is on culture rather than social structure. Not only are the goals and aims thought of as norms to be fulfilled, but the whole analysis in these terms portrays a kind of diffuse relationship between the individual and the social whole, with the behavior patterns of the former caught up by a process of social osmosis from the total society. No intermediaries like associations or institutions receive adequate attention in this picture; they are slurred over. On the other hand, Wirth's third and fourth categories of secession and militancy imply quite definite social structures and can hardly be conceived without explicit changes of groups and institutions in those structures.

In discussing Wirth's omission of vertical racism, I therefore ran into difficulty in applying his *cultural* categories to conditions where *structural* features were more relevant. This is why I found that normative pluralism, which explicitly refers to toleration of cultural differences, seemed irrelevant as an orientation of superordinates in "racial" interaction where structural restraints on social participation are so prominent.

What we really need at this juncture are more inclusive categories than Wirth's, expressing not only the distinction he recognized, but additional ones applicable to vertical racism. This will mean that such categories are broad enough to include both cultural and structural features of the situation. The answer, I believe, is to be found in the paired concepts of centripetal and centrifugal trends in social life.[8] Centripetal tendencies refer both to cultural trends such as acceptance of common values, styles of life, etc., as well as structural features like increased participation in a common set of groups, associations, and institutions. To keep the two aspects analytically distinct, it seems tenable to refer to the first as assimilation, and the second as incorporation.[9] Tentatively, Wirth's "militancy" could be included as an extreme centripetal tendency of the structural variety, since it is really a revolutionary demand that the minority take over authority structures and thus become major social participants rather than minor ones.

Conversely, centrifugal tendencies among subordinate groups are those that foster separation from the dominant group or from societal bonds in one respect or another. Culturally this most frequently means retention and preservation of the group's distinctive traditions in spheres like language, religion, recreation, etc., together with the particularistic values associated with them: Wirth's cultural pluralism. But in order to protect these values, structural requirements are needed, so there are demands for endogamy, separate associations, and even at times a re-stricted range of occupations. *In toto* trends like these may be only mildly centrifugal, calling for autonomy, separation, or federation; if they are more extreme, secessionist policy may clamor for a complete rupture with the larger social system.

In this reinterpretation of Wirth's analysis, it becomes possible to say that nearly every ethnic group, as part of a total society, will modally adopt either a centripetal or a centrifugal direction.[10] However, we must be careful not to identify integration with centripetal tendencies, or conflict with centrifugal. On the contrary, *integration involves satisfaction of the ethnic group's modal tendency, whether it be centripetal or centrifugal.* Some groups are better satisfied by autonomy, others by assimilation or full incorporation. Incidental confirmation of this apparently paradoxical conclusion comes from an Indian sociologist writing about his compatriots in Great Britain. First he tells about the integration of the Parsees into the fabric of Indian life, namely that "they have preserved their religion, culture, and their social identity. In contact with others, they act as a caste. By a paradox they have become integrated through voluntary segregation." He then adds, significantly, "This is the form of integration which Indian immigrants in the United Kingdom desire" (Desai, 1963, Preface).

So far we have focussed on the stance of the subordinates; what of the superordinates? Do they want the former to emulate them and/or associate more freely with them? If so, then the dominants look with favor on the subordinates becoming more alike, or joining in forms of cooperative action—a definitely centripetal preference. If, on the other hand, superordinates accede to the subordinates' demand for partial autonomy, or even insist that subordinates keep a well-defined social distance, this preference for some form of separation would be a centrifugal policy.

If we look at *both upper and lower groups in reciprocal interaction* rather than at subordinates alone (which is Wirth's approach) the implications seem clear: where both groups favor a centripetal policy, this will facilitate integration. I am saying still more: even if both groups favor a centrifugal policy, this too will foster integration, though of a different kind (such as "live and let live"). Integration is therefore promoted by *agreement* or *congruence* of views on centripetal aims or centrifugal aims. On the other hand, when there is disagreement or discrepancy of views so that superordinates favor centripetal policy while subordinates desire centrifugal (or vice versa) there will be endemic or intermittent conflict. This is illustrated in Figure 6 below. It must be emphasized that the terms "centrifugal" and "centripetal" when applied to subordinates, refer to views about *themselves*, but when applied to superordinates, refer to their views about *others* in the encounter.

A brief illustration for each cell will clarify the central features of Figure 6. Cell A can be symbolized by the example of Czech immigrants to the United States mentioned above. Not only did the Czechs have values similar to those of middle-class Americans but, on the whole, Czechs who migrated to the United States were quite eager to assimilate (centripetal goal); at the same time (early in the twentieth century) the great American public wanted the Czechs (and indeed all European immigrants)

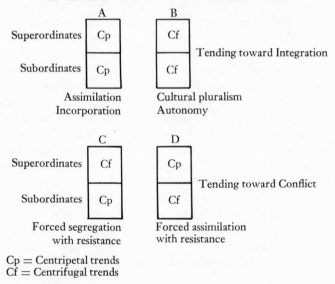

FIGURE 6. CONGRUENT AND INCONGRUENT ORIENTATIONS
TOWARD CENTRIPETAL AND CENTRIFUGAL TRENDS OF SUBORDINATES
AS VIEWED BY THEMSELVES AND SUPERORDINATES

A
Superordinates Cp
Subordinates Cp
Assimilation
Incorporation

B
Cf
Cf
Tending toward Integration
Cultural pluralism
Autonomy

C
Superordinates Cf
Subordinates Cp
Forced segregation
with resistance

D
Cp
Cf
Tending toward Conflict
Forced assimilation
with resistance

Cp = Centripetal trends
Cf = Centrifugal trends

to assimilate. Since the two orientations matched each other, this resulted in cultural integration. One of the few examples of cell B would be the French-speaking people of Switzerland who want sufficient autonomy and separateness to preserve their own language and customs (centrifugal aim); the superordinates in this case are constituted by the German-speaking people who form a majority but grant toleration and autonomy to French cantons (and Italian ones as well). Since both sides agree on a limited separation (live and let live—a centrifugal tendency) this represents another form of integration—looser and at least partly disengaged.

The situation of the Negro in the United States furnishes an instance of cell C, though the case is not as clear-cut as it once appeared. The superordinate whites with their ideology of racism have enforced at least a minimal amount of segregation on the subordinates (a centrifugal goal) while the minority on the whole opposed this by demanding desegregation and unrestricted participation in the greater society (centripetal aim). The resulting conflict led to new demands for separatism among minority leaders so today the simplicity of the C model is lost with subordinates taking a bi-modal stance; considerable disagreement on goals is now occurring, the moderates retaining centripetal aims (desegregation, integration) while a more radical element is pushing for centrifugal objectives (black nationalism, a separate community). Cell C therefore symbolizes the situation of the American Negro in the 1950s more than it does for the 1960s when minority goals are in process of transition.[11] In cell C, however, the ideology of the whites (superordinates) remains the same and is definitely centrifugal. Finally, the simplest cases of cell D are found in a number of European states like Prussia, Russia, or Hungary who, during the first decades of the twentieth century, tried to eradicate the language and culture of nationality groups within their domain (centripetal tendency) while the subordinates fought fiercely for their cultural autonomy (centrifugal aim). Conflicts resulting from these policy disagreements have had a long history on the Continent and are now emerging as a typical form of internal struggle in many new states of Asia and Africa.

There are several advantages to this paradigm. *First*, it focuses attention on both superordinates and subordinates simultaneously, making it possible to grasp the nature of their reciprocal interaction as a coeval event. This stereoscopic view enables us to transcend a one-sided preoccupation with the minority's reaction, considered by itself. *Secondly*, the paradigm is at a higher level of generality than Wirth's four-fold typology which, one suspects, is not exhaustive. The categories "centripetal" and "centrifugal," however, are sufficiently comprehensive so that they can encompass Wirth's distinctions along with others that could be added in the future. As later discussion will show, centripetal aims may involve not only ideological elements but forms of action in which both cultural and structural patterns coexist: emulation, cooperation, association, mutual participation—the forms are many. The same is true of centrifugal trends where some separation, detachment, exclusion, segmentalization, or withdrawal may take place. A *third* advantage of the paradigm is that it specifies social contexts that can serve as intervening variables in answer to the scientific query, "under what conditions?" So whatever independent variables are singled out for study (Cf. Introduction, p. 15 for the ones selected in the present volume) they will have different consequences in context A, context B, context C, or context D of the paradigm. These consequences will appear in different (often mixed) patterns of integration and conflict, which can then be specified and identified as dependent variables. The trends hypothesized on the right of the paradigm toward integration for A and B, or toward conflict for C and D, are based on what knowledge we have of these situations from the research literature, and as gross distinctions have a face validity that can serve as a springboard for future testing.

Summary

In this chapter I have focused attention exclusively on a two-group model with one group superordinate and the other subordinate. For convenience this can be designated as the *intergroup arena*. Following up the clue developed in the second chapter that conflict and integration are interrelated processes, I then explored three features of the intergroup arena in search of conditions associated with integration. The first probe examined variations in the legitimation of authority, a kind of single-factor analysis. The second turned attention to value differences, not as a separate variable, but in combination with power differentials and the alternatives in legitimation already reviewed—a multiple factor analysis. Finally came a scrutiny of the long range goals of interaction like assimilation, pluralism, etc. to determine the agreement or disagreement between superordinates and subordinates on the choice of policy for the latter. By collapsing these goals into more inclusive centrifugal and centripetal trends, I postulated a two-factor analysis of the problem. In each of the three cases, the logical possibilities were explored by means of a paradigm to give a panoramic view that would obviate the necessity of interminable inductive repetition. Each paradigm is at the same time a codified guide, a key to underlying assumptions, and a catalyst for perceiving new implications of political or ideological significance (Merton, 1957, 55), in the lively expectation of serendipity.

The exploration of legitimation problems by means of Figure 4 resulted in the following conclusions:

1. Agreement on complete legitimacy of the dominant group for the intergroup arena is least likely to occur on a mutual basis for both parties (Cell 1).
2. Assuming that concordance on views of legitimacy between both parties is a form of integration, the next most likely approximation is to be found in cell 5 where subordinates and superordinates both regard dominance as only partly legitimate. At least this is true on a purely logical analysis.
3. However we also found that the second most likely form of integration would occur (again, logically speaking) where the dominant group regards its power as legitimate and subordinates regard it as partly legitimate (Cell 2). Empirically speaking, however, we found this to be a strong contender for integration. As Lieberson's migrant subordination belongs here (the modal immigration case), we note that when this leads to assimilation, it veers toward cell 1 where consonance of views is very close. The chances for integration, while still contingent, seem relatively high in this case also.

4. Integration is least likely in Cell 3 where disagreement on legitimacy is sharpest.

5. By placing the cells in sequence, we develop a conceptual shorthand for picturing diachronic progression and typical recurrences like colonial occupations, slavery, and the sequences of migrant super- and subordination can be given conceptual clarity.

These recurrences furnish first approximations for historical study which will be given attention in Chapter 4.

In the second place, I attempted a multiple-factor analysis, keeping legitimacy alternatives the same while adding power differentials and value disparities, as in Figure 5. In this case the conclusions were: (1) integrative processes seem to be more successful where there is a large power differential combined with cultural congruity (sector B) rather than a situation with small power differentials and cultural congruity (sector D). However, though integration is the modal form for sector B, this probability vanishes when the "racial" feature is added. (2) One of the unsuspected by-products of Figure 5 is a set of inferences about race relations. Historically, vertical racism is associated with sector A where large power differentials are combined with cultural incongruities (particularly in early stages of contact); again, what I have designated as interposed racism is rather associated with small power differentials and cultural incongruity as in sector C. Finally, (3) residual racism is tentatively associated with sector B where the Nazi case stands out as a major exception to integration in that sector. We may advance the cautious hypothesis that the factor of racism heightens the probability of conflict and violence, even under conditions where integration seems likely on other grounds.

Third and finally came an analysis of the intergroup arena in terms of beliefs held by subordinates and superordinates about the final goal of their relationship. This analysis took Wirth's four-fold typology of minority goals as the starting point, noting that his first two, assimilation and pluralism, have primarily cultural dimensions, while his second pair, secession and militancy, implied structural features. By reconceptualizing his distinctions into two tendencies with both cultural and structural dimensions, it was possible to arrive at two opposed directional trends: centripetal and centrifugal. This eventuated in a four-cell paradigm, Figure 6, where one could view problems of integration and conflict in a quite different perspective. In this case it appeared (1) that agreement on long-range policy was associated with integration, both for cell A (agreement on centripetal aims) and cell B (agreement on centrifugal aims). It is worth remarking here that, unlike the previous analysis, empirical examples of A could well be more numerous than those of B, at least if we are thinking in cultural rather than structural terms. (2) In the case of cell C, where the subordinates prefer centripetal aims while the superordinates prefer centrifugal ones, we have the typical conflict of vertical racism. Conversely, the trend toward conflict in cell D, in which subordinates prefer centrifugal aims while superordinates want them to follow centripetal ones, has been connected with nationality and linguistic conflicts in Europe; it is also exemplified by the resistance to new forms of national unity by tribal, regional, and religious groups in Africa and Asia in recent years.[12]

In these three attempts to analyze the intergroup arena, we see repeatedly that the intervening variable (how the two parties view each other) proves crucial in distinguishing processes of integration and conflict. This, of course, is the main contention of the symbolic interactionists who maintain that the definition of the situation is really what determines its outcome. It is impossible to deny the weight of this argument which, incidentally, is strengthened by the analysis in the present chapter. However, in the chapters that follow, it will eventually become clear that social perception, while necessary as one determinant of conflict and integration, is nevertheless insufficient, per se, to account for them.

· NOTES ·

1. A suggestive four-fold typology of integration: cultural, normative, communicative, and functional is also advanced by Werner Landecker (1951). Although partial to his categories at first (Schermerhorn, 1967) I have tentatively concluded that his scheme is more relevant for global societal analysis than for assessment of ethnic relationships within a total system.

2. I am indebted to Professor W. E. Lawrence for calling attention to this example.

3. While Weber refers to an "imperatively coordinated group" in the singular, our application of the principle to intergroup situations flows naturally from the intrinsic discrepancy of power in both cases. For an elaboration of Weber's thesis, cf. Dahrendorf, 1959, 167 ff.

4. This capsule version cannot, of course, do justice to the many twists and turns that led up to maximal racism in Protestant hands. At the outset it differed little from the Catholic version though it was modified in time when it became a more extreme position. For some of the historical developments and their outcome, cf. D. B. Davis, 1966, 38 ff.; and 197 ff.; Toynbee, 1934, I, 211–12; Tannenbaum, 1947; S. M. Elkins, 1959; Mintz, 1961; Sio, 1965.

5. For an account of this progression, cf. Snyder, 1939. For greater detail on the Nazi ideology of race, the following are also important: Voegelin, 1933; Hertz, 1928; Arendt, 1951.

6. As the discussion in Chapter 4 will emphasize, this is more than a matter of "social definition" per se because it involves structural separation.

7. Though Ronald Taft once applied the term in precisely this way, *viz.*, "An even more subtle position exists where the majority group demands monistic assimilation from some groups and caste-like pluralism from another, e.g., the Southern States of the U.S.A." (Taft, 1953, 47). Presumably this refers to whites and Negroes in the American South. However, in a later article, Taft indicates a somewhat different position more consonant with the one adopted here (Taft, 1963, 279). At any rate, the term "pluralism" does not appear again with this unique connotation. (For the several meanings of the term "pluralism" see Chapter 4, pp. 122–24).

8. For the use of paired concepts in social research, cf. Bendix and Berger, 1959, 98.

9. This involves rejection of Gordon's term "structural assimilation" (Gordon, *op. cit.*, 71) as an unsuitable "meaning stretch." I believe that "structural incorporation" is preferable since it keeps the analytic boundaries clear.

10. While unanimity on goals is probably rare, modal trends are usually discernible. Occasional divergence from the mode may appear, however. For example, dissension in the ranks can produce an ambivalent reaction resulting in weak predominance of one mode or oscillation between modes (like the present controversy over "integration" vs. "black nationalism" among American Negroes). Or, paradoxical mixed modes may emerge where the employment of one policy may be used to implement its opposite, i.e., an entire group might seek greater political participation in order to protect its own autonomy; or it might threaten to secede in order to gain more participation.

11. Centrifugal goals have never been wholly absent among Negroes in the United States and have even been dominant during limited histori-

cal periods. Cf. Harold Cruse, 1967, and Lewis Killian, 1968, esp. the foreword by Peter I. Rose in the latter.

12. Simpson and Yinger catalogue the same phenomena from the standpoint of superordinates. Their "types of majority policy" include forced and permitted assimilation, pluralism, legal protection of minorities, peaceful and forced population transfer, continued subjugation, and extermination (Simpson and Yinger, 3rd ed., 1965, 20–25). In our Figure 6 above, all of these policies except assimilation would be categorized as centrifugal.

· REFERENCES ·

Arendt, Hannah, *The Origins of Totalitarianism.* New York: Harcourt, Brace & World, 1951.

Bendix, Reinhard, and Bennett Berger, "Images of Society and Problems of Concept Formation in Sociology," in Llewellyn Gross (ed.) *Symposium on Sociological Theory.* New York: Harper & Row, 1959.

Blumer, Herbert, "Industrialisation and Race Relations," in Guy Hunter (ed.), *Industrialisation and Race Relations, A Symposium.* New York: Oxford University Press, 1965.

Coser, Lewis, *The Functions of Social Conflict.* New York: Free Press, 1956.

Cruse, Harold, *The Crisis of the Negro Intellectual.* New York: Morrow, 1967.

Dahrendorf, Rolf, *Class and Class Conflict in Industrial Society.* Stanford: Stanford University Press, 1959.

Davis, David Brion, *The Problem of Slavery in Western Culture.* Ithaca, N.Y.: Cornell University Press, 1966.

Desai, Rashmi, *Indian Immigrants in Britain.* London: Oxford University Press, 1963.

Elkins, Stanley M., *Slavery: A Problem in American Institutional and Intellectual Life.* Chicago: University of Chicago Press, 1959.

Gordon, Milton M., *Assimilation in American Life.* New York: Oxford University Press, 1964.

Hertz, Friedrich O., *Race and Civilization.* New York: Macmillan, 1928.

Horowitz, Irving Louis, "Consensus, Conflict and Cooperation: A Sociological Inventory," *Social Forces,* 41 (1962), 177–88.

Killian, Lewis, *The Impossible Revolution?* New York: Random House, 1968.

Kroeber, A. L., *Anthropology.* New York: Harcourt, Brace, 1948.

Landecker, Werner S., "Types of Integration and their Measurement," *American Journal of Sociology,* 56 (January 1951), 323–40.

Lindgren, E. J., "An Example of Culture Contact without Conflict," *American Anthropologist,* 40 (1938), 605–21.

Merton, Robert K., *Social Theory and Social Structure.* Rev. ed. New York: Free Press, 1957.

Mintz, Sidney, Review of Slavery by Stanley M. Elkins, in *American Anthropologist,* 63 (1961), 579–87.

Moore, W. E., *Social Change.* Englewood Cliffs, N.J.: Prentice-Hall, 1963.

Redfield, Robert, *The Little Community Peasant Society and Culture.* Chicago: University of Chicago Press, 1963.

Schermerhorn, R. A., *These Our People, Minorities in American Culture.* Boston: Heath, 1949.

——, *Society and Power.* New York: Random House, 1961.

——, "Polarity in the Approach to Comparative Research in Ethnic Relations," *Sociology and Social Research,* 51 No. 2 (January 1967), 235–40.

Shibutani, Tamotsu, and Kiam M. Kwan, *Ethnic Stratification, A Comparative Approach.* New York: Macmillan, 1965.

Simpson, G. E., and J. M. Yinger, *Racial and Cultural Minorities.* 3rd ed. New York: Harper & Row, 1965.

Sio, Arnold A., "Interpretations of Slavery: The Slave Status in the Americas," *Comparative Studies in Society and History,* 7 (1965), 289–308.

Snyder, Louis L., *Race, A History of Modern Ethnic Theories.* New York: Longmans, Green, 1939.

Taft, Ronald, "The Shared Frame of Reference Concept Applied to the Assimilation of Immigrants," *Human Relations* 6 (1953), 45–55.

——, "Assimilation Orientation of Immigrants and Australians," *Human Relations* 16 (1963), 279–93.

Tannenbaum, Frank, *Slave and Citizen: The Negro in the Americas.* New York: Knopf, 1947.

Tiryakian, Edward A., "A Model of Societal Change and its Lead Indicators," in Samuel Z. Klausner (ed.), *The Study of Total Societies.* New York: Anchor Books, 1967.

Toynbee, Arnold, *The Study of History.* New York: Oxford University Press, 1934, Vol. I.

Voegelin, Erich, *Die Rassenides in der Geistesgeschichte.* Berlin: Junker und Dunnhaupt, 1933.

Weber, Max, *The Theory of Social and Economic Organization,* A. M. Henderson and Talcott Parsons (trans.). Glencoe, Ill.: Free Press, 1947.

Wiens, Harold J., *China's March Toward the Tropics.* Hamden, Conn.: Shoe String Press, 1954.

Williams, Robin M., Jr., "Some Further Comments on Chronic Controversies," *American Journal of Sociology,* 71 (1966), 717–21.

Wirth, Louis, "The Problem of Minority Groups," in Ralph Linton (ed.), *The Science of Man in the World Crisis.* New York: Columbia University Press, 1945.

3

§

Intergroup Sequences and Racism

Comparative investigation reveals ethnic groups ranging all the way from those well integrated by consensual norms uniting them with dominant or majority groups to those whose conflicts with superordinates are deep and seemingly irreconcilable. With dialectical caution, I shall not assume that the former lack the seeds of hostility nor the latter their mutual dependencies. However, in making comparisons, one cannot remain at the level of generality that has occupied our attention so far in this volume. From here on the focus will be on societies rather than society, to the inductive examination of the differences and similarities of the intergroup arena in one society after another. Furthermore it is now time to explore the reasons for these differences or similarities with our dual theoretical orientation as a general guide alerting the investigator to both pitfalls and opportunities. At first it can do no more than that, for in the inductive task, comparisons are needed that can be made at middle or lower levels of generality.

If, to take a crass example, a researcher set out to find parallels that apply equally well to Tamils in Ceylon, Muslims in Lebanon, Ibo in Nigeria, or Kazakhs in the Soviet Union, it would hardly be of much help to explore the comparative relevance of system analysis vs. the power-conflict model. The result would be an impressionistic taxonomy and not much more. It certainly would fail to uncover causal explanations and would come under justifiable criticism because it did not take into account the comparability, either of the ethnic groups themselves, or of the societies encompassing them. During the initial stage of exploration the immediate requirement is a more limited set of categories, what McKinney refers to as typologies of "problem relevance" that can serve as a bridge between more general theory and empirical observation (McKinney, 1966, 83, 96). The most obvious typology at the outset would be a classification of ethnic groups in terms of clearly defined characteristics. Unfortunately this does not seem feasible in the present state of our knowledge and, if the present mode of analysis is correct, such a categorization should be the culmination rather than the beginning of research. What seems more promising initially is an inquiry into the recurrent ways in which ethnic groups attain their status as subsections of larger societies.

This means that historical reality must receive primary attention. Harsanyi has made a cogent case for longitudinal analysis as an indispensable component of all sociological explanation, declaring:

> The fact that the social system is a dynamic system means that all problems in social science have an essential historical dimension and that in effect *the main task of social science is to explain historical development.*[1] . . . [Thus] the fundamental problem becomes a problem of comparative dynamics. The problem is to explain similarities and differences in the development over time of different societies or of different parts of the same society in terms of the initial conditions (i.e., the conditions prevailing at some arbitrary point of time chosen as the starting point of our investigation) and in terms of the subsequent external influences (boundary conditions) affecting their development. . . . Comparative dynamics . . . is based on the idea that different societies often show very different patterns of development, and its main objective is to explain these differences in development in terms of differences in the initial conditions and the external influences. (Harsanyi, 1960, 139, 140)

The implication, of course, is not that the sociologist or anthropologist must become a historian in the process. Many historians in the past have been so preoccupied with explaining the unique features of social change in a limited spatio-temporal sphere (Rickert's *einmaliq*) that they have shunned or distrusted the search for common features and generalizations. This is no longer as true as it once was but Harsanyi is probably correct in observing that "the reluctance of historians to offer explanations (except on rather superficial levels) for the course of social development is simply a matter of there being no worthwhile analytical theory they could have drawn upon" (Harsanyi, *op. cit.*, 139). Certainly the unique does not exhaust the possibilities of social change; both the unique and the general are features of social processes. If the unique is divorced from *any* classifying procedure, the scientific method disappears. What Kluckhohn and Murray say about the individual is likewise true for societies, epochs, institutions, and identifiable social processes: "Every man is in certain respects (a) like all other men, (b) like some other men, and (c) like no other man" (Kluckhohn and Murray, 1953, 53). What is more, he is all three *simultaneously*. To single out the unique as though it were insulated from the general is to falsify experience, abdicate the search for etiology, relinquish the quest for scientific validation, and pass over into the realm of the novelist and the biographer.[2]

In order to get on with the investigation, present concerns require categories or typologies of a middle range that single out *recurrent historical patterns* at a higher level of generality than the single events composing them. Such typologies are analytic constructs that subsume selected masses of data. I shall speak of these as sequential patterns or sequences of events that seem to be repeatable in various cultures.

The patterns of major importance for the current study can be designated as *intergroup sequences*. They are the recurrent patterns that appear in the interactions between subordinate ethnic groups and their corresponding dominant groups in one society after another. These sequential patterns differ from earlier cyclical stage progressions advanced by Park (1949, 150) and others in two important respects. First, they are farther away from the data and do not attempt to set out serial steps in which sequences occur, but deal in total outlines. They are *types* of sequence rather than *stages* of sequence. Whether they are found more often in one cultural setting or another is a matter for systematic exploration. Second, the methodological significance of the sequential patterns suggested here is quite different from that of earlier cyclical stages. In previous attempts like the "cycle of race relations," there appeared to be an implicit or latent belief that regularities at this level were the key to future generalizations. The present venture denies any and all such implications for the current formulation.[3] Rather it is suggested that types of sequence are contexts within which hypotheses may be tested for limited or broader invariance. Thus they are heuristic devices constructed to simplify historical progressions, used as steps toward the attainment of super-historical generalizations.

The Intergroup Sequences in Outline

What, then, are the sequential patterns of ethnic relations that appear and reappear in numerous societies? Five major types deserve mention: (1) the emergence of pariahs, (2) the emergence of indigenous isolates, (3) annexation, (4) migration, and (5) colonization.[4] A number of these break down into subtypes as will appear below, and a brief description of each type will clarify how it is conceptualized.

1. *The emergence of pariahs.* In a number of older Asian countries with rigid stratification systems: Tibet, Korea, Japan and India, the lowest stratum was composed of outcaste or untouchable groups who were defined as ritually unclean, their occupations degrading and hereditary, and their status severely segregated from many if not most community contacts. In such cases the position of such outcaste members was religiously defined as "inevitable, immutable, and in some way deserved" (Price, 1966, 9). With the coming of "modernization," both Japan and India officially abolished pariah status, Japan by legislative decree during the Meiji Restoration in 1871 and India in the Constitution of 1949 that established an independent state (Totten and Wagatsuma, 1966, 34; Isaacs, 1964, 48). Since their official emancipation, the Eta or Buraku of Japan and the Scheduled Castes or ex-

Untouchables of India have emerged as groups that are increasing their political consciousness and attempting to implement legal equality in the face of residual forms of discrimination still sanctioned in custom. Official decrees, while providing formal equality, have actually transformed them into minority groups oriented to the struggle for power.

2. *Emergence of indigenous isolates.* In the nations of Africa, Asia and Latin America, there is usually a "modernizing" sector of the population that initiates, energizes and directs economic and political development, while on the other hand there is a relatively passive sector either external to the mainstream of national modernization or only gradually caught up in it. The latter sector is composed of local units (villages, regional peoples, tribes, ethnolinguistic groups) that have limited communication with each other or the central national sector; relative isolation restricts their knowledge, experience and participation in the life of the wider society. When, however, the economic and political activities of the national elite penetrate the daily conduct of the isolates —initiating market exchanges, tax payments, wage labor, establishment of schools, political appeals for votes, etc.—these and other intrusions stimulate members of isolated groups by a process still poorly understood, to participate more and more fully in the activities of the society as a whole. Some such movement of indigenous isolates undoubtedly had its beginnings in colonial periods, but interest in this early development is only relevant here in the way it affects new relationships in the eventually independent states. Any awakening of insulated local or parochial peoples has a volatile outcome, at times transforming social organization. Now and then new associations will cut across ethnic divisions as has happened among African mine workers (Mitchell, 1960, 23), but at other times a new form of organization may strengthen or even arouse cohesion and militancy within a single people as happened with Karens in Burma (Geertz, 1963, 137–38). At all events the sheer increase in participation that characterizes the emergence of indigenous isolates has important repercussions for ethnic relations in the society as a whole. Subsequent discussion will return to this point.

3. *Annexation.* This is a recurrent sequence whereby a nation-state enlarges its borders by incorporation of adjoining areas

inhabited by people of different culture and/or historical origin. This can occur in one of two ways: by force (conquest or invasion); or by treaty-purchase. The first type of annexation has been endemic in Europe where, over many generations, it has resulted in the formation of so-called multinational states (Janowsky, 1945) and is especially relevant to the Soviet Union. In the United States it was exemplified in the forcible addition of a Spanish-speaking population of what later became southwestern states at the close of the Mexican War. The second type is illustrated by the Louisiana Purchase of 1803 which was a straight commercial transaction ratified by treaty. Though the purchase of Alaska in 1867 did not incorporate immediately adjacent regions into the United States, it illustrates a similar form of territorial expansion embracing (as did the purchase of Louisiana) extensive aboriginal populations.

I am distinguishing annexation from colonization (below, sequence 5) as contiguous vs. non-contiguous domination respectively, recognizing that the relations of subordination *may* be relatively identical in the two cases. Analytically, Georges Balandier finds the characteristic features of the colonial situation to be the separation of dominant and subordinate by race and culture (Balandier, 1965, 54). Ordinarily, annexation does not reveal such distinct differences, since adjacent peoples could easily be those of similar culture, related language, or comparable physical type. This has so often been the case in Europe that the European form of annexation is a sort of prototype for this sequence. Other things being equal, colonial situations display much more marked cultural heterogeneity and racial variation (as Balandier asserts) because the superordinates are far enough from home to be historically unrelated to their subordinates. On the other hand, where annexation follows close on the heels of colonization, as happened in the United States, the cultural and racial gap more closely resembles the one found in the sequence of colonization. So it is important to insist that annexation, as a separate sequence, has a pragmatic rather than an analytic justification, and its historical context must always be assessed before its consequences are calculated.

4. *Migration.* Here the overall pattern involves the movement of mass populations from a society of origin to a "host" society

of different language or culture, with some marginal cases where the shift in domicile takes place within the host society itself. Since the focus of the present inquiry is on the formation and perpetuation of ethnic minorities within a generally receiving society, our mode of classifying subtypes of migration in this case will differ from that of Peterson (1958) who takes account of the exercise of power over migrants at the point of *origin*. Interest here, however, centers on the point of *entry*, and on this basis it is possible to set up the sequence of migration as embodying a continuum of coercive control exercised by the receiving or host society. Proceeding from greater to lesser coercion then gives the following gradations:

a. Slave transfers to a receiving society
b. Movements of forced labor from one area of the host society to another
c. Contract labor transfers including the so-called "coolie trade"
d. Reception of displaced persons into a host society
e. Admission of voluntary immigrants into a host society

The last subtype corresponds to Lieberson's "migrant subordination" (Lieberson, 1961, 904). In each case some historical and cultural differences between the migrants and the members of the host society are more or less assumed.

At one extreme of the continuum are the slave transfers—the great bulk of them, in modern times, taking place between Africa and sections of the Western Hemisphere: the southern United States, the Caribbean, and Brazil (Cf. D. B. Davis, 1966). Slavery involves more continuous coercion than other forms of migration and this, of course, continues with day-to-day control of life activities after arrival; similarly, the operation of forced labor camps, as in the Soviet Union, embodies extreme forms of constraint, though somewhat less harsh than slavery itself (Fainsod, 1963, 432–33).

The pressures of compulsion are somewhat eased in the case of contract labor (including indentured forms) where the movement from one country to another follows the instigation of agents from either side. Many, if not most of these migrations have occurred in colonies where migrant labor has been shipped in for use in plantations or mines; the lot of these workers after arrival was sometimes little better than that of slaves, though at the end of a specified period, many returned to their original homes. Thus they subdivide into temporary and permanent residents. British Guiana and Trinidad imported such laborers from India, as did South Africa and Malaya, while Hawaii brought in Chinese, Japanese, Portuguese, and Filipinos. Contract labor crosses many boundaries in southern Africa for work in mines and factories. Following World War II, increasing numbers of southern Europeans and Algerians have supplemented the labor supply of France, Belgium, Germany, the United Kingdom, and Scandinavia. The control of such contract labor has been fairly strict and pervasive, shading off to the more permissive relations accorded to displaced persons.

In the case of displaced persons, societal control that is often severe at their point of entry, is usually relaxed thereafter, allowing the newcomers to seek out their own niche in the occupational system. Such migrants move in the wake of wars like the population transfers in Balkan nations after World War I, and movements of refugees across the borders of India and Pakistan after the convulsions of struggle for independence from British rule in the wake of World War II.

Finally, the mildest form of control is reserved for voluntary migrants, chiefly again at the port of entry and receding thereafter as they establish residence. At times the voluntary migration is to independent nation-states like the mass movement of Europeans to North and South America, Australia, New Zealand, and South Africa; on other occasions the migrations have had as their target dependent or colonial areas, as when the Chinese moved to Southeast Asia, the former Netherlands East Indies and the Philippines, or in the movement of Indians to Burma and South Africa, and the migration of Arabs, Syrians, and Lebanese to South, East, and West Africa during the colonial epoch.

5. *Colonization.* This sequence also includes postcolonial derivations which are especially significant for social development. Colonial patterns, unlike those of migration, postulate control of the territory by a nonindigenous people. Also in contrast with migration, the sequence of colonization varies along a different continuum; in this case it is a continuum of geographical extensiveness, i.e., the extent to which the territory is occupied by the

newcomers. Three degrees of such preponderance may be distinguished: limited settlement (and post-colonial derivatives); substantial settlement (and post-colonial derivatives); and massive settlement expanding to majority rule.

Limited settlement frequently occurs in tropical regions where the incoming colonials from temperate zones are not easily acclimated. At first the colonizers establish military superiority but remain a small ruling enclave surrounded by other peoples. Historically, this mode of limited settlement took three main forms, one in the land mass of Central and South America, one in the Caribbean, and one in Africa and Asia. In the first case, colonization was precapitalistic and the early Iberian settlement had its special features: it "decapitated" indigenous cultures and displaced them with its own, decimated whole populations with firearms and the white man's diseases, incorporated many of those who were left in larger landed estates or colonial towns, practiced extensive miscegenation with local groups, and eventually broke political ties with European rulers while maintaining strong cultural links. This type of limited settlement was a sort of *feudalistic amalgamation*, or ascendant merger.

The limited settlement in the Caribbean proved to be a more mixed type. Beginning as a genuine colonial form, it changed rapidly after indigenous peoples were destroyed and added massive slave populations. Hence the Caribbean areas combine features of colonialism with those of slavery and forced migration (in Latin America this was the exception rather than the rule). Throughout the West Indies plantations were run more by entrepreneurs than by aristocrats, a series of profit-making institutions run by Europeans on which the slaves and their liberated descendants became dependent. Whether independent of metropolitan rule or not, these areas remain today as territories of *residual dependency* upon capitalistic owners and managers. They are now, as they have been for generations, vestigal remains of an older socioeconomic system with limited settlement of Europeans continuing.

The third type of limited settlement in Africa and Asia began as enclaves of Europeans with commercial, mining, planting, and industrial interests carried on in an atmosphere of security maintained by military means. Here the rulers were, at least after the initial stages, separatistic or self-segregated without amalgamating with the surrounding peoples. There was little or no attempt to displace indigenous cultures, and in many ways the latter were encouraged or supported as an aid to security. Cooptation of local leaders for administration was frequent, though limited. This form of limited settlement may be called *paramountcy with selective permissiveness.* That is, such colonial regimes retained or accentuated the internal diverse groupings of tribal, regional, linguistic, or religious cohesion, creating a coercive balance between them. This balance of selective permissiveness was disrupted with independence, and the struggle to achieve a new balance is a dominant motif of many new states undergoing this sequence in their previous history. Here is a whole series of internal emergent ethnic groups orienting themselves to new political forms. Historically speaking, the derivatives of limited settlement often issue in the second sequence discussed above, i.e., the emergence of indigenous isolates.

In other cases the colonial progression resulted in more substantial settlement, stopping short of demographic or ecological ascendancy. Usually the land of the colony was sufficiently fertile and the climate salubrious enough to attract many farmers from the home country of the colonizers. These agriculturalists then appropriated large tracts for themselves, pushing original inhabitants into increasingly crowded areas. Newcomers then utilized the dispossessed for large-scale labor in farming, mining, or industrial enterprise, at lower mass levels. Notable instances have occurred in Algeria, Rhodesia, the Republic of South Africa, Angola, and perhaps Kenya. Substantial settlement generates a conflict of interest that often erupts into violence. At times this foreshadows complete independence of the indigenous peoples as in Algeria or Kenya, at other times it remains a latent but endemic source of suppressed conflict, as in South Africa and Rhodesia. For colonies of this type that have gained independence (Algeria and Kenya), they share with recently liberated colonies issuing from limited settlement, the task of establishing a new balance within or between internal ethnic groups.

The point is worth emphasis that substantial settlement does not *always* imply large population increases for the colonizers, but simply ample growth in their land holdings. Thus the incoming whites, as early as 1931, held nearly half the land in what was then Southern Rhodesia, though their share of the population was less than 5 per cent (Wills, 1967, 256; Balandier, op cit., 41). Today in South Africa, whites have less than 20 per cent of the population but occupy 87 per cent of the land (van den Berghe, 1967a, 53, 186).

Finally, colonization reaches its most extensive form with massive settlement; the newcomers eventually become an effective majority of the population and establish rule over the original inhabitants by virtue of sheer numerical size, though they may have won hegemony much earlier by superior arms. Empirically, of course, colonization of massive settlement is necessarily preceded by limited and substantial settlement in progression. Lieberson apparently refers to this third type of massive settlement in his category of "migrant superordination" (*op. cit.*). As a semantic choice, however, it seems preferable to reserve terms like "migrant" and "migration" for cases where the receiving society retains dominance. At any rate, colonization of massive settlement normally breaks with the mother country and establishes a separate sovereign state where newcomers and their descendants compose the majority of the population. Here the indigenous ethnics are totally engulfed—the relations are typified by those between whites and Indians in the United States and Canada, whites and Maoris in New Zealand, or whites and aborigines in Australia.[5]

Racism and the Intergroup Sequences

Each of these sequences, emergence of pariahs, emergence of indigenous isolates, annexation, migration and colonization has its own typical chain of consequences. Of the various recurrent consequences there are two that have crucial importance for ethnic studies: *racism* and *pluralism*. The present chapter deals with the first, the following chapter with the second.

Racism is an ideology that sees an invariable connection between cultural behavior and physical type. Hence it defines specific outgroups as having characteristic traits (usually detestable or in some way inferior) that are inherent outgrowths of their biological constitutions. While not all ethnic relations have a racist component, a great many do, and it is well at this point to make some distinctions between types of racism once more before relating the phenomenon to intergroup sequences.

It is quite likely that the most common form of racism is a doctrine of group supremacy or superiority couched in physical terms—as Ruth Benedict puts it, "the dogma that one ethnic group is condemned by Nature to hereditary inferiority and another group is destined to hereditary superiority" (Benedict, 1943, 98). This is the sort of racist belief that accompanies and rationalizes a dominant power position of substantial magnitude, where the contrast between upper and lower statuses is clear and unmistakable. Metaphorically speaking, this is vertical racism with the upper incumbents looking down at the lower and characterizing them as inferior, relatively or absolutely. Where the distinction is relative, vertical racism is minimal, i.e., appearing without rigid segregation; where the distinction is absolute or extreme, it is possible to speak of maximal racism and its manifestation is the compulsory separation of segregation or apartheid.

To take a different situation: where several ethnic groups of distinctly different physical appearance coexist in the same territory without any one of them monopolizing a power position, a kind of mutual or reciprocal ethnocentrism results, with each group stereotyping the others in its own way. While it is the cultural practices of the "others" that have salience, these are eventually attributed to their unique inheritance, i.e., are racially imputed. Since there are several groups making an attribution, no one of them can unilaterally impose its views on the rest, as happens in vertical racism; now the notion of racial superiority, plurally asserted, becomes relativistic and loses its capacity to polarize the society into clearly defined uppers and lowers. To continue the metaphor, this is horizontal racism, differing substantially from the vertical form described above.[6]

The Emergence of Pariahs and Racism

In the first sequence of emergent pariahs the situation is one of caste or semicaste. Strictly speaking this does not have racist consequences since it is not physical appearance per se that sets off the pariah group. It is quite possible and fairly common for a Buraku in Japan or a member of a scheduled caste in India to "pass" into the wider community without being detected by reason of color or physiological characteristics. In a tightly organized and highly institutionalized society, however, the real danger in passing comes from fear of detection where manners, dialect differences, or tracing of family lines (in marriage arrangements) reveal the origins of the passer. In such cases the stereotype of the lowly, filthy, unclean outcaste is immediately applied; the passer is avoided, shunned or ostracized in innumerable ways, subject to loss of job or promotion, denied residential opportunities in the larger community and so forth. All the components of racism are present except that of the physical symbol—the inherent inferiority, the ascriptive status, the assigning of psycho-social characteristics to biological inheritance, and the enforced endogamy. In a sense this is racism without race and it is significant that George DeVos and Hiroshi Wagatsuma (1966) refer to the Buraku as "Japan's Invisible Race" in characterizing their position. However, this lacks the features of true racism, not merely because visible phenotypical marks are unimportant, but also because, in both Japan and India the position of the outcastes has been molded and institutionalized over many centuries resulting in occupational specialization in "unclean" activities regarded as ritually polluting in the religious tradition. Racism as it appears elsewhere (particularly the vertical type) is the product of recent encounters in the movement of people (slavery, colonization) and status distinctions are not embedded in age-old traditions. They are newly constructed definitions clearly based on color and physical appearance that have been institutionalized since the seventeenth century rather than over a millennium. In the case of emergent pariahs, then, the consequence is outcasteism but not racism, and the former has the patina of ancient custom belonging to a well-established system; in comparison, racism is a parvenu.

The Emergence of Indigenous Isolates and Racism

This second sequence is deliberately limited to the type of pattern occurring in new states following World War II, though its antecedents in colonial regimes must at least be taken into account.

As newly regnant elites or dominant groups are beginning the process of legitimizing their position, social changes attending the entry of indigenous isolates on the stage of public life present a theme with variations. Such previously secluded groups are at times compelled, at times attracted, or at times aroused by grievances sufficiently to break out of their local insularity and participate in the wider societal life.

How such emergent groups are defined will depend on the interweaving of numerous intergroup components in the existing situation. For instance, cultural differences between social units may be relatively insignificant but the size of the previously isolated group may be so minute that it has been swept into a larger whole, first by alien colonials and next by alien neighbors who continue to manage its affairs by taxation, legislation and administrative fiat. Naturally, "the smaller the unit, the fewer the resources" (Mair, 1963, 116), so if, in the judgment of larger tribes or ethnic groups, the smaller unit is not viable by itself, it "must be" kept in a larger national whole whose resources will support a viable state. In Africa where this pattern is frequently repeated, the attitude of ascendant larger units in respect to those of smaller size is often one of condescension but can hardly be given a racist label. In India, however, where the cultural gap between dominants and subordinates is much greater (for example, the case of Hindus on one side and aborigines on the other) this has brought about postures of superiority among Hindus that encompass a melange of ideas—the aboriginals are uncouth because they are primarily hunters and not farmers, they must be avoided as outside the pale of caste respectability, they are secretly admired for their martial virtues, while scorned for their dark complexions (Chaudhuri, 1965, 68 ff.). It would not stretch the evidence too far to call this a sort of *pseudoracism*. On the other hand, Burma displays a wider variety of differences among its peripheral units with some like the Karens acculturated to cosmopolitan ways by British administrators and missionaries, others like the Arakanese converted to Islam, some ethnolinguistic groups like the Chins being easily overrun while others in contrast like the Shans maintain substantial autonomy through the exercise of power by local chiefs (Geertz, 1963, 136–39). With dominance uncertain and changeable, it would be an error to speak of racism, even of the horizontal variety, in the Burmese context. Yet in the quite different atmosphere of Sarawak where "economically more advanced Chinese (31 per cent) or the politically more experienced Malays (18 per cent)" are set over against some 50 per cent of the population distributed among a number of tribal peoples of simple organization and nonliterate culture (Hanna, 1962, 164 ff.) the prevailing ideology seems to run the gamut from pseudoracism to horizontal racism.

Summing up the sequence of emergent indigenous isolates, it would be possible to say that the consequences of this pattern seldom issue in racist attitudes but in a few exceptional cases can encompass such a wide range of plural peoples that the responses at least verge on the more moderate forms of racism.

Annexation and Racism

The sequence of annexation is also relatively free from the consequences of racism. This may be because adjacent peoples are, on the whole, less likely to have marked physical differences than inhabitants of more distant regions. There are, however, some exceptions to this: (1) where one people has migrated long distances in the recent past to colonize their present territory; or (2) where one power is rapidly expanding its borders, empire fashion, and therefore encounters people who differ notably in both culture and appearance in the farther reaches of territorial expansion. The United States meets both of these conditions in the annexation of Spanish Americans from Mexico since American settlers from Europe were recent newcomers and their new country was in an expansionist phase when the annexation took place. Hence some vertical racism developed but of a milder and minimal variety in this case. Another example that fits the second exception above is the expansion of Russia, both Czarist and Soviet into Siberia and Central Asia during the nineteenth and twentieth centuries. However, though encounters with Mongols, Tartars, Bashkirs, Kalmucks and Kazakhs came rapidly, this did not seem to result in vertical racism of any sort, and even horizontal racism seems improbable. Walter Kolarz asserts:

> Absence of racial pride and prejudice is thus for Russia not a revolutionary principle, but is both the natural prerequisite of

the growth of the Russian Empire and the natural outcome of
centuries of racial intermixture . . . The Soviet regime may have
transformed anti-racialism into a dogmatic principle, it may
have formulated this principle legally and politically, but Russian anti-racialism is no Bolshevik creation, it is a component
part of Russian history (Kolarz, 1952, 6).

Parenthetically it is worth remarking that annexation by treaty-
purchase in the case of the United States did not so much *produce*
racism in its train but simply transported into new territory an
inheritance of racism already resulting from prior colonization
with its subjugation of Indians by whites.

Forced Migration (Slave Transfers) and Racism

In the modern world, at least, slavery has had more pronounced
racist consequences than other intergroup sequences. To begin
with, slave transfers are clearly the most coercive forms of migration so there is a close correlation between exploitative power
and racism. This is especially true in plantation economies where
a highly stratified occupational structure makes up a hierarchy
of control with top authority in the planter, delegated authority
in the overseer (both being white) and the heavy menial labor is
performed by black slaves differentiated from the master race.
Though the plantation is an authoritative community of those
who issue commands on one side of the racial line and those who
obey them on the other, it is softened by paternalism and particularistic relations (van den Berghe, 1967, 31–33). The "inferior"
race is regarded as one needing constant supervision, care and
management, while the plantation is dubbed a "race–making"
institution by later observers. Slave plantations have been most
common in the Western Hemisphere throughout the southern
United States, the West Indies, and Brazil.

At this point it is necessary to call attention to the fact that
some of the intergroup sequences overlap or converge. Even
though an initial distinction is already drawn between migration
(slavery being the most coercive type) and colonization, this
distinction is a function of the dual relation posited between a

single dominant group and a single subordinate group. To illustrate:

FIGURE 7.   UNITED STATES CASE

A. INTERGROUP SEQUENCE: COLONIZATION (*Massive settlement, sub-type*)

INCOMING GROUP   *INDIGENOUS POPULATION*

Dominant group   Subordinate group

Europeans ⟶ American Indians

B. INTERGROUP SEQUENCE: MIGRATION (*Slave transfer, sub-type*)

HOST SOCIETY   *INCOMING GROUP*

Dominant group   Subordinate group

Whites of European origin ⟶ Black Africans

While intergroup sequences A and B are separable analytically and refer to different dual relations in each case, one between European colonists and Indians, the other between whites and Negroes, they nevertheless merge historically since the two sequences took place in much the same time period. There is another overlap demographically since the whites who formed the major dominant group vis-à-vis the blacks, also composed a sizeable part of the European colonists vis-à-vis the Indians. Thus the dominant group was the same in both cases, but relative to each subordinate bore a different relation. There is, however, another important connection. During early American history when settlement was only on the way to being massive, and frontier conditions were relatively typical, the incoming colonists, seeing the value of cash crops, made their first attempts to procure mass labor for plantations by enslaving the Indians—a process that failed utterly. A more drastic attempt to use forced Indian labor in the West Indies proved an even greater debacle (Berry, *op. cit.*, 102–03). Thus the failure to impose forms of disciplined mass labor in one intergroup sequence brought about a shift to another sequence with a different set of subordinates to fulfill the same economic purpose.

Edgar Thompson's comments on this are enlightening:

> The planter resorted to the importation of outside laborers not only because the native population was numerically insufficient

but . . . because it was difficult or even impossible to obtain a satisfactory degree of control over people who were at home in the local environment. The familyless man or woman recruited in some distant place and transported to a plantation region where he found himself in strange surroundings and among strange peoples was more easily made dependent upon an employer. Thus the native Negro in many parts of Africa is regarded as a very unsatisfactory plantation laborer, but in early Virginia he was regarded as superior not only to the native Indian but also to the white indentured servant. With imported laborers, usually familyless, the control situation changed in favor of the planter. It is easier to fit unattached individuals into their proper places in the organization of plantation work. (Thompson, 1939, 185)

A merger of colonization with slavery was therefore a frequent occurrence in the New World with the racism of each reinforcing the other; yet slavery seems to have played the major role in making racial lines rigid. Here still another distinction must be made. Brazil imported between three and five million slaves from Africa for labor on the sugar plantations (van den Berghe, 1967, 61), where native Indians proved less adaptable to forced labor as in North America. In this society, racism was much more mild, deserving the title of "minimal racism" already mentioned in chapter 2. There were several reasons why the impact of slavery and the plantation system had weaker racist consequences in Brazil. In the first place the early colonists were mainly single men who took American Indian women first as mistresses, later as wives, thus setting a trend toward a mestizo population where intermixture of people having noticeable color variations became fixed in the mores sanctioned by both church and state. The Catholic conception of the slave and master as equal in the sight of God, frequent miscegenation with slaves and extensive manumission resulted in a less rigid caste line than was found in North America. Furthermore the large number of mulattoes and others of intermediate color shades, had its influence and in addition, access to higher educational advancement early in the nineteenth century enabled many to enter professional status and this was coupled with the growth of prestige in urban centers where mulattoes had increasingly mobility opportunities (Pierson, 1955, 435–37). Thus the form of racism resulting from slavery in Brazil has been muted rather than harsh and people actually change their racial identity (Harris, 1964, 59). However, modern industry and the rise of competitive relations apparently heightens racism. As van den Berghe puts it, "At present, however, Brazil may be more aptly described as a racial purgatory than as a racial paradise" (van den Berghe, 1967, 75).

Contract Labor, Voluntary Migration, and Racism

In addition to slave transfers other types of migration must also be considered. In the case of contract labor it is quite apparent that resemblances to slavery are more significant than similarities to other forms of migration. The distinction between slave labor and contract labor is not always clear empirically since the latter often involved force and compulsion. The legal or analytical differences between the two may be important, but one must recognize that contract labor runs the gamut from enforced servitude without chattel ownership to carefully stipulated intervals of work obligation terminated abruptly when contracts end. Also contract laborers divide again into (1) those who renew contracts or remain at their jobs without a formal contract, (2) those who remain in the country but seek other employment, and (3) those who return to their homes in another land and are therefore temporary sojourners. Nor are these fixed categories since many in each of the three classifications change their minds and opt for other alternatives as changing conditions affect them and their perceived opportunities.

In the nineteenth and early twentieth centuries the great bulk of contract laborers have been passive migrants whose passage has been arranged by agents in Southeast Asia, Pacific regions and Africa. Their destination has (like the slaves) been the plantation or, in a smaller number of cases, mines, both of them economic complexes of colonial societies with limited settlement. Like the slave labor societies of the United States, the Caribbean and Brazil, plantation owners in Southeast Asia, the Pacific, and Africa found it more economically rewarding to ship in foreign workers than to make use of the indigenous population. But while natives in the Western Hemisphere were soon decimated to a vanishing point, this was less true elsewhere because indigenous groups frequently formed a solid mass surrounding minority enclaves of foreign plantation workers. Not infrequently this led to multiracialism as a permanent pattern both during and after colonial rule, i.e., societies like Malaya, Ceylon, Fiji, Hawaii, Mauritius, Reunion, and others. On the whole, dominant white colonialists developed differential racial definitions for incoming workers and the indigenous peoples. Such racism was not strongly stereotyped and took considerable account of cultural variations. In fact the racial label came to be indiscriminately employed for each group distinct from the colonial masters, the whole process reaching its apogee in Hawaii "where Germans, Norwegians, Portuguese, and Spanish, although sharing a common European and Christian heritage with the British and American planters of the Islands, have consistently been treated as distinct racial groups and have so been classified in the official census as long as their place within the Island economy was primarily on the plantation" (Lind, 1955, 58–59).

The impact of contract labor on racist features of society is also apparent in the Caribbean in a limited number of areas where multiracialism has appeared in somewhat different form. With the great bulk of the population consisting of Negro slaves, the coming of Emancipation created a situation where plantation and estate owners gave inducements to the newly freed slaves to work for wages at their old occupations. Where there were virgin lands for the former slaves to occupy and develop as petty farmers, the rewards for remaining on the plantation were not sufficient and the consequent dearth of estate labor led to the importation of East Indians to fill the gap. "This led to the characteristic multi-racialism of places like Trinidad, Surinam and British Guiana" (Braithwaite, 1965, 32).

The combination of contract laborers with voluntary migrants has compounded the features of multiracialism in Southeast Asia. Some of the voluntary migrations there even preceded the colonial era as in the case of the Chinese who spread into Indonesia, Malaya, Thailand and the Philippines at an early date (Purcell, 1966) though the pace of their migration quickened noticeably when these areas were colonized by Europeans (Hunter,

1966, 60). A similar influx of voluntary migrants from India found their way into Burma and Malaya under the umbrella of British colonial rule (Mahajani, 1960) and in their case presented more clear-cut physical differences from the indigenous people than the Chinese throughout Southeast Asia. However both the Indians and Chinese, whether plantation and mine workers on the one hand, or entrepreneurs and merchants on the other, are even today regarded as immigrant racial minorities (Hunter, *op. cit.*, 8–9). It is worth mentioning that the consequent features of racialism during the colonial period were more decidedly vertical as distinguished from the significantly horizontal racism that developed after independence. This issue will receive more attention in the discussion of colonization below.

In Africa the most significant influx of contract laborers were imported as indentures from India into Natal by agents who were paid a capitation fee for every able-bodied worker they could secure; the indentured laborers were utilized on sugar plantations, railways, dockyards, coal mines, municipal services and domestic labor in lieu of the Zulu who were unwilling to serve in such confining occupations. At the close of their period of indenture, the great majority of Indians remained in South Africa in spite of government inducements to leave, either continuing in the same line of work or finding other employment. Somewhat later they were joined by voluntary migrants from India under ordinary immigration procedures and set up numerous commercial establishments. These later immigrants formed only about 10 per cent of the total Indian community in Natal (Hilda Kuper, 1960, 1–10) and hence were stereotyped with their fellow nationals in a common racial category of relatively low degree. In the many-tiered society of South Africa they came to occupy an intermediate racial position between whites and Africans, vulnerable to hostility from both sides (Van der Horst, 1965, 127–28)[7] though only about 3 per cent of the South African population. While their demographic proportion relative to Africans was smaller, migrants from India formed an intermediate racial status throughout East Africa as well, and outnumbered whites by two or three to one before independence (Hollingsworth, 1960). Likewise, migrants from the Levant became commercial middlemen in a number of sub-Saharan areas (Coleman, 1958, 47).

In most cases of voluntary migration, racial labels or assigned statuses are not imposed upon the newcomers. However, where the host society has a previous history of slavery or colonization, with concomitant racial ideologies, these may carry over to color the perception of the immigrant who is then defined in racial terms. Such has been the case in Britain where immigrants from Commonwealth areas of Asia, Africa, and the Caribbean have entered (Rose, 1967), and the United States in those cases where it received Asian immigrants as well as some from south of the border (Schrieke, 1936; Burma, 1954).

Colonization and Racism

Certainly since the seventeenth century the connection between colonization and racism is so close that exceptions are rarer than the rule. There seems to be almost an irresistible force that crystallizes racist attitudes in the colonial situation where domination of a people in a distant land with strange customs and unfamiliar appearance heightens the contrast between ruler and ruled. As one first-hand observer has put it:

> France is unquestionably one of the least racialist-minded countries in the world; also colonial policy is officially anti-racialist. But the effects of the colonial situation inevitably make themselves felt, so that a marked racialist attitude appears side by side with the official attitude, and, indeed, in spite of it. Even the administration officials themselves, although they apply France's pro-native policy humanely and conscientiously, are nevertheless subject to the psycho-sociological laws and unless they are men of exceptional calibre, come to adopt attitudes which are coloured with racialism. Those outside the administration, of course, have no appearances to keep up. (Mannoni, 1950, 110)

In comparison with other colonial rulers of the eighteenth to the twentieth century, the French, in the eye of scientific observers, have actually been somewhat freer of racist ideology than many other colonials. Yet if Mannoni is right, this presumed tolerance was nullified by the imposed hierarchy of daily living experience in the colonial situation; *a fortiori* the pressure would appear to be even more impelling in other colonies.[8]

While colonization promoted racism in the long run, the historic path toward that end had many twists and turns. In the dramatic expansion of Europe after the fifteenth century, early contacts of explorers, traders, and adventurers with the peoples of Oceania, Asia, Africa, and the Americas awakened such diverse responses and counter-responses that generalities are hardly possible. First encounters precipitated every conceivable sort of reaction: supernatural awe, fascination, friendliness, gift exchange, barter, misunderstandings, conflict, and deadly hostility—each governed by unique circumstances (Frazier, 1957, Chap. 2). Technological and military superiority of the invaders, even when accompanied by awareness of color contrasts, does not fully account for the ensuing racism and, in particular, distinctions between the minimal racism of Iberian colonies and the maximal racism so often found elsewhere. To explain this it is necessary to introduce a third element, namely, patterns of sexual relationship across intergroup lines.

In brief, the thesis is this: miscegenation may augment and crystallize what is at first a potential sentiment of racial superiority, actualizing racism to at least a minimal degree when group dominance is already coupled with visible color difference. Contrary to widespread popular belief, miscegenation is in no way a proof of racial tolerance; only intermarriage holds that distinction. But miscegenation (which overwhelmingly takes the form of concubinage) is simply the sexual aspect of superordination where dominant-group men exploit subordinate-group women.

During their first stages of development, colonial societies with a surplus of males in the ascendant group not only had a considerable history of miscegenation, but in later stages tended to take one or the other of these two alternatives: (a) develop an increased volume of intermarriage with subordinate women; or (b) develop an increased volume of marriage with dominant-group women—the latter depending on transport of such females to the colony as an adjunct to permanent settlement.

In the preinstitutionalized form of colonialism, miscegenation became common in many regions of the world, often mixed with traces of alternative (a). It occurred in New Zealand where early settlers not only consorted with Maori women but married them in order to get protection and preference in trading (Wright, 1959, 73). It was manifest in Australia where a considerable half-caste population of mixed English and aborigines came into existence (Clark, 1958, 13). The early history of South Africa reveals extensive concubinage and occasional intermarriage in the Cape regions (MacCrone, 1937, 42 ff.). By 1960 the offspring of such mixed unions constituted nearly a tenth of the total South African population (van den Berghe, 1967, 102). Similarly in India, the first English settlers had frequent sexual attachments with Indian women; some remained "single" but kept zenanas, some formed unions with half-castes, while "marriage with colored women was accepted as the normal course" (Spear, 1963, 13). Initial colonial practice in Indonesia displayed the same tendencies "thanks to the tacit recognition given to two hallowed Dutch colonial institutions: barracks concubinage and the planters *njai* (housekeeper) . . . In the later days of the East India Company there were more illegitimate births out of Christian fathers than legitimate ones, while in the middle of the nineteenth century concubinage was an accepted part of the mores of the city of Batavia and the illegitimate spouse received the same respect as the legitimate one" (Van der Kroef, 1953, 486). Perhaps the most extreme case occurred in Mexico where the Spanish colonists never formed even 3 per cent of the population, yet concubinage was so prevalent (with intermarriage running second) that mestizos became the dominant element, constituting as much as four-fifths of the total in the mid-twentieth century (van den Berghe, 1967, 45).

In sum, where alternative (a) became the typical pattern and intermarriage the predominant mode, racism was mild or minimal, as shown by the experience of Mexico, Brazil, and other Latin American countries. On the other hand, with alternative (b), the immigration of women to the ruling group stimulated exclusivist claims to the men of that group and this intensified racist ideology. As two leading historians comment about India, "It must be confessed that the growing number of English women who began to settle in India with their husbands increased the tendency of the white population to form . . . a caste" (Thompson and Garratt, 1934, 465). An even more forthright statement comes from an observer of French colonialism:

> The colonial woman is, as it were, the feminine counterpart of Prospero, but—and it is an astonishing fact—in Madagascar the European women are far more racialist than the men . . . At

least one element in this feminine racialism is over-compensation for an inferiority complex similar to that of *nouvelles-riches* in Europe, whose relations with their domestic servants and social inferiors bear the stamp of over-compensation. There is undoubtedly some sexual tinge to it too; the white woman is constantly trying to impress it on the white man's unconscious that there can be no possible comparison between herself and the Malagasy woman. (Mannoni, *op. cit.*, 116)

In accounting for maximal racism as a consequence of alternative (b), it is therefore necessary to *chercher la femme*. The alteration of the sex ratio in the ruling group and the increasing role of colonial women in decision making must be given due recognition. But it is because of the pervasive effects of such changes on the social system that they become important. Before the righting of the population balance among the colonial rulers, they mingled more freely with the indigenous population; furthermore, in the everyday life of the colonies, the spheres of official and informal relations more often overlapped, interactions were more fluid, and the reciprocal recognition of individuality on both sides of the line had more chance to develop. With the closure of family relations in the ruling group, this started a chain reaction which separated ruler and ruled in personal-social relations everywhere except in administration and the marketplace. Lines between superordinates and subordinates became hardened and fixed with consequent loss of personal differentiations. Color distinctions began to blot out other distinctions and racism became the defining perception of the social field.

As these relations became more permanent and institutionalized, the colonial system becomes a dual or bifurcated one. As one authority has bluntly put it:

The color line, indeed, is the foundation of the entire colonial system, for on it is built the whole social, economic, and political structure. All the relationships between the racial groups are those of superordination and subordination, of superiority and inferiority. There is no mistaking this pattern for one of mere segregation or separation with equality. The color line is horizontal, so to speak, and cuts across every colonial society in such a way as to leave the natives in the lower stratum and the whites in the upper . . . Throughout the colonies, we find a system of group discrimination and subordination, and natives are judged and treated, not on the basis of individual worth or ability, but as members of an undifferentiated group. Although other elements are involved, the heart of the colonial problem is the native problem, and the native problem is a racial or caste problem. (Kennedy, 1945, 308)

It is time to ask again: why did the Spanish colonies (with Mexico as the prime example) never develop racism to any considerable degree while other colonies were rife with it? Among these other colonies, of course, were the English settlements on the Atlantic seaboard whose encounter with the American Indians is another case in point. This example really furnishes a third variation or alternative in addition to the first two, for in the New England colonies the newcomers came as *completed families* in contrast with the Spanish settlers who were principally single men.[9] So family enclosure in the New England colonies, coupled with the Chosen People complex of the religious ideology established sharp boundaries between the colonists and the Indians who then were defined in racist terms. In the Spanish colonies, however, there was no appreciable influx of women from the home country (Morse, 1964, 129). Other convergent factors tended to unify rather than separate the two populations in Latin America. One was the entire disruption of the native economy and the forcible placement of Indians in haciendas and Spanish-type towns where they became utterly dependent on Spanish grandees, overseers and administrators. An additional factor was cultural imperialism that attempted to destroy all vestiges of indigenous beliefs and practice by imposing Spanish language, customs, and conversions to Roman Catholicism (van den Berghe, 1967, 43, 44). This Hispanicization proceeded so rapidly and thoroughly that racial differences lost their significance as time went on and cultural distinctions eventually predominated.

On the whole, then, colonization in the post-Columbian world has, with the exception of the Spanish case, been closely linked with racism and like the plantation is a kind of "race-making" phenomenon. Within this broad category are individual or regional variations but they do not seem to be correlated with limited, substantial, or massive settlement so that they need separate treatment. There is, however, one related problem referred to above as "postcolonial derivatives" which still requires attention. Since decolonization has its major consequences in the structural rather than the racial features of societies, it is important to include both matters in the discussion of pluralism which now claims our attention.

· NOTES ·

1. Italics added. The italicized phrase makes an extreme claim which is not necessary to Harsanyi's main argument; it seems quite sufficient to contend that it is an *essential* task of social science to explain historical development without making it the *main* task, and that is the position taken in this book.
2. Kurt Lewin stated the point unequivocally, "Problems of individual differences . . . and of general laws are clearly interwoven. A law is expressed in an equation which relates certain variables. Individual differences have to be conceived of as various specific values which these variables have in a particular case. In other words, general laws and individual differences are merely two aspects of one problem; they are mutually dependent on each other and the study of one cannot proceed without the study of the other" (Lewin, 1950, 243).
3. It is true that Berry (1958) on the one hand, and Shibutani and Kwan on the other (1965) insist on the limited nature of cyclical uniformities in their works. However, they are content to leave the issue there as an undigested remnant from the past, standing alone in splendid isolation. They furnish no bridge between these and a theoretical formulation that could facilitate further exploration.
4. The writer would like to acknowledge the counsel of Marie Haug in the formulation of these sequential types.
5. While the main concern here is with European colonialism, this does not imply disregard of non-European cases such as Japanese in Korea, Malays in Madagascar, or Arabs and Persians in East Africa.
6. Cf. the related discussion on such types above, Chap. 2, pp. 73–77.
7. There is some discrepancy in the evidence on the relative social distance of Indians, Colored, and Africans from the dominant whites (van den Berghe, 1965, 255–56).
8. It is an interesting sidelight that the most passionate indictment of colonialism yet to appear has come from a Negro subject of French rule in Martinique, one who was apparently fully assimilated into French culture by finishing his medical and psychiatric studies in France. In vehement French he excoriates colonialism and all its works with special barbs at the French. The author, Frantz Fanon, has called his book *The Wretched of the Earth* (1963) and it has become favorite reading for both the new left and the black nationalists in the United States during the 1960s.

9. It is true, of course, that in Virginia and farther south, most men in the colonial settlements were single. Social adaptation to this problem, however, was unique and effective: boatloads of women from England were eventually brought in to balance the two sexes. The premium on women at first was very great and some writers have seen in this the historical origin of southern "chivalry." It is worth noting in passing that there is no Pocahontas legend in the northern colonies. For one account, cf. Calhoun, 1919.

· REFERENCES ·

Balandier, Georges, "The Colonial Situation," in Pierre L. van den Berghe (ed.), *Africa, Social Problems of Change and Conflict.* San Francisco: Chandler, 1965.

Benedict, Ruth, *Race, Science and Politics.* New York: Viking, 1943.

Berry, Brewton, *Race and Ethnic Relations.* 2nd ed. Boston: Houghton Mifflin, 1958.

Braithwaite, L. E., "Race Relations and Industrialisation in the Caribbean," in Guy Hunter (ed.), *Industrialisation and Race Relations.* London: Oxford University Press, 1965.

Burma, John H., *The Spanish-Speaking Groups in the United States.* Durham, N.C.: Duke University Press, 1965.

Calhoun, Arthur, *A Social History of the American Family.* 3 vols. Cleveland: Clar, 1919.

Chaudhuri, Nirad A., *The Continent of Circe.* New York: Oxford University Press, 1965.

Clark, Colin, *Australian Hopes and Fears.* London: Hollis & Carter, 1958.

Coleman, James S., *Nigeria, Background to Nationalism.* Berkeley: University of California Press, 1958.

Davis, David Brion, *The Problem of Slavery in Western Culture.* Ithaca: Cornell University Press, 1966.

De Vos, George, and Hiroshi Wagatsuma, *Japan's Invisible Race.* Los Angeles: University of California Press, 1966.

Fainsod, Merle, *How Russia is Ruled.* Rev. ed. Cambridge, Mass.: Harvard University Press, 1963.

Fanon, Frantz, *The Wretched of the Earth,* Constance Farrington (trans.). New York: Grove Press, 1963.

Frazier, E. Franklin, *Race and Culture Contacts in the Modern World.* New York: Knopf, 1957.

Geertz, Clifford, "The Integrative Revolution," in Clifford Geertz (ed.), *Old Societies and New States.* New York: Free Press, 1963.

Hanna, Willard A., *The Formation of Malaysia.* New York: American Universities Field Staff, Inc., 1962.

Harris, Marvin, *Patterns of Race in the Americas.* New York: Walker, 1964.

Harsanyi, John C., "Explanation and Comparative Dynamics in Social Science," *Behavioral Science*, 5, No. 2 (1960), 136–46.

Hollingworth, Lawrence W., *The Asians of East Africa.* London: Macmillan, 1960.

Hunter, Guy, *South-East Asia, Race, Culture and Nation.* London: Oxford University Press, 1962.

Isaacs, Harold R., *India's Ex-Untouchables*. New York: John Day, 1964.

Janowsky, Oscar I., *Nationalities and National Minorities*. New York: Macmillan, 1945.

Kennedy, Raymond, "The Colonial Crisis and the Future," in Ralph Linton (ed.), *The Science of Man in the World Crisis*. New York: Columbia University Press, 1945.

Kluckhohn, Clyde, and Henry A. Murray, "Personality Formation: the Determinants," in Clyde Kluckhohn and Henry A. Murray (eds.), *Personality in Nature, Society and Culture*. 2nd ed. New York: Knopf, 1953.

Kolarz, Walter, *Russia and Her Colonies*. New York: Praeger, 1952.

Kuper, Hilda, *Indian People in Natal*. Natal, South Africa: University Press, 1960.

Lewin, Kurt, *Field Theory in Social Science*, ed. Dorwin Cartwright. New York: Harper, 1950.

Lieberson, Stanley, "A Societal Theory of Race and Ethnic Relations," *American Sociological Review*, 26 (December 1961), 902–10.

MacCrone, I. D., *Race Attitudes in South Africa*. London: Oxford University Press, 1937.

McKinney, John C., *Constructive Typology and Social Theory*. New York: Appleton-Century-Crofts, 1966.

Mahajani, Usha, *The Role of Indian Minorities in Burma and Malaya*. Bombay: Vor & Co., Publishers Private Ltd. Issued in New York under the auspices of the Institute of Pacific Relations, 1960.

Mair, Lucy, *New Nations*. Chicago: University of Chicago Press, 1963.

Mannoni, D., *Prospero and Caliban, The Psychology of Colonization*. New York: Praeger, 1950.

Mitchell, J. C., *Tribalism and the Plural Society*. London: Oxford University Press, 1960.

Morse, Richard M., "The Heritage of Latin America," in Louis Hartz, *The Founding of New Societies*. New York: Harcourt, Brace & World, 1964.

Park, Robert E., *Race and Culture*. Glencoe, Ill.: Free Press, 1949.

Petersen, William, "A General Typology of Migration," *American Sociological Review*, 23 (June 1958), 256–66.

Pierson, Donald, "Race Relations in Portuguese America," in Andrew W. Lind (ed.), *Race Relations in World Perspective*. Honolulu: University of Hawaii Press, 1955.

Price, John, "A History of the Outcaste: Untouchability in Japan," in George De Vos and Hiroshi Wagatsuma (eds.), *Japan's Invisible Race, Caste in Culture and Personality*. Berkeley: University of California Press, 1966.

Purcell, Victor, *The Chinese in Southeast Asia*. 2nd ed. London: Oxford University Press, 1966.

Rose, Peter, "Outsiders in Britain," *Trans-Action*, 4, No. 4 (March 1967), 18–23.

Schrieke, B. J. O., *Alien Americans: A Study of Race Relations*. New York: Viking, 1936.

Shibutani, Tamotsu, and Kian M. Kwan, *Ethnic Stratification*. New York: Macmillan, 1965.

Spear, Percival, *The Nabobs, A Study of the Social Life of the English in Eighteenth Century India*. London: Oxford University Press, 1963.

Thompson, Edgar T., "The Plantation: The Physical Basis of Traditional

Race Relations," in Edgar T. Thompson (ed.), *Race Relations and the Race Problem*. Durham: Duke University Press, 1939.

Thompson, Edward J., and G. T. Garratt, *Rise and Fulfillment of British Rule in India*. London: Macmillan, 1934.

Totten, George O., and Hiroshi Wagatsuma, "Emancipation: Growth and Transformation of a Political Movement," in George De Vos and Hiroshi Wagatsuma (eds.), *Japan's Invisible Race, Caste in Culture and Personality*. Berkeley: University of California Press, 1966.

van den Berghe, Pierre L., "Toward a Sociology of Africa," in Pierre van den Berghe (ed.), *Africa, Social Problems of Change and Conflict*. San Francisco: Chandler, 1965.

———, *Race and Racism*. New York: Wiley, 1967.

———, *South Africa, A Study in Conflict*. Berkeley & Los Angeles: University of California Press, 1967a. (First paperbound ed.)

Van der Horst, Sheila T., "The Effects of Industrialisation on Race Relations in South Africa," in Guy Hunter (ed.), *Industrialisation and Race Relations*. London: Oxford University Press, 1965.

Van der Kroef, Justus M., "The Eurasian Minority in Indonesia," *American Sociological Review*, 18 (October 1953), 484–93.

Wills, A. J., *An Introduction to the History of Central Africa*. 2nd ed. London: Oxford University Press, 1967.

Wright, Harrison M., *New Zealand 1769–1840: Early Years of Western Contact*. Cambridge, Mass.: Harvard University Press, 1959.

4

𝕎

Intergroup Sequences
and Pluralism

The word "pluralism" is plagued with many meanings in the writings of social scientists. At least four uses of the term may be distinguished, the last two of which are correlative or mutually implicated:

1. *An ideological designation.* In this sense, pluralism is a sort of doctrinal belief usually ascribed to an ethnic minority group whose members assert the desirability of preserving their way of life even though it differs markedly from that of the dominant or majority group. As Wirth puts it, "a pluralistic minority is one which seeks toleration for its differences on the part of the dominant group" (Wirth, 1945, 354). This is the meaning referred to in chapter 2 (see p. 75) where pluralism is referred to as a centrifugal tendency in Figure 6. In the literature of ethnic and race relations, this tendency is denoted both by "pluralism" and "cultural pluralism" interchangeably. Since the usual reference in this case is to an ideology of what *ought to be*, I propose here an alternative term and shall speak of it from now on as *normative pluralism*.

2. *A political designation.* As used by the political scientists especially, pluralism refers to the multiplicity of autonomous

interest groups and associations which bring pressure to bear on the making and implementing of political decisions through political parties, lobbies, or the use of mass media. The interests represented are conceived in the broadest terms and may include sectional or regional demands, the claims of business organizations, organized labor, farm blocs, professional groups like medical or bar associations, veterans' groups, reform groups, and the like. This term may be used in a purely descriptive sense but at times goes beyond this by attempting to show how this contributes to the functioning of democracy as opposed to totalitarianism. When such plural associations and organizations function in relative independence of the state they prevent the latter or even any single private source of power from gaining monopolistic weight; they help to train citizens in the political skills necessary for carrying on the democratic process; they accustom men to accept the legitimacy of opposition. They serve as a mechanism for dissemination and communication of ideas; and their intermediation between government at the top and the citizen at the bottom prevents the agglutination of masses which can be easily swayed by waves of ephemeral or destructive enthusiasms (cf. Kornhauser, 1959). We shall refer to this henceforth as *political pluralism*, a term, by the way, which is often regarded as incompatible with a one-party state.

3. *A cultural designation.* Here ethnic groups come into focus when one or more have a language, religion, kinship forms, nationality, tribal affiliation, and/or other traditional norms and values embodied in patterns that set them off from dominant or majority groups; this is cultural pluralism, as used here. Cultural differences can also vary independently of the stratification system from one society to another. In the case of Switzerland three major ethnic groups maintain relative cultural distinctiveness without marked inequality.[1] In Canada the balance is tipped with those of English ancestry predominating over those of French affiliation (cf. *Royal Commission on Bilingualism and Biculturism*, 1967). In the case of South Africa the stratification levels are more extreme with two cultural groupings in the upper level (English and Afrikaans), and at least nine or more African groups of varying sizes—language being the criterion—with the following four ethnic groups at the bottom of the numerical scale:

Tsonga, Swazi, Ndebele, and Venda (van den Berghe, 1967a, 291). In South African society it is race that produces a harsh overlay defining the major stratification pattern, relegating cultural features to a secondary place. Partly for this reason, the coloured or mixed population is separately defined, though in terms of language and custom they are predominantly Afrikaans with a minority of English speakers.

This form of cultural pluralism, then, may be regarded as analytically separable from race, or from any special type of status position. Empirically, however, it is sometimes combined with the first and always (excepting the Swiss case) combined with the second.

Nevertheless, as already observed above, culture and social structure are virtual Siamese twins, with each implicated in the other. So if a cultural group has its own special set of norms, they will ipso facto define certain institutions or patterns that separate the members of that group structurally from adjacent groups, at least in some minimal way. This brings us to:

4. *A structural designation.* A multicultural or multiethnic society is by implication a society with plural structural units. These units have different cultures or subcultures and, correlatively, are segmented or compartmentalized into "analogous, parallel, non-complementary, but distinguishable sets of institutions" (van den Berghe, 1967 mimeo, 3), at least in their most pronounced form.[2] Such societies with plural structures form a continuum. At one extreme of this continuum is monopoly of power by a single dominant group governing and regulating one or more other ethnic groups through a coercive political institution which is the only common and unifying institution in the society. In every other respect the institutions of kinship, religion, the economy, education, recreation and the like are parallel but different in structure and norms. Ordinarily this is compounded by differences in language and sometimes by race as well. The distinguishing feature is institutional pluralism and duplication which assures that members of each ethnic group playing roles in their own institutions have most of their social participation restricted to interaction with those of their own group, meeting those of other ethnic groups only fleetingly or occasionally in impersonal contacts, or as Furnivall put it, chiefly in the market-

place. This extreme form is the prototype for what M. G. Smith calls the "plural society" and what we have here termed "ethnic groups" he speaks of as "cultural sections." In his words, "Generally these cultural sections are highly exclusive social units, each constituting an area of common life, beyond which relations tend to be specific, segmental, and governed by structural factors" (M. G. Smith, 1960, 768). Such a distinction differs in emphasis and scope from the way Milton Gordon speaks of structural pluralism. In the latter case subordinate ethnics have primary relations in their own group and secondary relations outside it (Gordon, 1964, 235ff.). Thus Gordon's meaning is a broader one than the one adopted here overlapping the latter somewhat. The two usages do not contradict but rather supplement each other.

This exclusiveness of social participation regulated by institutional rules and standards for each cultural unit is a variable and not a fixed category, i.e., there may be more or less exclusiveness. For this variable we prefer the term *degree of enclosure;* the greater the degree of enclosure among the cultural sections, the greater is the potential for purely coercive integration and the lesser the possibility for consensual integration. Value systems are separated one from the other and the society "hangs together" only by compulsion channeled through a single common political institution buttressed by whatever legitimation it may receive from the subjugated plural subordinate groups.

One step removed from this extreme would be a dominant group controlling both the polity and the economy with the latter furnishing sustenance for people in several cultural groupings. This, as noted above (pp. 26–27) is the case in South Africa where the industrial complex with its money economy weaves a web of imperious necessity that binds people of different sections together with an integument that political force alone could not accomplish, though in this case the two institutions reinforce each other's integrative functions. The degree of enclosure in South Africa is modified somewhat by common participation in a shared economic institution.

At the opposite extreme where minimal enclosure occurs we can have several ethnic groups which share participation in a number of institutional orders—economic, political, recreational, educational, while still maintaining some cultural features that are variants on a historically related theme. In the case of kinship patterns, Smith remarks on the situation in the United States: "Marriage and the family vary among Greeks, Italians, and Irish in content rather than form, in their affective quality rather than in their social function, sanctions and norms . . . Unless ethnic traditions present incompatible institutional forms, they are, like social class patterns, stylistic variations within a common basic way of life, analytically similar to Linton's alternatives." This extreme of minimal enclosure impresses Smith as qualitatively, rather than quantitatively different from the maximal type so he designates the former by a special name. He continues, "Thus ethnic variations, like class styles, may produce cultural and social heterogeneity, but do not involve pluralism" (Smith, 1960, 770–71). Here we cannot accept his argument *in toto*. Although it is quite logical to recognize the difference between historically related cultures and historically unrelated ones, and to insist that the latter display more institutional enclosure than the former, this does not mean that historically related cultural groups lack institutional enclosure vis-à-vis each other. The case of the Greeks in the United States is an excellent example; while their kinship institutions are historically related to those of other countries in the Mediterranean basin and to other Christian populations farther north, it has been the Greeks who have clung to endogamy with more tenacity than perhaps any European ethnic group in the United States and this is definitely an exclusionist policy that still sets the group apart. To a lesser degree, their participation in the Orthodox rather than the Roman Catholic church creates another institutional enclosure that separates them from interaction with others, *even though these two religious institutions are variants on a common Christian theme.*

It thus seems more plausible to accept van den Berghe's thesis that "in most cases . . . social or structural pluralism is simply another facet of cultural pluralism" (van den Berghe, 1967 mimeo, 4). Hence I prefer to speak of maximal or minimal enclosure in the sense of a continuum with degrees rather than to speak of one extreme as pluralism and the other as heterogeneity in the manner of M. G. Smith.[3] Furthermore it seems best to employ the term heterogeneity as a synonym for pluralism rather than to give it a more restricted application to one end of the continuum as Smith does. As a matter of policy it is too much to expect that a term in such general use and with such general application will have to be dropped except when its denotation is much narrower. There is much to be said for a policy that does not require social scientists to learn entirely new meanings for familiar terms, especially when this seems unnecessary.

To sum up: the fourth meaning of pluralism is structural and this is correlative to the third meaning which is cultural. While these two may be analytically separated, they have a dialectical relation of mutual implication in the empirical world. When we refer to structural pluralism we are focusing on institutional differences in ethnic groups which separate or enclose them from dominant or majority groups in terms of social participation. Hence we may also speak of this as *social* pluralism which designates the same dimension of the problem. Social or structural pluralism varies from maximal to minimal forms which can be conceptualized as degrees of enclosure with indicators like endogamy, ecological concentration, institutional duplication, associational clustering, rigidity and clarity of group definition, segmentary relations of members with outsiders, etc. (van den Berghe, 1965, 78–79).

As used here, the term heterogeneity will be used indifferently to indicate either cultural or social pluralism and since this is consonant with its present use, no further justification is necessary.

However the analytical distinction between cultural and structural pluralism serves to warn against premature satisfaction with designating any society superficially as heterogeneous without further specification. One further caveat is needed. The structural dimension of pluralism prevents the investigator from taking the cultural factor by itself as though it were the whole picture; this has been done uncritically in the past by anthropologists who placed the entire emphasis on acculturation or cultural borrowing (Herskovits, Malinowski, Linton) or the sociologists who conceptualized assimilation in much the same way (Znaniecki, Park, and the Chicago school). This approach has played down the features of power and conflict which appear in societies whose structural features have been maximally different. Also, the overemphasis on the cultural has centered so exclusively on individual or family acculturation that it has lost the macrosociological view which is necessary for a full-blown comparative analysis.

It remains now to ask, what have been the effects of the five intergroup sequences: emergence of pariahs, emergence of indigenous isolates, annexation, migration, and colonization on the pluralistic composition of societies in the modern world? In answering this question I shall place more emphasis on structural pluralism than cultural pluralism, without neglecting the latter entirely. And account must be taken of the racial divisions already noted above.

Emergence of Pariahs and Pluralism

In the first place, the emergence of pariahs does not *create* problems of parallel structure, since these are already present in the society. It does, however, raise serious questions about the perpetuation of that structure as a result of the new legal dispensations ostensibly promoted to weaken or destroy it. Wherever such legislation grants formal legal rights for full civic and social participation, new conflicts arise over implementation and enforcement of government enactments. Much more research is needed to discover the shifts in institutional enclosure; it is especially important to explore participation in such key institutions as the economy to note the changes in occupational clustering, or the polity where there may be mobilization or lack of it. The data on these problems are quite unsatisfactory and require more thorough investigation on a comparative basis.

Emergence of Indigenous Isolates and Pluralism

This sequence appears in the "developing countries" and requires careful analysis. Although the process of change undergone by such ethnolinguistic groups has received abundant attention from anthropologists, it is usually placed in a conceptual framework that puts primary stress on the shattering of traditional modes of life (with its consequent disorganization) or to the forms of acculturation arising from reciprocal exchange between peoples when contacts increase. In most of these studies the focus is on adjustments made at the individual level by members of the simpler cultures (Cf. Spicer, 1952). In the present volume the field of analysis overlaps with familiar studies of "modernization" that trace the changes occurring in the transition from "traditional" to "modern" organization. It is precisely here that a shift of attention is required to the larger outlines of national societies facing problems of integrating whole populations into a "modern" configuration, and it is this movement that sweeps ethnic enclaves into the total process transforming the entire society into "something new and strange." The mode of approach most appropriate is to view this major change as one of ever-increasing social participation.

Gino Germani's analysis of this situation is so pointed that it bears repetition here:

> . . . in "traditional" types of society there is a considerable majority of the population whose participation is circumscribed with respect to geographic surroundings (limited to small communities); occupation (isolation in the economic sector); nonparticipation in decision-making (absence in political activity); and knowledge, experience, and enjoyment of the material and non-material benefits of general culture (as occurs when a considerable proportion of the inhabitants is limited to the confines of their respective ethnic backgrounds). The so-called industrial society is characterized by a high degree of mass participation in the majority of social activities. . . . In general terms, the causes which have produced the breakdown of the traditional pattern are well known and might be mentioned in passing. They consist of the growing penetration of the national society into considerable layers of the population which have, in one form or another, remained isolated, the break-up of local communities, disappearance of the enclosed or isolated economies and their growing incorporation into the national economy; transformation of traditional forms of work into wage labor, either by the establishment of industries or by changes in the primary, agricultural, or extractive sector, and hence disappearance of old "primary" or community forms of social relationships in the sphere of work as well as in other sectors such as

the life of the community, its means of recreation; growth of means of transportation and greater accessibility of the "central" zones from the peripheral areas; universal penetration of mass means of communication; increasing educational facilities and their dissemination among larger sectors of the population; disequilibrium in population, caused by persistent high birth rates and falling death rates. These and other phenomena disrupt the traditional order on a scale not comparable with what has occurred in past centuries. (Germani, 1964, 394, 399)

As indigenous isolates become more intensive participants in the life of the modernizing society, their degree of enclosure

FIGURE 8. STAGES OF INCREASED PARTICIPATION

Communication Dimension

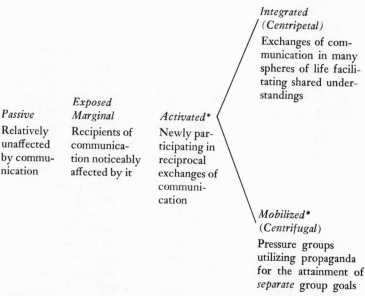

Integrated
(Centripetal)
Exchanges of communication in many spheres of life facilitating shared understandings

Passive
Relatively unaffected by communication

Exposed Marginal
Recipients of communication noticeably affected by it

Activated*
Newly participating in reciprocal exchanges of communication

Mobilized*
(Centrifugal)
Pressure groups utilizing propaganda for the attainment of *separate* group goals

* This is a deliberate departure from Germani's terminology which follows that of Deutsch in calling the intensive forms of participation in modern society "mobilization." For this I have substituted "activation." I believe that the study of intergroup relations will be clarified if Blalock's conception of "mobilization" comes into general use. Thus Blalock asserts, "power is a multiplicative function of two very general types of variables, *total resources* and the degree to which these resources are *mobilized* in the services of those persons or groups exercising the power" (Blalock, 1967, 110). Hence I prefer "activation" as a neutral term for intensive participation, and "mobilization" to symbolize the use of power resources as sanctions.

(the dimension of structural pluralism) might be expected to diminish, while their relationship to the superordinates (modernizers, on the whole) will change significantly. However, the increasing contacts between upper and lower groups has dialectical rather than singular results, i.e., they turn out to be *either* centripetal or centrifugal as noted in Figure 6, chapter 2 (see p. 83). If centripetal, the indigenous isolates will not only lose their seclusion but incorporate norms and institutional patterns of the superordinates while being admitted to membership into the latter on some regularized basis. If centrifugal, increased participation will trigger a new self-consciousness on the part of subordinates along with withdrawal and separatism that accom-

Institutional Dimension

Passive
Minimal economic or other exchanges with outside groups

Exposed Marginal
Market exchanges, payment of taxes, some group labor for dominants. Sporadic or intermittent schooling for a few children in educational system of dominants

Activated
Large scale entrance into modernizing societal occupations, political roles and educational sphere

Integrated (Centripetal)
Acceptance of limited autonomy for subordinates by superordinates

or

Incorporation of subordinates by populistic political process

or

Step-wise integration of subordinates on individual basis as persons enter institutional systems at higher levels

Mobilized (Centrifugal)
Subordinates' use of newly available economic, political, and educational resources as tools for gaining *separate* group goals

pany the awakening. This recoil phenomenon not only refreezes a pluralistic structure that has begun to thaw, but produces heightened sensitivity to symbols of inequality or inferiority that would never have occurred during isolation; these symbols become rallying points[4] for group demands and group action in the direction of autonomy, federalism, special legal privileges or "protections," rebellion, or secession.

The continuum of increased participation characteristic of the modernizing process can only be suggested in rough outline. It may clarify the picture somewhat to separate analytically two of the elements that are compounded empirically. In Figure 8 this is done, with the pattern of increasing communication outlined separately from the patterns of institutional incorporation for the sake of exposition.

The assumption behind this rough sketch is that processes of integration or conflict become discernible for indigenous isolates only after a certain threshold of activation. Hence there may be a series of ethnic groups in a given society that are in different stages of the participation curve. Such appears to be the case in Burma where a number of the "hill people" are either passive or exposed marginals, while others like the Chins, Karens, Kachins, Shans, and Mons are not only more complex in social organization (kingdoms, feudal principalities) but, in colonial days were under the direct rule of the British in so-called "excluded areas" while central Burma experienced indirect rule and therefore lesser direct contact with the British (Trager, 1966, 80). But the larger ethnic groups who had more sustained contact with colonial rulers imbibed many nationalistic ideas; the Karens especially received extensive Western influences from Christianizing missions and schools (Trager, *op. cit.*, 103). World War II with its alternate occupation of Burma by British, American, Chinese, and Japanese troops heightened outside influences and spurred nationalist sentiment. The larger ethnic groups in upland areas participated in the drive for Burmese independence but regarded it in terms of their own separate autonomy. No sooner did the country at large gain independence than Karens, Shans, Kachins, and others staged numerous revolts in behalf of separate sovereignty, and their resistance in one form or another has continued ever since (Trager, *op. cit.*, 60–82; 95–139). As Hunter remarks, "The transition from civil war to politics was never fully achieved; the central power of the army was left to impose a unity which politics had failed to create" (Hunter, 1966, 18).

However the process of mobilization, as shown on the above diagram, is only one alternative. In Latin America the trend has been noticeably toward integration of the third type listed under the institutional dimension. As Mishkin puts it, "In reality, the two groups merge . . . the various levels that comprise Peruvian national culture are fluid in character, each spilling over into the next. Any segment of the population curve will contain groups representing various degrees of Indian and mestizo status. The same individual may be considered Indian from one point of view or to be classified as a mestizo from another" (Mishkin, 1946–48, 413). In this case activation operates through regulatory mechanisms, accepted on both sides, by which the process of integration is transmuted into selective individual mobility into the upper group. Educational achievement is the chief mechanism regulating this movement but the process is complicated, of course, by population pressures on the land, excessive migration to urban peripheral slums, and the inability of the developing economic system to absorb the migrants. It is significant, however, that this is not socially defined so much as an "Indian problem" but simply a problem of poverty. If mobilization occurs here, it is in the direction of proletarian revolution rather than an "Indian rebellion." This is again a function of the incorporative, miscegenative feature of the Latin American societies as already noted.

Annexation and Pluralism

Annexation has, of course, been a perennial mode of conquest practiced throughout the world. Here interest is limited to modern manifestations as a mode of incorporation into the nation-state. And since the nation-state in its contemporary form is a recent development, dating from the eighteenth to the earlier part of the nineteenth century, account must be taken of the impact of nationalism on *previous* annexations as well as the effects of annexation that have occurred subsequent to the rise of nationalism with its unique idea of the national state. It is impossible to trace the development of this idea in the fullness it requires; the task has already been accomplished by Kohn (1955) and many others.

A brief overview will be sufficient here. The idea of nationalism with its corresponding conception of the nation-state seems to have been established in Western Europe where it first found its fullest embodiment in England and France who arrived at it in quite different ways. It was in these two countries that "just as the king had required undivided allegiance in the days of royal supremacy so the sovereign nation-state of the nineteenth century expected not only loyalty to the state but also identification with the language, culture and mores of the majority" (Janowsky, 1945, 17). The notion of man's freedom identified with nationalism spread like an ideological prairie fire from this time on, and had as its chief components the ideas of sovereign independence of people with homogeneous characteristics—common language, history, literature, religion, or culture, the state as the embodiment of the people's will, equality expressed in the electorate with the numerical majority as the ruling element, and this new social form of nationality as "the source of all creative cultural energy and economic well-being" (Kohn, 1955, 10). When these ideas spread to central and eastern Europe, with their long histories of repeated annexations and delayed national unifications, the ideological impact of nationalism had fateful consequences because of its central idea that uniformity and homogeneity were good while any form of pluralism was bad. This led certain dominant powers with annexed sectors: Russia with Ukrainians and Poles or Prussia with Poles, for example, to insist on enforced uniformity and an attempt to obliterate the language and culture of their subject peoples.[5] Normative monism was the order of the day for dominant powers speaking in the name of nationalism. However, their subjects also appealed to the same ideology in the name of freedom: if uniformity was good and pluralism was bad, then they asserted their autonomy as nations and demanded separation, independence and the right to set up new sovereign states with their *own* uniformity and homogeneity (Janowsky, *op. cit.*, 20–22, 23–28). Such annexed peoples having their own language and set of institutions, their awareness of a common historical past, and an awakening to the possibility of a new independent status under the potent influence of the nationalist ideal, came to be known as nationalities rather than nations.[6] The more loosely organized Austro-Hungarian Empire never attempted to organize an overarching national state but the wave of nationalist ideology from the west transformed their annexed peoples into nationalities—Czechs, Hungarians, Croations, Serbs, etc. The treaties of Versailles and Trianon after the first World War recognized the rights of self-determination for nationalities, many of which became full-blown nations as a consequence. However, because of the impossibility of drawing national boundary lines with the exactitude demanded by the norm of homogeneity, the ideal of the nation-state was incompletely realized and the emerging states produced a new set of annexations *de facto* where sections or portions of adjacent national or nationalities of different language, culture or religion were incorporated in an otherwise unitary state. It was during this period that the term "minority" came into general usage as a synonym for nationality groups in the post-Versailles crop of new Central European nations and the notion of minority rights became a belated supplement to the idealistic demand for national self-determination which proved to be an illusory attempt at creating uniform states.[7]

Thus annexed populations, some from the prenationalist era, some from the period before World War I, some from the period between the two World Wars, and some from the era after World War II constitute centers of cultural and social pluralism within European nations today. The structural consequences of this pluralism have not been given the attention they deserve and constitute not only an unfinished task for comparative ethnic relations but one that has scarcely begun. Unfortunately, the clamor of normative and policy considerations has been so great that they have drowned out the more objective task of analysis. Furthermore, since language has been the most salient distinguishing mark of the plural constituents, this has given cultural features the most prominent place instead of structural characteristics. We do not have a very clear idea of the degree of enclosure actually existing in such pluralistic centers though we find some clues in the Swiss case on the one hand and the Soviet example on the other.

These two types are both called "multi-national states," by Janowsky (1945, 35ff).[8] The Swiss case is a political federalism of linguistic equality influenced by the French Revolution; the Soviet case is a centralized party state with unitary installation and control of uniform core institutions (political, economic) together with linguistic freedom and grades of formal representation on an ethnic or nationality basis—the outcome of the Communist revolution. These may be called equalitarian and tutelary federalism respectively. In both cases there is ecological concentration of linguistic groups but while this creates small, compact communes in Switzerland, it permits much larger scattered settlements in the vast stretches of the Soviet Union where mobility has led to much greater mixing of peoples. In both Switzerland and Great Russia, the annexations for the most part preceded the era of nationalism; the Swiss area was a Germanic country till the eighteenth century where German rulers overran smaller pockets of French and Italian speaking people. Only under the influence of the French Revolution did the German majority which persists to this day enter into a confederation union allowing linguistic equality at the central state level and autonomy of French and Italian cantons who then had their own forms of local government, schools, and churches (historically related in cultural terms) maintained in their own language. While this constitutes a genuine cultural pluralism, the structural enclosure is at an intermediate level, varying with the economy. Where pastoral and agricultural pursuits predominate and are highly local in character, social pluralism is more pronounced, but where industrialism and the tourist trade have been linked with national institutions the integrating effects are much greater. Thus structural pluralism varies from canton to canton. The Russian case is still more complicated and deserves special, though necessarily brief treatment.

The spread of Russian domination into both Siberia and Central Asia was started under the Czarist regime and completed under Soviet auspices. While in a technical sense this may be conceptualized as annexation, it is equally possible to regard it as colonization and some of the leading scholars define it in this way. Thus Walter Kolarz entitles a leading work *Russia and Her Colonies* (1952) and highlights the colonial relations between the Soviet government in Moscow with the subject peoples of Central Asia; likewise Seton-Watson describes the imperial features of Soviet rule and shows a number of parallels between this and colonial practice in Asia and Africa (1964). But the distances between the central government and the outlying districts were far more vast than those existing in Central Europe which meant that in Russia the chances for coming in contact with historically unrelated cultures was much greater. We have already noted that this did not result in racialism for the Russians and hypothesize that an important reason for this was that Russians *thought* more in terms of annexation of adjacent areas, and less in terms of the stark contrasts that were characteristic of overseas colonizers. However it seems at least defensible to classify Russian expansion under our category of annexation while recognizing many of its colonial features or practices.[9]

Since the cultural characteristics of the many peoples brought under Russian rule were so often highly dissimilar to those of the Great Russians, the structural elements show an approach to maximal enclosure of the different ethnic groups, especially in nomadic, or semi-nomadic economy on the one hand, and Muslim religious practices on the other. The Czarist regime practiced cultural imperialism by Russification, i.e., by trying to force non-Russians to become Russians in language and in tribute from puppet leaders. The Soviets had a different aim, namely the triumph of communism as a politico-economic system. Recognizing that this could not be accomplished swiftly, the Soviets set up administrative units with different degrees of participation at the national level: "fifteen fully fledged Soviet Republics, . . . sixteen Autonomous Republics, nine Autonomous Provinces, and ten National Areas "with a few still lower forms of autonomy" (Kolarz, 1955, 191–92). These varied apparently on the basis of their potential collectivization and communization, or, in other language, on their degree of social and economic development. Those at the top had the highest literacy, the greatest amount of industrialization and urbanization, and the greatest number of indigenous leaders with managerial skills and Communist party sympathies. The system of Communist rule had a manifest and latent tendency, the former emphasizing federation, linguistic and cultural autonomy, and the acceptance of local leadership in public affairs. Both Lenin and Stalin recognized the rights of autonomy and the legitimacy of self-determination for emerging "nations" (Janowsky, *op. cit.*, 79, 81) among whom they included the multiple ethnic groups of Central Asia. During the early period of Soviet rule, this principle which contrasted so favorably with the Russification policy of the Czars received approving comment from many students of ethnic relations, of whom Janowsky is a prominent example (*op. cit.*, Chap. VI).

The latent features of the Soviet regime were more veiled and did not appear with full clarity until the full force of integration policy was revealed. After thirty years of what was openly asserted to be a transitional phase, these formerly latent totalitarian tendencies are coming into the foreground. One feature is the ideology of the "elder brother," a term applied to the Great Russians conceived as the vanguard of the working class standing in a tutelary relationship to the non-European peoples of Siberia and Central Asian republics, migrating to the more "backward areas" to become the elite "as skilled industrial workers, as managers of the newly founded state enterprises, as officials staffing the inflated bureaucratic machine, as teachers in schools and higher educational institutions, and also as policemen and public prosecutors . . . It led to the foundation of largely Russian industrial towns and workers' settlements and to the strengthening of the Russian and European character of existing Asian towns" (Kolarz, 1955, 199). Structurally this means the importation of new institutions with new alien personnel and superimposing them upon an indigenous traditional matrix. The parallel with colonial practice in Asia and Africa is striking; in both cases political and economic institutions are the entering wedge, the vanguard of control, and the levers of change that discipline large sections of the population in new patterns of work and organized effort and the goals of that effort are defined by outsiders. With only minor changes, Furnivall's description of colonialism in Asia can well be applied to the Russian case, viz., "The cult of efficiency merely built up a monumental Western skyscraper on Eastern soil, with the natives in the basement; all inhabited the same country, but the building was of a different world, the modern world, to which the ordinary native had no access" (Furnivall, 1941 quoted in Hunter, *op. cit.*, 61–62).

Thus the apparent permissiveness and tolerance of the Great Russian elite in allowing the use of separate national languages (the manifest policy) is only superficially similar to the colonial practice of indirect rule with its encouragement of "native" practices that are left undisturbed. The Soviet pattern is far too dynamic to rest at this point. The elite of communism are to be transforming agents and their accession to local cultural or linguistic practices is but a first accommodative stage in the future victories of a world-embracing system. Thus even in these first stages, "The Communist leaders are in fact perfectly willing that Kirghiz, Udmusts, White Russians or any other nation should use their own language, in public or in private, provided that they express only Communist ideas with it" (Seton-Watson, *op. cit.*, 17). The fact that "native languages" are nearly as popular today as they were forty years ago is therefore not a reliable sign that a long-range policy of unification is failing (Pipes, 1964, 4 ff.) but that normative pluralism is being used as an instrument for long range ends which will be accomplished as the Communist politico-economic complex expands and incorporates ever greater masses of the people. The latent policy can only be stated in future terms. It is summarized succinctly by Kolarz as follows:

> According to Communist doctrine, the blossoming of national cultures—national in form, socialist in content—is to prepare a further higher stage of development when national groups are to disappear as distinct cultural and linguistic entities and be fused "into a single common socialist culture with a single common language." This is the official Stalinist doctrine to which the Communist Party of the Soviet Union has been committed since its Sixteenth Congress in 1930, when Stalin outlined the idea of "one socialist world—one culture—one language." (Kolarz, 1955, 208)

The Soviet form of annexation, then, has the effect of creating pluralist structures for the nationalities with the eventual aim of superseding them. The nature of these structures and their transformations constitute a fascinating area for future investigation, especially when compared with that of emerging nations of Africa and Asia. Our present ignorance of these pluralistic structures is practically total and one can only hypothesize that the degree of enclosure varies from almost complete separation to strong interpenetration—the evidence will not be available until there is freedom for international research in the Soviet Union. Our present data only indicate that cultural pluralism is still vigorous in Central Asia. Thus an anthropologist who has done pioneering research in the area reports:

> . . . the peoples of Central Asia have retained the patterns and values of their own traditional cultures. They have been selective in their borrowing of new elements and have modified these to fit into their own way of thinking and behaving. Such proffered elements as do not fit into their own patterns are rejected. The peoples of Central Asia have learned from the liquidations of the 1920's and the purges of the 1930's not to resist with violence innovations they find unacceptable. They have, however, learned to follow quietly their own cultural inclinations despite legal enactments and the urging of agitators. (Bacon, 1966, 208)

How rapidly totalitarian *dirigism* will be able to overcome this resistance is still a moot question.

In the Middle East a perennial process of annexation has been present for centuries, manifested locally in chiefdoms expanding to incorporate other chiefdoms and oases, with successful rebellions producing new chiefdoms eventually provoking new rebellions. Outside, these smaller concentric circles were the larger encircling dominions like the Ottoman Empire annexing both Arab and non-Arab peoples, and, during the period of Ottoman decline, the temporary rise of French and British empires displacing the rulers of that day. The nation-states attaining independence after World War I inherited the annexations of the past much as the new nations of Central Europe did in the same period and as a result of the same nationalistic wave of popular feeling. The residual populations from these earlier waves of annexation showing the greatest cultural contrast with their new nationalistic rulers in Iran are the Turks of Azerbaidjan, the Turcomans, the Kurds, the Arabs, and the Armenians. In Turkey of the present reduced size there is also a large contingent of Kurds. Among the Arab nations Syria has the greatest number of non-Arab inhabitants, again the Kurds. This people, having their own Indo-European language, and a common set of cultural traditions and practices (overlaid by formal adherence to Islam) are divided among Turkey, Syria, Iraq, and Iran and have developed a strong nationalistic aspiration of their own, "but it is still limited in its effect by the persistence of tribalism, which is still a stronger force than nationalism among the Kurds" (Hourani, 1947, 38). In the Middle Eastern nations as a whole one would therefore expect to find the most pronounced structural pluralism as a typical set of relations separating the Kurds from the dominant majority of the four nations mentioned.

While nationalistic claims among minorities in the Arab countries are rare, the principal pluralities are chiefly religious (Berger, 1962, 253). The spread of Islam was accompanied by a semiofficial tolerance for the religious bodies historically related to the Muslim faith, Judaism and Christianity, while the adherents of these religions were granted autonomy as *millets*, especially in the Ottoman Empire. A millet was a closed community of believers with a chosen leader having sacerdotal and secular power. Aided by a council, the head of the millet had control of churches, education, marriages, civil rights, cemeteries, and similar spheres of action on the basis of autonomous millet law. Both Christian and Jewish communities had such millets, thus establishing a marked structural pluralism. As Hourani puts it, "these groups formed closed communities. Each was a 'world' sufficient to its members and exacting their ultimate loyalty. The worlds touched but did not mingle with each other; each looked at the rest with suspicion and even hatred . . . They were all marginal, shut out from power and historic decision" (Hourani, *op. cit.*, 22). With the emergence of new middle eastern nations after World War I, the tradition of closed communities continued; this ended for Jews at the close of World War II as the importation of anti-Semitism from Nazi forces proved threatening and the establishment of Israel as a separate state provided a visible haven. The vast majority of Jews in the Arab world eventually migrated to the latter (Berger, *op. cit.*, 256, 260). The extent to which the structural separation of Christian communities still exists is in need of further exploration and research. Other forms of pluralism in the Arab world would have chiefly to do with internal variations within the Muslim faith and while these are significant cultural variations, their structural importance appears to be secondary with the possible exception of Iraq where Orthodox Sunnis are more urban with leading positions in the economy and polity, while the heterodox Shiites are primarily agriculturalists (Berger, *op. cit.*, 257).

Migration and Pluralism

Taking slave transfers into account as one major type of sequence, we can advance a provisional generalization that chattel slavery (in the Western world at least)[10] generally tends to produce plural societies. The division between master and slave usually hardens into two separate segments. The extent of the institutional differences in the two stratified divisions is a function of the cultural homogeneity of the slave group on the one hand, and the break-up of consanguineal ties by individual sale of slaves to different masters on the other. Thus the institutional differences between the culture of the masters and that of the slaves will be greatest where slaves of the same ethnolinguistic unit are concentrated together and where relatives are not separated by sale or transfer. On the other hand, institutional differences will be at a minimum where slaves from many ethnolinguistic units are thrown together and where individuals are sold to different owners regardless of familial ties. The first condition was approximated in Haiti, Trinidad, and Brazil, the second in the United States. This institutional difference which may create a sharper cleavage at first is subject to other forces with the passage of time. Thus the structural separation of the two groups that was definitely marked at first in Brazil was quickly modified by miscegenation and manumission as noted above, both these factors producing a gradated series of color variations, hastening the acculturative process, and erasing the rigid lines between the two groups (though it left some pockets of vestigial cultural distinctions in isolated groups). In the United States the process was reversed. Though there was miscegenation, it was accompanied with very little manumission so that intermediate racial types were relegated to the slave population, thus keeping the dividing lines intact. Since the indiscriminate sale of individual slaves was common, acculturation proceeded rapidly but in a restricted milieu that was unrepresentative of American culture as a whole. In this case we have a derivative phenomenon of subcultural variations among Negroes that can be attributed to their special position in a plural slave society. Van den Berghe speaks of this as cultural drift and calls it secondary cultural pluralism resulting first from deculturation and then from selective acculturation in a structurally plural segmentation produced by racial definition and separation (van den Berghe, 1967, 135). Since race is an independent factor it apparently has the special power to produce its own form of social pluralism which is a high degree of *enforced* enclosure typified by the segregated status of Negro life in the United States. Considering that the American Negro has only minor differences in culture when compared with other Americans, it makes sense to say that here we have "a nearly pure case of deep structural pluralism with little cultural pluralism" (van den Berghe, mimeo. 1967, 4).

The impact of slavery in the West Indies took a somewhat different course, partly because the white masters were a tiny colonial oligarchy having no reinforcing majority to support them, as was the case in the United States, and also experiencing a much earlier abolition of slavery as an institution. In the British Caribbean particularly, the steady practice of miscegenation, coupled with structural demands for bourgeois and white collar workers led to a polarization of societies into three rather than two sections with somewhat less sharp distinctions than those found in the southern United States. The top segment is white, including directors, managers, planters, and the upper echelons of business enterprise. The intermediate segment is of mixed color and fills the occupations chiefly of the non-manual type in offices, stores, banks, schools, and some service establishments. At the lowest level are the blacks who are plantation workers, small farmers, and industrial workers that are the great bulk of the population. Racial lines separate the three sections into units with fairly high enclosure interacting chiefly with those of their own unit. Until recently the whites held both political and economic power, but:

. . . as power was transferred from London, the form and status of these Caribbean governments continued to change, and so did certain sectors of their intersectional networks. The historically dominant upper section lost political power to that immediately below. These two upper sections developed a symbiotic association. Together they promoted the development of federal government and ideology, a process which itself involved further changes in the form and status of these . . . societies. (M. G. Smith, 1965, 320)

Because of the relatively sharp cleavage between the two upper sections and the lowest one the future is problematic and depends on convergences of interests (*Ibid.*, 319), which is to say at least problematic if not unlikely.

The sequence of contract labor transfers can also be illustrated in the Caribbean where it complicates the picture already given. This has deepened the pluralistic structure of these societies, especially in Trinidad, Guyana and Surinam. The incoming tide of East Indian laborers has swelled their sector of the population to perhaps 40 per cent in Trinidad and 50 or more per cent in Guyana (*Ibid.*, 11). The potentials for conflict between the Creoles and Indians, each tightly enclosed in its own network of institutions and associations while competing or jockeying for power in the political arena have been admirably analyzed in the case of Guyana (Despres, 1967), and though the pluralistic structure has received less attention in Trinidad and Surinam, the Creole-Indian conflicts already occurring in Trinidad are perhaps only portents of future instability. In South Africa where the contract labor population of Indians and their descendants have occupied an intermediate structural position, they have become the target for attack by Africans at the lowest structural level. It is significant that "the most violent racial outbreak which has occurred in South Africa was in the Durban riot of 1949 in which Africans murdered a number of Indians and looted and burned Indian property" (Van der Horst, 1965, 128). This pattern of conflict with Indians has occurred in East African countries as well.

The demographic ratios have a correlative importance and the proportion of the contract laborers to the total population must be taken into account. Where their numbers, augmented by natural increase, approaches 50 per cent or more of a population, without other significant divisions, the structural separation precipitates severe conflicts, particularly when voting rights open the way for communal[11] mobilization (Laponce, 1957). This has not only happened in Guyana but to an even more pronounced degree in Fiji where Indian indentured labor on the sugar plantations has grown numerically from minority to majority status at just the time when the franchise is initially available to all. In an agricultural economy where indigenous Fijians have title to 80 per cent of the land, while the East Indians have a majority of the electorate, predictions of explosive conflict to come are not too difficult (Mortimer, 1960, 305–06). Throughout Southeast Asia, however, the presence of imported laborers has had lesser demographic consequences. In Burma where Indian contract laborers were only part of a larger group including commercial immigrants, the Indian population was only about 7 per cent of the nation, decreasing to about 3 per cent today. Since they have been concentrated in the capital city, their visibility is heightened, making them the target of Burmese nationalistic hostility. The structural features of their separate community life separates them rather sharply from the Burmese (Mahajani, 1960) but as an identifiable unit of contract laborers they have not existed separately from the shopkeepers and money lenders with whom they form a separate enclave. In Malaya the contract laborers from India formed a much larger proportion of all Indians and a greater percentage of the total population than in Burma (14 per cent). Their specialized role in the economy and their comparative segregation on plantations and in rural camps, not only lowered their visibility but insulated them from the mainstream of urban and industrial, as well as political life. Only since independence have they formed a political organization which has joined the ruling Alliance party as a kind of junior member. Partly because of their small numbers and low economic status, partly because of the greater preponderance and weight of the Chinese community whose competition is more feared, the Indians in Malaya, maximally enclosed though they may be, have precipitated relatively little conflict and are "a tolerated minority" (Hunter, 1966, 55–56).

The waves of contract laborers that found their way to the plantations of Hawaii, particularly from Japan, China, and the Philippines, formed structurally enclosed communities for a time with relatively minor conflict since at first they were segregated from more public life. Though it might have seemed predictable that such ethnic units would eventually come into marked collision with each other, this did not seem to occur. Lind explains this by two factors: first, that a more urban and industrial economy penetrated the islands of Hawaii than was the case in Malaya, enabling workers of different national or racial groups to find opportunities when they left the plantations; and second, the greater spread of the equalitarian ethos in Hawaii (Lind, 1955, 63–67). To these we should probably add a third factor that presupposes those of Lind, namely, that ethnic groups entered a sphere of economic participation that drew them into a common whole *before* they attained the franchise. Had these two factors been reversed, the situation could well have been quite different.[12]

The movement of voluntary migrants to other lands has had varied pluralistic effects. In countries where the culture and institutions of the newcomers were historically related to that of the host society and where physical differences were not great enough to be given a racial definition, even temporary residence in ecologically distinct colonies proved but a transient pluralistic structure eroded by larger social forces. Such was the case with European immigrants to the United States where groups of the same linguistic and geographical origin came to be defined in terms of nationality even before their homelands attained the full stature of nation-states.[13] The break-up of the structural and cultural differences go hand in hand and tend to shift from one generation to the next. It is the structure of primary groups that retains its hold the longest since the host society resists incorporation at this level and the ethnic group clings to it partly out of customary preference and partly as a compensation for lack of entry into the outer sphere (Gordon, 1964, 70–71). Political conflicts in the electorate soon find accommodation in the "balanced slate" where mobilized power finds differential expression roughly comparable to the ethnic representation (Banfield and Wilson, 1963, 38–44).

On the other hand where racism has permeated popular thinking in the host society and the immigrants have culture and institutions historically unrelated to that of their hosts *and* physical differences that are easily defined in racial terms, both social and cultural pluralism find a prominent place and the degree of enclosure for incoming ethnics is doubly enforced (from within and from without) as was the case for the Japanese during their early sojourn in the United States. This pluralism, however, was shattered in their case by a set of fortuitous circumstances that cannot be followed here (see Schermerhorn, 1949, 199–224). A similar structural pluralism has enclosed other oriental groups and, to a lesser degree, Mexicans and Puerto Ricans as well.

Immigration parallels with those of the United States have occurred in Australia during recent years, so far as European ethnic groups are concerned, with perhaps a larger number settling in rural regions. Due to the proliferation of large-scale farming in Australia an unusual number of newcomers have settled on ranches in solidary workers' settlements under the direction of British-descended Australians or, in other cases, have organized their own ethnic agricultural communities (Price, 1963). The structural features of this extensive cultural pluralism remain to be investigated.

In the Orient the most extensive voluntary migrations have been those of the Chinese into Thailand, Malaya, Indonesia, the Philippines, and a number of smaller countries (Purcell, 1966). Though originally most of the immigrants were peasants, they were oriented toward a money economy, toward thrift and achievement through capital accumulation and through cash cropping, mining, trading, and merchandising soon raised themselves into a sort of middle class status which has characterized Chinese communities as a whole. At the same time family solidarity, the cohesion of each dialect group, and the highly organized associational life of the Chinese gave a high degree of enclosure to their communities which combined paradoxically with dynamism, flexibility and compromise in relations with non-Chinese in external relations. The structural separation into an intermediary position has raised intermittent storms of violence against the Chinese as against the East Indians in Africa. Structural features of pluralism have been provisionally analyzed for Malaya (Freedman, 1960); extension of this analysis on a comparative basis for other Southeastern Asian societies is definitely called for. Other factors intervene here also and will be touched on in the discussion below.

Colonization and Pluralism

In portraying this sequence, it has already been noted above that it may be conceptualized on the one hand in terms of relative demographic preponderance of the colonizers (limited settlement, substantial settlement, or massive settlement) and in terms of postcolonial derivatives. It is important to recognize at the outset that colonial societies are the *classical form* of plural societies, i.e., what are termed here societies with maximal enclosure of ethnic groups. Having the colonial case clearly in mind, Smith describes its characteristic element as follows, "The dominant social section of these culturally split societies is simply the section that controls the apparatus of power and force and this is the basis of the status hierarchies that characterize pluralism . . . When the dominant section is also a minority,[14] the structural implications of cultural pluralism have their most extreme expression, and the dependence on regulation by force is greatest" (M. G. Smith, 1960, 772, 774).

Such a society should not be characterized by the term hierarchical, for this too often presupposes a structure arising from non-coercive differentiation in which the higher positions are functionally more important and are validated by pervasive consensus.[15] A better term would be *hierocratic;* this implies a structure of domination in which one cultural section[16] with its own set of segmentary institutions imposes its rule upon one or more other cultural sections, each with its own set of segmentary and historically unrelated institutions which remain at least partially intact during the period of reign. In the colonial case (particularly the instances of limited and substantial settlement) maximal enclosure occurs on both sides of the boundary lines separating superordinate and subordinate sections.[17] Here we have "a social structure compartmentalized into analogous, parallel, non-complementary, but distinguishable sets of institutions" (van den Berghe, 1967 mimeo, 3). The integration of such a society is clearly not consensual but coercive with the political institution the central organ in the hands of the dominant cultural section, actually the only institution that in any sense unites all groups.

Secondarily the ruling section may establish economic institutions that incorporate some members of other sections but not all. Cultural pluralism as well as social pluralism is characteristic of subordinate sections whose autonomy in this respect is clearly marked. When there are two or more subordinate sections, the relations between them are "segmented, utilitarian, non-affective, and functionally specific" (van den Berghe, *ibid.*), also potentially hostile, and the conflict being augmented by differential treatment accorded them by the ruling section which in turn maintains this differential balance by regulatory measures, administrative decisions, or legal enactments. Thus, they become institutionalized. Relations between subordinate sections and the dominant section are of a dependent status, jockeying for favors, with latent conflict on one side, and coercion, paternalistic administrative neutrality, with latent favoritism on the other. This highly unstable system is dependent on the successful legitimation and institutionalization of political domination, buttressed by the spread of interdependence as the dominant section extends its economic institutions over wider and wider spheres of activity among indigenous populations.

As noted in the Latin American case, the colonial section in Mexico almost completely destroyed the cultural and social autonomy of the Indians, not only by liquidating the leaders but by transplanting Indians to encomiendas and towns, where they were incorporated as laborers in a new economy, by miscegenation, and by converting them to a different religion which integrated them more fully into a unitary whole with their conquerors. This process which reached an extreme in Mexico, had less efficacy elsewhere, and perhaps least in the countries that now have the largest Indian components, Bolivia, Paraguay, Peru, Ecuador, and Guatemala. Here the two institutions of the state and religion had their integrative dominance while economic institutions did not keep pace. Miscegenation, too, had lesser effects, stopping short of its wider extension in Mexico. It now became the dominant mestizo group (perhaps "section" is too strong a term for it, though not for the Indians). In the case of Guatemala, Manning Nash has this to say:

> . . . only a part of the population is fully aware of the national
> entity, participates significantly in its cultural and social life, or

has control over resources and communications of nationwide scope or impact. That part of the population which carries the national variety of culture is in fact the national society; it is scattered throughout the national territory; it is the link between the nation and other nations in the world and is the segment of the population in whom political control is vested and within which political control is contested. It is also that part of the population whose economic decisions have national repercussions. (Nash, 1957, 826)

This part of the population is, of course, the ladino (elsewhere in Latin America the mestizo) and the implications for social pluralism are plain. In the Spanish American case, the usual lacuna between the colonial period and the postcolonial derivatives of independence is not as sharp as it was in Asia or Africa, because the mestizos in Latin America were the spearhead of the independence movements, and their structural relationship to the Indians remained constant both before and after the break with European rule. Cultural ties with Spain remained as strong as ever. Moreover the national revolutions of the Spanish colonies were, for the most part, both preindustrial and preurban.

The colonization process in Asia was of quite a different character. There the colonial powers of the seventeenth and later centuries entered territories where both mainland and maritime kingdoms and empires had flourished in the past with long histories of cultural and social pluralism and their attendant conflicts. What the Europeans brought with them was new weapons, new organizations of economic units, and new forms of political administration resting on the first two. By means of these techniques the colonial power imposed a superstructure on the indigenous culture or cultures, a superstructure instrumental to economic gain and rationalized in terms of it. Whether that gain comes from raw materials at the lowest possible cost (an earlier stage) or from market outlets for finished goods (a later stage) or a combination of the two, the colonial power treats the whole society as an economy, and the members of that society in instrumental terms (Hunter, 1966, 61). If local labor seems unfitted for these tasks, indentured or contract labor is brought in and the pluralism of the society is thereby artificially increased; in many of these areas "European colonization changed its composition" (Hunter, *ibid.*, 60). The need for middlemen, for merchants and traders to speed up the processes of transfer and shipment "required the introduction of large numbers of people more used to a higher and technical culture and to a money economy than were the peasantry on the spot" (Hunter, *ibid.*, 61) which led to attraction of Chinese in ever larger numbers. Each colony became more populated and more pluralistic as time went on, and in each case it became true to say that "the union is not voluntary but is imposed by the colonial power and by the force of economic circumstances; and the union cannot be dissolved without the whole society relapsing into anarchy" (Furnivall, 1948, 307).

The structural pluralism of the Asian and Southeast Asian colonies was clearly hierocratic, usually with a plentiful number of subordinate sections related to each other and to the ruling sections in the pattern already noted. In a three-fold plural structure of Europeans, immigrants or contract laborers, and native residents, it was the latter who raised the banner of nationalism and independence and who became the section incorporating the new rulers. Furnivall's prediction of relapse into anarchy was then borne out, to a lesser degree than he apparently expected but with many severe breakdowns in any case. However it is more important to explore the structural reasons for this than to accept it as a mere datum.

In the colonial structure the indigenous sections were at the bottom in economic institutions and to a lesser degree in political as well, though a few nationals had places in the bureaucracy. In the structure of the independent society that followed, the native sections were catapulted to the top in the political structure with scant experience in policy decision-making. However, in the economic sphere they had very little foothold and turned against those who occupied the remaining echelons of economic power.

> For the effect of creating a virtual monopoly of key functions —commercial, financial, industrial—in the hands of immigrant groups must be seen through the eyes of young nationals who have often completed their higher education overseas and become passionately nationalist. With new political weapons in their hands, the young nationalists turned them against the Chi-

nese who still possessed residual economic power. Job reserva-
tion aimed against Chinese has been frequently imposed by
legislation (Thailand, Vietnam, Cambodia, Burma, Indonesia)
. . . (Hunter, 1966, 68–69)

From another angle the sudden change from dependent to
independent status for the societies in question disrupted the
coercive bonds that held them together. The rapid substitution
of an internal authority weakly legitimated for a more compulsive and tightly institutionalized relationship released centrifugal
forces previously held in check. Sections formerly oriented upward to a quasi-judicial, unrelated, and relatively neutral power,
bypassing each other in this relationship, now faced each other
as antagonists with only one of their own number as the court
of appeal. Without consensus to substitute for externally imposed
coercion, the appeal to power and strength became overwhelming. With swift expansion of the franchise, this was one of the
channels through which conflict was directed but it proved insufficient. As equalitarian ideology spread rapidly, almost anything could become a symbol of privilege or deprivation. It
could be the numerical ratio of one's own section in the bureaucracy, in the cabinet, in the political party, or the trade union.
It could be the number of schools in "our" district as compared
with "theirs." It could be the extent to which one language is
given autonomy or preference in comparison with another. It
could be employment rates or unemployment rates, or the ratio
in lucrative or prestigeful occupations. Occupational clustering
in the various sections, under the impact of the equalitarian demand and increased urbanization becomes subject to the demand
for "normalization" of each group's representation across the
board. All these become criteria for legitimizing the new government, and by association, demands on the section with which
that government is identified. Conversely, the new ruling section
uses its power to offset its previous deficiencies and buttresses
them with new privileges to make their dominion secure. Endemic conflict is therefore the order of the day.

The colonial pattern in Africa was both similar and different.
For present purposes it is important to note four differences
within the otherwise similar hierocratic plural societies: (1) there
was probably a greater cultural gap between the colonizers and

the colonized than existed in Asia;[18] (2) there was a much smaller proportion of immigrants and contract laborers in Africa; (3) there was a greater proportion of colonies of substantial settlement in Africa than in Asia; (4) the African colonies came at a later historical epoch. What were the effects of these four factors?

With respect to the first item, the cultural distance between Europeans and Africans made for a reinforcement of European culture and language as the imposed norm in a more pronounced manner. Few were the colonial administrators in Africa who learned the language of their subjugated peoples, and in many cases there was no extant literature as a vehicle for this learning.

> African cultures, elaborate as they were later found to be by anthropologists and historians, were dismissed by colonial rulers as too primitive to respect or preserve, not least because techniques were of the lowliest and religions unlinked to the major known religions of the world. Moreover, the multiplicity of small tribes in Africa, with their individual cultures, gave little choice to missionaries and administrators but to instill Western language, Christianity, some variety of European outlook and values throughout the continent to as many Africans as their influence could touch. (Hunter, 1966, 62)

This may also have been the reason for the greater hardening of the racial gap in Africa than was the case in Asia.

Since, in the second place, the African colonies had fewer migrants and contract laborers from overseas, the problem of ethnic groups in intermediate positions is less salient and appears in massive forms only in South Africa, as already noted. In the colonial period, the lack of an intermediary group to accelerate the process of profit taking by Europeans led to a more direct rather than indirect relation with Africans and either to specially devised methods of training the latter in the desired skills (a relatively slow process) or the recruitment of still more Europeans for these tasks. In either case the hierocratic relationship was dual and sharply vertical, in contrast with the three tiered colonies of Southeast Asia. In the postcolonial period of independence, Africans, in most cases had no foreign element to attack as former collaborationists with their rulers. Pluralities of tribal or national groupings often fused together by the dominant colonials,[19] now vied with each other for political and economic supremacy, but all were "charter members" and not aliens.

Thirdly, the spread of substantial colonial settlement in Africa was unique to that continent and did not appear in Asia. The hierocratic structure of plural society is greatly strengthened when the ruling section is composed of permanent residents rather than temporary ones. When the settler population has second or third generation inhabitants,[20] they begin to form a social system of their own with a full set of institutions: political, economic, educational, religious, and eventually regard these as autonomous. Still forming far less than half the total population of the society, the European settlers eventually came to regard it as their own society to the extent of taking responsibility for declaring independence, as in South Africa and Southern Rhodesia. Conflicts of interest are greatly augmented between sections in these societies and may be expected to continue. This is a direct carry-over of colonial plural structure into what is ostensibly a nation-state of the more usual type. Coleman speaks of "competitive parties within the oligarchy" (Almond and Coleman, 1960, 555), while van den Berghe has coined the apt term of "Herrenvolk democracy" (van den Berghe, 1967, 109). The compartmentalization of South Africa into plural sections is by far the most extreme form of its kind. The segmenting of English, Afrikaans, Coloured, Asian, and African furnish an example of institutional duplications and sharp group boundaries unparalleled in the rest of the world. These sections coalesce into two major divisions on racial lines with whites controlling the polity and economy, excluding nonwhites from political participation in the central government while restricting access to any but the lower rungs of the economy. In the attempt to reverse the process of merging into what would be a politically unified group on the part of the Africans, the whites have established Bantustans or reservations for Africans where tribal ways of life are encouraged and revived (or so is the attempt) (van den Berghe, 1965, 510).

In the fourth place, African colonization came much later in time than the Asian, the former occurring chiefly in the nineteenth century. By this time, industrialism as an economic system had taken firm root in Europe and its insatiable demand for minerals which proved to be especially plentiful in south and central Africa led to an overspreading network of gigantic mining enterprises dwarfing not only similar ones in Asia but in other parts of the world as well. The social organization of Africans in industrial labor forces attained a magnitude that went well beyond the smaller groups resident on plantations even in a highly rationalized agriculture. The suddenness and rapidity of industrialization catapulted the African through stages of change in a few generations that had taken Europe centuries to develop, the difference being that in Europe this was a gradual indigenous development in which the spread of skills and managerial competence was internal; in Africa the whole complex was imported and imposed from an external source while the African himself was restricted to unskilled levels of participation.

The mixed ownership and control of the giant corporations took many forms in the colonial era; some were privately managed by owners from a single European country; some by capitalists from several European countries (supranational); some were partly or wholly owned by colonial governments, others by European governments. A great many of these companies had interlocking directorates dubbed as the "Cape-to-Katanga team." The coming of independence for new nation-states where Africans took over the political institutions meant a loss of control over such corporations as in the Congo where transfer of government jurisdiction over mining interests was made three days before independence. In Northern Rhodesia the mining companies had private mineral rights independent of the colonial government as a part of a larger complex connected with South Africa. When the territory became Zambia, these rights remained undisturbed. In Southern Rhodesia, where a white government purchased the mineral rights, this has been one of the most potent obstacles to the winning of political power by the Africans (Wolfe, 1963). It is undoubtedly one of the major components creating a "Herrenvolk democracy" in both South Africa and Southern Rhodesia, and a significant factor helping to explain the tenacity of colonial government in Angola, which holds large blocks of shares in diamond deposits. Participation at unskilled levels of these industries has kept Africans dependent on European managers, engineers and other specialists to keep them running, thus reinforcing

hierocratic tendencies in such new nations as the Congo and
Zambia.

Summary

After reviewing ethnic relations in terms of recurrent intergroup
sequences that appear in many societies the following may be
said: first and foremost it appears that the great bulk of ethnic
group formations attain subordinate or minority status as the
result of coercive subjugation by dominant groups. There are
some exceptions among voluntary immigrants, emergence of
pariahs, and some contract laborers, but proportionately they
are not the mode. Considering the prevalence of annexations in
Europe and the Middle East, slave transfers in North America,
the Caribbean, and Brazil, and world-wide colonization in Asia,
Africa, North and South America, evidence shows conclusively
that the overriding relationship has been one of force and compulsion. Two implications follow from this conclusion: (1) studies
of ethnic relations based chiefly on data from voluntary migrations
cannot serve as the model or foundation for ethnic relations as a
whole;[21] (2) some form of power or conflict theory has the first
claim to relevance in approaching ethnic relations historically.[22]
Compulsion or constraint is a key factor for most analyses of
the field. It may be supplemented but not displaced when considering societies as wholes which will occupy attention in the next
chapter.

Another conclusion, already entailed by the first but in need of
emphasis is that vertical racism as described above is always a
product of coercive domination. The reverse, however, is definitely *not* true for, as we have seen, the brutal conquests of
Spanish America resulted in either mild or nonexistent forms of
racism, and the types of annexation practiced by Russia did not
result in a color line or racist ideology.

An analysis of pluralism has made it almost tautologous to say
that the major types of intergroup sequence necessarily give rise
to greater or lesser institutional enclosure for ethnic groups
occupying subordinate status. The apparent exception that occurs
with the emergence of pariahs is only superficial since a high

degree of enclosure *precedes* their emergence. The sequence of colonization produces as we might expect, maximal structural enclosure where historically unrelated cultures come into contact, and this results in severe conflicts. As van den Berghe puts it, "Generally, the more pluralistic the society as a whole and the political institutions in particular, the more tyrannical the polity" (van den Berghe, mimeo. 1967, 7). Highly pluralistic societies also predominate among the new states, for an independent analysis shows that "the more extremely plural a nation, the more likely it is to have achieved independence after 1945; two thirds are new nations since World War II" (Haug, 1967).[23] These are societies under former colonial rule, indicating that postcolonial derivations carry over much of the pluralistic structure inherited from their colonial past. In the sequence of annexation there appears to be relatively high but not maximal enclosure, with nationality, linguistic and religious differences being most prominent. Here, however, we deal with "charter member" minorities who claim preemptive right to native soil where they have been resident, sometimes from time immemorial (E. C. Hughes and H. M. Hughes, 1952). It is quite otherwise with contract labor transfers where the subordinate ethnics are aliens. Here there is variable structural enclosure (from high to intermediate) without the legitimation of historic residence. Also noted in the case of slave transfers is the variable enclosure depending on the rigidity of group definition which was greatest in the southern United States, somewhat less in the Caribbean, and least marked in Brazil. With the sequence of voluntary migration, social or structural pluralism is again variable, being least in evidence when historically related cultures are juxtaposed, but considerably greater when unrelated cultures come into contact and the dominant group has a previous history of racist ideology. Also important is the relatively marked social pluralism that follows migration into colonial areas (the overseas Chinese).

While each of the intergroup sequences shows a reciprocal relationship between two groups only, namely a dominant group and a subordinate group, the situation is complicated when two or more sequences occur in the same society, often at different time periods. Thus colonization sets up a one-to-one relation between colonizers and indigenous groups, but the former may import slaves at a later period precipitating the second sequence of slave transfers. Consequently, from the standpoint of the society as a whole, there is a compounded effect of both colonization and slavery. In other cases the compound is colonization with contract labor. So there are various permutations of annexation and voluntary migration, colonization with contract labor *and* voluntary migration. Space does not permit a discussion of these mixed or multiple sequential types here; one can only say that a great many societies display plural sequences in different time periods. The conclusion must be that while sequential analysis is an important first step, it must be rounded out by investigation of societies as wholes. It is to this exploration that we now turn.

· NOTES ·

1. In this sense Switzerland represents an embodiment (and the only one, to our knowledge) of the desired goal for normative pluralism.
2. The historical antecedents of the conception "plural society" cannot be presented here for lack of space. The original idea was formulated by Furnivall (1948) and then made its way into anthropological writings. A later and more refined version of the notion which had profound ramifications for anthropological theory was presented by M. G. Smith (1960) and entered the stream of sociological thought in van den Berghe's works (1965; 1967). Many other writings, especially among Africanists are devoted to development and analysis of the topic but they cannot be followed here.
3. Vera Rubin raises the same difficulty about Smith's position in a critique of his paper when she remarks that "It is difficult to determine, however, from Smith's formulation, when an institutional variation is a life style and when it is a 'basic way of life'" (Vera Rubin, 1960, 781).
4. Geertz mentions the following as "poles around which parapolitical vortices" tend to form: the use of native languages, electoral enumerations, political party participation, differential productive capacity of groups, educational opportunities and policies, religious issues, regional loyalties, census statistics, historiographies, and related others (Geertz, 1963, 119–30).
5. Needless to say, both Czarist Russia and Prussia adopted only *selective* features of nationalism, i.e., uniformity without democratic participation.
6. In our terminology, referred to as ethnic groups (with national claims, however). Francis draws an important distinction between nationality and nation in Europe (both ideas arising in the wake of nationalism). As he defines them, nations are theoretically sovereign in the determination of their political destiny while nationalities are subject to a

superimposed political authority in greater or lesser degree (Francis, 1965, 180). Notice that the latter implies structural pluralism.

7. A discussion of this process in terms of *normative* pluralism will be found in a previous article (Schermerhorn, 1959).

8. Janowsky also includes South Africa as another example but since he restricts attention to the ruling white groups only, excluding the African majority, we omit this illustration as insufficiently inclusive. Furthermore it fits in more naturally with our sequence of colonization below where it will receive further attention.

9. Kolarz puts this in the opposite way: "While practically all European nations were devoting their energies to the colonization of the Americas and other overseas territories, the Russians colonized the vast spaces adjoining their own living space" (*op. cit.*, 1).

10. We are not discussing domestic slavery here—a type that appeared in scores of African societies and throughout the Middle East as well. It is worth noting that such domestic slavery did *not* lead to the structural rigidity so common in Western chattel slavery. For example, the Hausa Fulani custom was to convert the slave to Islam and adopt him as a ward who not only became an intimate part of the household, but learned the technical skills of Hausa culture and became rapidly assimilated. There were even slave administrators and slave generals (M. G. Smith, 1965, Chap. 6).

11. The term "communal" has come into general use in Asian regions to denote collectivities of religious, linguistic, national, or caste nature defined as a homogeneous whole and exerting their power as a unit in political affairs. It thus overlaps our definition of ethnic groups without being identical with the latter. Except for the caste designation the term "communal" almost always refers to the units of structural pluralism which have a median to high degree of enclosure.

12. We are omitting here the temporary sojourn of foreign workers whose entry and exit into other nations rises and falls with the economic cycle. Of the hundreds of thousands of southern European workers who have made their way as far north as Scandinavia few studies have been made. First steps have been taken at Munich among students of Emerich Francis. For example: U. Kurz, *Partielle Anpassung und Kulturkonflikt. Eine soziologische Untersuchung der Gruppenstruktur und des Anpassungsverhaltens in einem italienischen Arbeiterlager Münchens*, Münchner Dissertation, 1964. For a more comprehensive but less recent account of the situation in France, see Alain Girard and Jean Stoeltzel, *Français et immigrés*, Paris, Presses Universitaires de France, 1954; Andrée Michel, *Les Travailleurs Algeriens en France*, Paris, Centre National de la Récherche Scientifique, 1956.

13. Such "nationality groups" in the United States are designated as "secondary minorities" in Francis' discussion and subdivided into two types: those who come from rural into urban environments where they take on individualistic patterns; and those who migrate from rural settings abroad to rural settings in the host country remaining more solidary

than individualistic. These he distinguished from primary minorities who usually do not migrate but constitute simpler peoples subjugated by conquest, rural folk groups annexed or incorporated into a national socioeconomic whole, a more complex society (or a portion of it) incorporated into a still larger nation, and a collective solidary folk group migrating to another territory (Francis, *op. cit.*, 134–35).

14. "Minority" is used here in a simple numerical sense.

15. This is what Durkheim envisaged in the following passage: ". . . every society is despotic; there is nothing artificial in this despotism; it is natural because it is necessary, and also because in certain conditions societies cannot endure without it. Nor do I mean that there is anything intolerable about it. On the contrary, the individual does not feel it any more than we feel the atmosphere weighing on our shoulders. From the moment the individual has been raised in this way by the collectivity, he will naturally desire what it desires and accept without difficulty the state of subjection to which he finds himself reduced" (Durkheim, 1957, 61).

16. Because of the maximal enclosure characteristic of such social units, I am following M. G. Smith and using the term "section" instead of "ethnic group" to mark the rigidity of separation. However, in our usage, a section is simply a maximally enclosed ethnic group.

17. This effect may be heightened where the dominant group defines the boundaries in terms of race, as noted above. However it is better to keep the categories of race and structural differences analytically distinct since they can vary independently. "It is quite true, by and large, that modern plural societies are multi-racial, and that these racial groups tend also to be culturally distinct, but this is by no means always the case, as the cultural diversity of the American Negroes and the distinction between *évolué* and *indigène* in Africa makes clear" (M. G. Smith, 1960, 775).

18. This statement, of course, does not apply to North Africa. Unless otherwise noted, throughout this whole discussion "Africa" refers to Sub-Saharan Africa rather than the entire continent.

19. The South African case eventually took a different turn and will be mentioned later.

20. Rhodesia, a major example, is also a haven for retired Europeans as well, thus adding an element strongly wedded to the status quo (Hunter, 1962, 170).

21. This type of restriction, though occasionally violated, is what limts the work of Francis (1965) and in another way of Shibutani and Kwan who state that "all systems of ethnic stratification begin with some kind of migration" without sufficient qualitative distinction between slavery, colonization, and other forms of population movements, and overlooking annexation where there may be no migration at all (1965, 148).

22. This has given rise to the author's preliminary conceptualization of the relationships *exclusively* in terms of power (Schermerhorn, 1964) a view now recognized as insufficiently dialectical.

23. Haug's study is based on Banks and Textor's *Cross-Polity Survey* (1963) with five indicators used to designate pluralism: language, race, religion, sectionalism, and interest articulation by nonassociational groups. This survey covered 114 societies ("polities").

· REFERENCES ·

Almond, Gabriel A., and J. S. Coleman (eds.), *The Politics of Developing Areas*. Princeton, N.J.: Princeton University Press, 1960.

Bacon, Elizabeth E., *Central Asians Under Russian Rule, A Study in Culture Change*. Ithaca, N.Y.: Cornell University Press, 1966.

Banfield, Edward C., and James Q. Wilson, *City Politics*. Cambridge, Mass.: Harvard University Press, 1963.

Banks, Arthur S., and Robert B. Textor, *A Cross-Polity Survey*. Cambridge, Mass.: M.I.T. Press, 1963.

Berger, Morroe, *The Arab World Today*. New York: Doubleday, 1962.

Blalock, H. M., *Toward a Theory of Minority Group Relations*. New York: Wiley, 1967.

Coleman, James S., "Conclusion," in Gabriel A. Almond and J. S. Coleman (eds.), *The Politics of Developing Areas*. Princeton, N.J.: Princeton University Press, 1960.

Despres, Leo A., *Cultural Pluralism and Nationalist Politics in British Guiana*. Chicago: Rand McNally, 1967.

Durkheim, Emile, *Professional Ethics and Civic Morals*, Cornelia Brookfield (trans.). London: Routledge & Kegan Paul, 1957.

Francis, Emerich, *Ethnos and Demos*. Berlin: Duncker & Humblot, 1965.

Freedman, Maurice, "The Growth of a Plural Society in Malaya," *Pacific Affairs*, 33 (1960), 158–68.

Furnivall, J. S., *Progress and Welfare in Southeast Asia*. New York: Institute of Pacific Relations Research Series, 1941.

———, *Colonial Policy and Practice*. London: Cambridge University Press, 1948.

Geertz, Clifford, "The Integrative Revolution," in Clifford Geertz (ed.), *Old Societies and New States*. New York: Free Press, 1963.

Germani, Gino, "Social Change and Intergroup Conflicts," in Irving L. Horowitz (ed.), *The New Sociology*. New York: Oxford University Press, 1964.

Gordon, Milton M., *Assimilation in American Life*. New York: Oxford University Press, 1964.

Haug, Marie, "Social and Cultural Pluralism as a Concept in Social System Analysis," *American Journal of Sociology*, 73 (November 1967), 294–304.

Hourani, A. H., *Minorities in the Arab World*. London: Oxford University Press, 1947.

Hughes, Everett C., and Helen MacGill Hughes, *Where People Meet: Racial and Ethnic Frontiers*. Glencoe, Ill.: The Free Press, 1952.

Hunter, Guy, *The New Societies of Tropical Africa*. London: Oxford University Press, 1962.

———, *South-East Asia, Race, Culture and Nation*. London: Oxford University Press, 1966.

Janowsky, Oscar I., *Nationalities and National Minorities*. New York: Macmillan, 1945.

Kohn, Hans, *Nationalism: Its Meaning and History.* Princeton, N.J.: Van Nostrand, 1955.

Kolarz, Walter, *Russia and Her Colonies.* New York: Praeger, 1952.

———, "Race Relations in the Soviet Union," in Andrew W. Lind (ed.), *Race Relations in World Perspective.* Honolulu: University of Hawaii Press, 1955.

Kornhauser, William, *The Politics of Mass Society.* New York: Free Press, 1959.

Laponce, J. A., "The Protection of Minorities by the Electoral System," *Western Political Quarterly,* 10, No. 2 (1957), 318–39.

Lind, Andrew W., "Occupation and Race on Certain Frontiers," in Andrew W. Lind (ed.), *Race Relations in World Perspective.* Honolulu: University of Hawaii Press, 1955.

Mahajani, Usha, *The Role of Indian Minorities in Burma and Malaya.* Bombay: Vor & Co., Publishers Private Ltd. Issued in New York under the auspices of the Institute of Pacific Relations, 1960.

Mishkin, Bernard, "The Contemporary Quechua," in Julian H. Steward (ed.), *The Handbook of South American Indians,* II. Washington, D.C.: Bureau of American Ethnology, Bulletin 143, 1946–1948.

Mortimer, M., "Thunder in Fiji," *Contemporary Review,* 197 (1960), 305–07.

Nash, Manning, "The Multiple Society in Economic Development: Mexico and Guatemala," *American Anthropologist,* 59 (1957), 825–33.

Pipes, Richard, "The Forces of Nationalism," in series of articles entitled as a whole, "Soviet Colonialism: Does it Exist?" *Problems of Communism,* 13 (1964), 1–6.

Price, Charles A., *Southern Europeans in Australia.* Melbourne: Oxford University Press, 1963.

Purcell, Victor, *The Chinese in Southeast Asia.* 2nd ed. London: Oxford University Press, 1966.

Royal Commission on Bilingualism and Biculturism, *Report, General Introduction,* Book I, *The Official Languages.* Ottawa: The Queen's Printer, 1967.

Rubin, Vera, "Discussion," in *Annals of the New York Academy of Sciences,* 83, Art. 5 (January 20, 1960), 780–85.

Schermerhorn, R. A., *These Our People, Minorities in American Culture.* Boston: Heath, 1949.

———, "Minorities, European and American," *Phylon,* 20 (Summer 1959), 178–85.

———, "Toward a General Theory of Minority Groups," *Phylon,* 25 (Fall 1964), 238–46.

Seton-Watson, Hugh, "Moscow's Imperialism," in series of articles entitled as a whole, "Soviet Colonialism: Does it Exist?" *Problems of Communism,* 13 (1964), 1–24.

Smith, M. G., "Social and Cultural Pluralism," in *Annals of the New York Academy of Sciences,* 83, Art. 5 (January 20, 1960), 763–85.

———, *The Plural Society in the British West Indies.* Berkeley: University of California Press, 1965.

Spicer, Edward H. (ed.), *Human Problems in Technological Change, A Casebook.* New York: Russell Sage Foundation, 1952.

Trager, Frank M., *Burma from Kingdom to Republic, A Historical and Political Analysis.* New York: Praeger, 1966.

van den Berghe, Pierre L., "Toward a Sociology of Africa," and "Race

Attitudes in Durban, South Africa," in Pierre L. van den Berghe (ed.), *Africa, Social Problems of Change and Conflict.* San Francisco: Chandler, 1965.

———, *Race and Racism.* New York: Wiley, 1967.

———, *South Africa, A Study in Conflict.* First paperbound ed. Berkeley and Los Angeles: University of California Press, 1967a.

———, "Some Analytical Problems in the Study of Plural Societies." Mimeo., 1967.

Wirth, Louis, "The Problem of Minority Groups," in Ralph Linton (ed.), *The Science of Man in the World Crisis.* New York: Columbia University Press, 1945.

Wolfe, Alvin W., "The African Mineral Industry: Evolution of a Supra-National Level of Integration," *Social Problems,* 11 (Fall 1963), 153–64.

5

❦

Societies as Contexts

In the previous chapter it became plain that the consequences of intergroup sequences for racism and pluralism differed in various parts of the world. In pursuing the reasons for such differences we are inevitably led to consider the types of societies in which such changes take place. Surely, intergroup encounters and the relations that develop from them are not self-subsistent phenomena but take their shape and form to a marked degree from the social organization and directional processes of the societies in which the encounters take place. The trajectories of such sequences must be understood within larger fields of forces. These are, in brief, total societies as contexts.

What we today regard as national societies have had a long history with roots extending into the past for several centuries but assuming characteristic institutional forms since the eighteenth century. The various nations of the world have reached this point of crystallization, some earlier, some later, but in spite of their current variations, what are now regarded as modern societies differ from their predecessors in several important respects. These may be listed as follows:

1. The most powerful government positions are no longer a function of hereditary privilege.[1]

2. Productive activities are either moving away from or generally divorced from domestic work.
3. A money economy is displacing or has fully displaced a subsistence economy.
4. Forms of labor are increasingly or wholly rewarded by wages and salaries.
5. Increases in transportation facilities spread a network of connections between sectors of the population formerly separated or isolated; this makes for greater accessibility of central zones to peripheral areas.
6. Mass media have made some forms of instantaneous communication possible; this has furnished common symbolic or ideological perspectives for increasingly large segments of the population.
7. There has been a penetration of national influences, both political and economic, into all regions and local sectors. On the whole this operates through the agency of urban centers which are growing in both size and importance.
8. The provision of educational facilities for the population is widely recognized as a responsibility of government and extension of such facilities continues.
9. Extensive linkage with other countries through foreign trade, transportation, and communication networks is a prominent feature, reproducing on an international scale what is already taking place on the national.[2]

Whether societies are communistic or capitalistic, developed or undeveloped, democratic or authoritarian, they share these characteristics in the contemporary world. Those becoming nation-states most recently may have smaller proportions in wage labor, less extensive communication systems, and perhaps only the beginning of a comprehensive educational system. But the commitment is clear, the direction is discernible, and the outlines of a "modern" society can be definitely distinguished from what preceded it.

It is worth mention in passing that these characteristics have, to an appreciable degree, been imports from Europe when they occur elsewhere. As Rustow points out, "nearly all non-European countries have been subject in the last five hundred years to shorter or longer periods of European penetration—whether in the form of conquest and colonial domination (America, Africa, Australia, and much of Asia), foreign exploitation of natural resources (Saudi Arabia), conquest by an indigenous offshoot from a European ideology (Communist China), or self-directed and rapid Westernization (Japan, Turkey)" (Rustow, 1963, 60).

The attentive reader will have noticed that in this highly generalized outline of contemporary societies, some important characteristics have been omitted. In presenting the common, shared features of modern societies, it has, of course, been necessary to leave out a number of factors of central importance simply because the variability is too great to allow for inclusion at this level of generality. For example, nothing is said about industrialization or urbanization which are highly significant at certain levels of analysis. Nor is there any mention of political participation by the citizenry which is so important when attention is focussed on democratic processes.[3] Some reference will be made to these in due time.

Descending to an intermediate level of generality, it is worth noting once again that every society is (1) like no other society, (2) like some other societies, and (3) like all other societies in our universe of discourse. So far, concern has been with the third level alone, i.e., with the common features of all modern societies. In the long run, the task of comparative research is to establish generalizations at this level, if possible. However, past experience shows that this is only an ultimate or terminal possibility that has little likelihood of success if, in the first stages of exploration, societal differences are completely disregarded on the assumption societies are essentially alike.

Suppose, for example, that on the basis of the argument in previous chapters, the following hypothesis is advanced: "the higher the degree of enclosure of the ethnic group coupled with a high degree of control over its scarce rewards by a dominant group, the greater the conflict." Conversely this might read: "the lower the degree of enclosure coupled with a lower degree of control over its scarce rewards by a dominant group, the greater the integration." While such hypotheses have an initial plausibility, little argument is necessary to show that such propositions would give indifferent or negative results if tested indiscriminately with Tamils in Ceylon, Muslims in Lebanon, Indians in Peru, Ibo in

Nigeria, or Kazakhs in the Soviet Union. In the present state of our knowledge it is hardly possible to draw meaningful parallels across the board at this universal level without being forced back first to the classical methodological question, "under what conditions?"

The search for these conditions has been a latent, though significant, part of the argument in the two immediately preceding chapters where intergroup sequences have been distinguished. Concern for the question is now explicit and manifest in the question, "what types of society show predictable variations in these relations?" By classifying societies at the outset, it becomes possible to specify the contexts in which generalizations of this sort may or may not be valid. Only if some such classification is available can one make "a systematic specification of which theories and propositions hold for all societies, which for only certain types of societies, and which for only individual societies" (Marsh, 1967, vii).

The problem of classifying societies at the intermediate level is a formidable one; well aware of the temerity involved in making such a selection, and broaching the task with proper tentativeness, I propose two modes of classification interrelated with each other. The *first* is a grouping of societies into sectors or regions sharing a roughly similar historical sequence and cultural relatedness; the *second* is a structural categorization based on the relative dominance of political over economic institutions or vice versa. Each is examined in turn.

Sector or Regional Classification

The most neutral name for the first classification is *multinational sectors*. Some, though not all of these divisions are regional and in such cases can be referred to as multinational regions. It is assumed that comparability of societal conditions is greater for nations within a single sector than for nations in different sectors. At the outset we distinguish eight multinational sectors as follows:

1. *Western European nations and the derivative neo-European complex.*[4] This includes not only the nations of Western and non-Communist Europe but Canada, the United States, Australia,

New Zealand, and Israel. In all of these nations there is a capitalist or mixed economy. The franchise and constitutional forms of government predominate. Labor movements have modified the distributive features of the economy by pressure on employers or by political action. In most cases there is a high degree of urbanization and industrialization with smaller proportions of the labor force in agriculture than are found in other sectors. The Gross National Products of these nations rank highest in comparison with other sectors. Likewise each nation in the Western European complex has an extensive communications network and a correspondingly high degree of literacy and education for its citizens. The polity is legitimized by custom and widespread political socialization. In nearly all cases the transfer of political office is well institutionalized. There is a wide range of occupational differentiation with a historic trend toward increase in the middle of the distribution; occupational roles evolve toward greater distinctness and specialization at most levels. For the majority of adults, the bulk of their activities are economic or domestic with infrequent or intermittent participation in the political process. Voluntary associations independent of political control are widespread, showing greater participation at middle and upper levels of the stratification system. Formal political equality is combined with actual economic inequality, permitting those of great wealth to have disproportionate and relatively decisive control over key elements of various institutions. In general, the values of those in the middle range of occupations tend to be the dominant and hence integrating values of the society, reflected in the communication channels, in educational, religious, political and economic institutions.

2. *Eastern Europe: the Communist states.* In this division are the U.S.S.R., Poland, East Germany, Czechoslovakia, Hungary, Rumania, Bulgaria, Yugoslavia, and Albania. By revolution or precipitate military action, each of these countries has undergone a sudden restructuring of its entire system, spearheaded by an oligarchical tightly organized Party controlling the polity and, through it, the economy. While the industrialization of these states shows variable levels, agriculture is less technologically developed and utilizes a larger percentage of the labor force than occurs in Sector 1. Legitimation of the polity depends less upon custom than upon control of the mass media by Party or govern-

ment sources. Considerable relaxation of centralized control is a sort of cumulative trend in Yugoslavia, Rumania, and Czechoslovakia. Transfer of political office is not fully institutionalized. There are two major spheres of mobility, the Party hierarchy and the wider occupational system. The former is subdivided again into the activists, the governmental incumbents, and bureaucratic managers of the economy, while the latter has the range of most industrial systems with some modifications. Mobility is potentially more rapid in the Party than outside of it. Communications systems are somewhat less pervasive than in Class 1, reaching the urban populations completely and the rural incompletely. Literacy and education run from medium to high, depending on the country. Organized interest groups unsupervised by the state do not exist. Planned programs and ideology of Party and government serve as the integrating links of these societies.

3. *Iberian societies of the Eastern and Western Hemisphere.* Here are the "mother countries" of Spain and Portugal, together with their former derived colonies in Central and Latin America. While European and non-European states of this category form obvious subclasses, there are a number of important common elements that serve to bind all of them together. Perhaps most important is the late retention of feudal relations and the delayed appearance of middle classes that are endemic throughout.[5] Likewise the bond of language has created a greater linguistic homogeneity in this sector than any other. The juxtaposition of a few industrial centers with regions having an immobile peasantry exacerbates internal conflicts both in Europe and Latin America.

> The uneven economic and social development of a relatively industrial and advanced Spain and a rural Spain, with problems characteristic of many underdeveloped countries, contributed to make the social conflicts of the thirties so explosive. As in some Latin American countries the successful industrial-capitalist development in some areas is threatened by the revolutionary potential of a backward rural social structure that perhaps requires basic changes politically imposed rather than the result of spontaneous economic development. (Linz and de Miguel, 1966, 278)

Urbanization is uneven, running from medium to low, with large segments of the population engaged in agriculture. The military is a major instrument of internal government in many of these societies while transfer of political power is on the whole weakly institutionalized. *Personalismo* or loyalty to a commanding leader rather than to specific policies is a dominant, if fluctuating form of political integration. The level of literacy runs from low to high, clustering around a medium position.

The American subdivision of this sector has a variable growth of a mestizo population, sometimes greater, sometimes smaller than an indigenous Indian group. Wars of independence from colonial control, political participation, and economic development have been carried on chiefly by mestizos, supplemented by immigration from Europe. Gross National Product per capita is modally low and the occupational range is narrow compared with highly industrialized nations; there are a number of gaps in middle distribution. Communications systems lack wide coverage; the media affect the urban centers without penetrating far into rural regions.

4. *Caribbean societies*. This would include most of the islands with their wide variation in autonomy plus Guyana, British Honduras, Surinam and French Guiana. The common resemblances here are more difficult to portray although all territories have a background of colonial conquest and some development of a plantation economy with imported slaves or indentured workers whose descendants, for the most part, now occupy lower economic and status positions. The majority of the islands and territories have a cash crop economy of agriculture (with some mining) controlled by European managers or planters and laborers drawn from former slave or indentured populations. Nearly all of the territories have "multiracial" populations of various sorts, with considerable numbers of Amerindians in British Honduras, Guyana, Surinam, and French Guiana, while significant elements of East Indians appear in Trinidad and Guyana. Probably the greatest diversity of ethnic elements occurs in Surinam. For the rest the bulk of the population consists chiefly of African Creole groups with many color shadings. Political forms range from downright colonial rule in British Honduras to modified control by metropolitan powers in the Virgin Islands (U.S. and Great Britain), Grenada, Dominica, and St. Vincent (Great Britain), Martinique, Guadeloupe, and French Guiana (France), Curaçao, Aruba, Bonaire, and St. Maarten (Netherlands), or com-

plete independence in Antigua, Jamaica, St. Lucia, Trinidad, Guyana, Barbados, Dominican Republic, Haiti, and Cuba. Puerto Rico's "commonwealth" status has the substance of independence but special political and economic ties with the United States. Whatever the political condition of all these territories may be (not all of them being full-fledged states), economic dependence on cash crop exports controlled by Europeans and Americans is ordinarily sufficient to ensure political control by a white elite (except for Cuba, Haiti, and the Dominican Republic). With a frozen economy of relatively static agriculture, low industrialization and urbanization and rapid population increase, it seems likely that social mobility for most of the population is glacially slow; this has led to considerable emigration (chiefly to Great Britain and the United States). Since status position is so often linked with color shadings, mobility over generations occurs with miscegenation, and preoccupation with genealogies is a pervasive pastime. Attempts by people of color to rise in the social scale comes to an abrupt halt at the top of the pyramid where whites of European extraction hold undisputed sway by ascription. At this level, the line becomes castelike.

Variations from the mode appear in Haiti, the Dominican Republic, Puerto Rico, and Cuba. Haiti has a similar agricultural economy but has reversed the color combinations after throwing off the European yoke, so that those of darker shades have practically gained preeminence. The polity is a dictatorship with paternalistic claims. The Dominican Republic resembles the Latin American countries even more than other Caribbean nations and is a marginal case, approximating the societies in Sector 3 (Iberian). While Puerto Rico is also predominantly Spanish, it has, under the sponsorship of the United States, rapidly industrialized with dominance of foreign capital, growing away from a plantation economy; its polity is constitutional and representative. Cuba is as fully Hispanicized as the Dominican Republic and Puerto Rico but has today the characteristics of Communist nations mentioned above—superimposed on a tropical plantation system with quite limited industrialization.

5. *Non-Communist Asia and Southeast Asia.* This includes the nations from Afghanistan on the northwest to the Philippines on the east with Japan sufficiently distinct from the others to be

excepted from the modal features of the sector as a whole. In characterizing the Asian nations, it is important to recognize historic trends before the colonial era that have recurred again. Most of the societies in earlier as well as later eras experienced a succession of invasions and conquests by alien rulers of different culture and religion. By the time the last of these overlords, the Europeans, arrived, acquiescence, toleration, and acculturation to customs and traditions of the rulers had become a way of life— at least until the ideology of nationalism finally aroused whole populations and upset the colonial order. However the bifurcation of societies into peasant villagers and highly cultivated elite of capital cities remained; after independence, the latter became not only Westernized political leaders but economic planners as well. With only limited industrialization and urbanization, the masses still live on the land and engage in simple agriculture. Communication networks blanket the urban centers but have little impact on the villages, thus perpetuating the gulf between them. Popular franchise partly fills this gap in some countries as political candidates appeal to the peasantry and bring national concerns to local populations. But political roles tend to be diffuse rather than differentiated; leaders often command personal loyalty as blank checks for future favors, playing down their stands on specific issues. Conversely, citizens tend to identify with leaders or groups rather than upon policy. The old drama of political rivalries observed from afar becomes the new drama of audience participation, with the expressive function of politics overriding problem solving. On the whole, political institutions take responsibility for economic development; the allocation of resources to the "private sector" or the "public sector" determines the direction taken by the economy. In general, literacy and educational levels are medium to low, and a feverish drive to establish new educational institutions outruns the skilled personnel to man them. Legitimation of recently established political authority is often weak, and the transfer of political power is not always institutionalized.

As already mentioned, Japan is an exception to these trends, having a high degree of industrialization, urbanization, and a literacy rate unmatched in Asia. Thailand also departs from the mode in two respects: she has not had a colonial past, and also does not have an economy controlled and managed by government.

6. *Communist Asia.* This comprises China, North Korea, and North Vietnam. While the number of states is negligible, demographically this sector has decisive importance since it contains about a third of the world's population. The inclusion of North Korea is problematical since Chinese documents now refer to the area as one of the "nationalities" to be integrated into the Han communist state, while on the other hand, recent news accounts report gestures of the North Korean authorities toward autonomy. The rest of the area has either experienced colonial or quasi-colonial domination, and has attained independence through diverse forms of military action. In general, the same sort of politico-economic complex appears here as the one noted in the Communist states of Eastern Europe, with the Party as the de facto ruling elite and the political institution acting as its organ. Industrialization is still in its early stages, urbanization is moderate to low, and the vast majority of the labor force is in agriculture, now collectivized in China but far less so in North Vietnam. Communication networks are far more effective in urban than in rural areas, and in China have more impact on the eastern section than on the rest. Literacy is medium to low with great expansion of schools at all levels combined with a notable shortage of trained teachers. Vertical mobility is, for the most part, enlistment or recruitment of citizens by the bureaucracy into positions having high priority in economic development, therefore chiefly planned or cooptive. Policy is legitimized through educational channels and systematized propaganda. Transfer of political power is not institutionalized. Internal conflict over control of the Party machinery in China may presage changes in the polity but fluid conditions make this problematical for the time being.

7. *The Middle East and North Africa.* This group of states comprises the Muslim strongholds outside of Asia from Morocco on the west to Iran on the east. We exclude here the sheikdoms and principalities of the Arabian Peninsula and Persian Gulf as well as the artificial "oil states" of Kuwait, Bahrein and Qatar as lacking many characteristics of national-states, while including Saudi Arabia and Yemen. Turkey is a marginal case which could

be placed either in the neo-European complex or the Middle East. It has been Westernized without foreign intervention, unlike its neighbors to the south, but its previous imperial connection, Muslim faith, and its army function of guardian for the revolution link it more clearly with the Middle East where it properly belongs.

Throughout the area as a whole, the nomadic tradition in which successful rebellions produced new sheikdoms or kingdoms which in turn produced new rebellions, is a pronounced social pattern that persisted through the "colonial" era and into the present epoch of independence. This was a sort of societal substratum that persisted beneath the surface of the overarching unity of the Islamic *umma* on the one hand, or the decaying Ottoman empire on the other. The almost simultaneous timing of Ottoman decline with Western entry with the mandates that proved to be a disguised colonialism precipitated a series of nationalisms. "Greek nationalism led to Armenian, Armenian to Turkish, and Turkish to Arab" (Hourani, 1963, 48). There is also, in the newly emerging nations of the Arab world a continual tension between nationalism on the one hand and a subterranean pan-Islamic trend that often surfaces in a general Arab solidarity. The economy is handicapped in most of these nations by extensive desert regions that permit only 4 per cent of the total land area to be cultivated; landlords still control major sections of farm lands outside of Egypt, Tunisia, Syria, Iraq, and Iran. About three-fourths of the populations are still engaged in agriculture, industry is barely nascent, and there is a limited communications network having scant impact on the villages. Probably the modal political regimes are traceable to coups d'état, followed by an organization of mass support and a planned economy, giving the impression of "revolutions from the top." Legitimacy of rule is largely engineered by propaganda, control of the mass media, and slowly developing educational systems. Transfer of political power is weakly institutionalized, on the whole. While there are parliamentary institutions, they are not necessarily representative. Urbanization is low, with initiative for economic development coming from urban centers, particularly the capital and the governmental hierarchy resident in it. Literacy and educational systems have not penetrated far beyond the urban centers. Except in Tunisia and Morocco, civil and military roles are often fused; the army, serving as a vanguard, often performs the roles of a political party.

8. *Sub-Saharan Africa.* This embraces the nations from the Sahara to the Cape of Good Hope. The historical realities of colonization have affected all these states except Ethiopia and (marginally) Liberia. As for the rest, Angola and Mozambique remain at the colonial stage, while Rhodesia and the Republic of South Africa remain, each in its own way, impacted in a unique but frozen form of latent colonial substance combined with manifest forms of independence. Most countries have a diversity of preliterate tribal[6] groupings, each with its own traditions and customs, together with a smaller number of areas with "great and little traditions." While in Asia, the latter predominate, Africa has a disproportionate number of the former. Colonial regimes superimposed a limited number of boundary-defined territories, administrative networks, military order, a competitive money economy, a European educational system, and an ideology of racial superiority. Nationalist movements for independence gave rise to some mass parties with charismatic leaders who maintained a dynamic unity after independence; in other cases, leaders from Westernized sectors rose or were catapulted into positions of authority in the new states. In both cases, independent governments of the new nations face the dilemma of directing the economy into new channels of development requiring arduous and disciplined work habits, and simultaneously winning legitimacy for an emerging political order. Urbanization, while spreading widely, is still in its early stages (with the possible exception of Nigeria) and industrialization is sporadic and still mostly in the control of alien elements. The economy is relatively fragmented at a wide range of technological levels while the great mass of the population remains in agriculture. However, in many areas, migration to and from the cities produces a turnover workforce, now agricultural, now industrial, a factor which supplements and strengthens an otherwise restricted communications network. Transfer of political power is, on the whole, weakly institutionalized, often punctuated by tribal claims for hegemony. Literacy is relatively low, and the spread of educational institutions is rapid at primary levels while receding at secondary or upper levels. In several cases there is weak civil

control of the military, the latter then becoming an independent source of authority in government, making or unmaking a given regime. There is also a marked tendency in most countries for one-party political regimes to show greater stability than multi-party ones. South Africa and Rhodesia constitute exceptions to the above trends, both belonging to a neo-European complex resembling the societies of Sector 1 at upper stratification levels, and colonial societies below. It is in these two nations that indus-trialization has made its greatest strides, giving them a special profile as will be seen in the tables below.

While it might be possible to add a final category of Oceania, this island region remains residual here for the following reasons: (1) many if not most of the Polynesian, Melanesian, and Micro-nesian areas cannot be classified as nation-states; (2) colonial, mandated, or protectorate status for a number of islands are be-wilderingly variable; (3) centralized authority in the "naturally" clustered islands is so fragile and unstructured as to preclude systematic analysis. For some time in the future, we shall be de-pendent upon local case studies, as in the past. However, it seems premature to relate these, at the present stage, to a sector like the others. There may be reference later to island clusters at the stage of emerging national states, however.

The following table presents a few salient features of the sectors for rapid comparisons. (See Table 1, pp. 178–81.)

We turn now to the second classification of societies. Unlike the first which categorized them in terms of cultural-historical sectors having related development, the second is primarily struc-tural or cross sectional, centered on here-now relationships in the present tense. For the purposes at hand, none of the familiar dichotomies is quite suitable, i.e., between developed and "de-veloping" nations, communist vs. capitalist countries, or demo-cratic vs. nondemocratic states. What is needed here is a more generic distinction rooted in sociological or institutional analysis. In order to do this, we make an initial primary assumption which is: in contemporary societies, economic and political institutions have the commanding positions in social life.[7] Hence the reciprocal relationship between political and economic institutions is the root problem of the modern age, one whose solution is still in suspension. Recognizing this as the core of societal analysis, we propose that societies be roughly classified in terms of their answer to this question—the relation between or the relative dominance of the polity or the economy in social organization. There appears to be a great divide between the societies that answer the question in favor of the polity and those who take the opposite tack. In one case the political organs control and direct the economy, while in the other, economic organizations set the guide lines within which the polity operates. In the latter, market forces have a recognized autonomy of their own, even in a welfare state, while in the former, the state *organizes* the economy to serve overarching ideological goals. Since we have no names to designate these types, let us refer to the societies in which political institutions dominate the economic, somewhat inelegantly, perhaps, as the pol-ec societies, while those of the opposite type would then be ec-pol societies. Under these rubrics it becomes plain that the structural resemblances between Communist nations on the one hand, and a sizeable number of new states planning "development" with forced-draft methods in the Old World,[8] put them in the pol-ec category. As David Apter has noted, many of the "autocratic new nations use a Leninist party and governmental structure as well as the language of socialism" (Apter, 1963, 61).

It is quite apparent, even upon cursory analysis, that there are sector differences observable within these categories. In communist societies, for example, the pol-ec trend is at one extreme of a continuum with state enterprise, collectivization, and government monopoly of foreign trade and exchange relations being the modal pattern. However, nations of sectors 5 and 8 (Asia and Africa) qualify for the pol-ec category in less extreme form. It is still germane to call them pol-ec societies where the government's management of the economy leads or directs production, investment, and trade, both domestic and foreign, even though there is a substantial private sector. In Myrdal's terms, economic planning in such countries is not only centralized but "programmatic," i.e., it is as complete and comprehensive as the political authorities can make it, even though they lack the controls of nationalization (Myrdal, 1968, 739).

On the other hand, ec-pol societies are not so much characterized by *lack* of planning as by "unprogrammatic" or "piecemeal" planning, much of which develops gradually in response to interdependencies of the market, oligopoly, or the distributive system (Myrdal, *op. cit.*, 738–39). The interests and initiatives of private

I. Sector 1. Western European Nations and the Derivative Neo-European Complex.

Society	GNP per capita (in dollars)	Per cent of labor force in agriculture	Per cent literate	Marsh's Index of Differentiation**
Greece	340	48	80	31.0
Italy	516	29	87.5	41.3
Austria	670	32	98.5	51.3
Israel	716	15	93.7	48.0
Finland	794	46	98.5	47.5
Netherlands	836	11	98.5	58.0
West Germany	927	14	98.5	68.4
France	943	26	96.4	57.5
Denmark	1057	23	98.5	55.7
Norway	1130	26	98.5	55.2
Great Britain	1189	5	98.5	84.6
Belgium	1196	10	96.7	74.5
New Zealand	1310	16	98.5	58.0
Australia	1316	14	98.5	72.7
Sweden	1380	13	98.5	62.7
Switzerland	1428	12	98.5	51.6
Canada	1947	12	97.5	89.9
United States	2577	10	98.0	109.4
	Range 340–2577	Range 5–48	Range 80–98.5	Range 31.0–109.4
	Mean 1182.3	Mean 20.1	Mean 96.2	Mean 62.0

II. Sector 2. Eastern Europe: The Communist States.

Society	GNP per capita (in dollars)	Per cent of labor force in agriculture	Per cent literate	Marsh's Index of Differentiation**
Albania	175	72	60	—
Yugoslavia	265	67	77	26.2
Rumania	360	70	89	21.8
Bulgaria	365	64	85	23.0
Poland	475	57	95	45.8
Hungary	490	38	97	36.8
East Germany	600	19	98.5	62.8
U.S.S.R.	600	48	95	41.4
Czechoslovakia	680	38	97.5	65.5
	Range 175–680	Range 19–72	Range 60–98.5	Range 21.8–65.5
	Mean 335	Mean 52	Mean 88.2	Mean 40.4

* Figures obtained, unless indicated, from Bruce M. Russett *et al.*, (eds.), *World Handbook of Political and Social Indicators*, 1964. The order in which nations are listed is from the lowest to the highest Gross National Product (GNP) per capita.

** Marsh's Index represents the extent of a society's differentiation from a simple, preliterate form, and is calculated from a formula that takes per cent of labor force in nonagricultural pursuits, and gross energy consumption per capita in megawatt hours as base variables. For an explanation of the way he derives this formula and the resulting index, see Robert Marsh, *Comparative Sociology*, 1967, pp. 332ff.

III. Sector 3. Iberian Societies of the Eastern and Western Hemispheres.

Society	GNP per capita (in dollars)	Per cent of labor force in agriculture	Per cent literate	Marsh's Index of Differ- entiation
Bolivia	99	72	32.1	21.4
Paraguay	114	55	65.8	22.6
Nicaragua	160	68	38.4	16.7
Peru	179	60	47.5	23.0
Ecuador	189	53	55.7	23.5
Guatemala	189	68	29.4	17.1
Honduras	194	66	44.0	13.8
Salvador	219	63	39.4	19.5
Portugal	224	48	55.9	29.6
Mexico	262	58	50.0	29.3
Colombia	263	55	62.0	24.8
Brazil	293	61	49.4	26.3
Spain	293	50	87.0	31.4
Panama	329	54	65.7	26.9
Costa Rica	357	55	79.4	24.1
Chile	379	30	80.1	40.6
Uruguay	478	37	80.9	39.7
Argentina	490	25	86.4	45.4
Venezuela	648	42	52.2	39.0
	Range 99–648	Range 25–72	Range 29.4–87.0	Range 13.8–45.4
	Mean 282	Mean 53	Mean 57.9	Mean 27.0

IV. Sector 4. Caribbean Societies.***

Society	GNP per capita (in dollars)	Per cent of labor force in agriculture	Per cent literate	Marsh's Index of Differ- entiation
Haiti	105	83	10.5	11.0
Surinam	142	65	72.5	26.2
Barbados	200	29	91.1	—
Guyana	235	47	74.0	35.2
Santo Domingo	239	56	59.9	23.5
Jamaica	316	49	77.0	29.2
Trinidad	423	25	73.8	44.9
Cuba	431	42	77.5	40.0
Puerto Rico	562	24	81.0	37.6
	Range 105–563	Range 24–83	Range 10.5–91.1	Range 11.0–44.9
	Mean 294	Mean 53	Mean 68.5	Mean 30.9

*** Incomplete. Figures for many islands and territories not given.

V. Sector 5. Non-Communist Asia and Southeast Asia.

Society	GNP per capita (in dollars)	Per cent of labor force in agriculture	Per cent literate	Marsh's Index of Differentiation
Afghanistan	50	85	2.5	12.0
Mongolia	50	71	57.5	—
Laos	50	90	17.5	9.6
Burma	57	70	47.5	19.2
Pakistan	70	65	13.0	16.7
India	73	71	19.3	20.3
South Vietnam	76	75[a]	17.5[b]	16.8
Thailand	96	82	68.0	13.7
Cambodia	99	80	17.5	15.3
Ceylon	129	53	63.0	28.8
Indonesia	131	61	17.5	20.5
South Korea	144	70	77.0	14.7[b]
Taiwan	161	50	54.0	32.4
Philippines	220	59	75.0	20.9
Japan	306	40	98.0	41.5
Malaya	356	58	38.4	26.3[c]
	Range 50–356	Range 40–90	Range 2.5–98	Range 9.6–41.5
	Mean 127	Mean 55	Mean 42.7	Mean 20.5

[a] All figures with an a are taken from *Production Yearbook 1958*, FAO, Rome, and quoted in Marsh, *op. cit.*, Appendix 1.
[b] These figures are for both north and south divisions of the country taken together, since separate divisions are not broken down in the statistics.
[c] Refers to the Federation of Malaya.

VI. Sector 6. Communist Asia.

Society	GNP per capita (in dollars)	Per cent of labor force in agriculture	Per cent literate	Marsh's Index of Differentiation
North Vietnam	55	75[a]	17.5[b]	16.8
North Korea	68	80[a]	77.0[d]	14.7
China (Mainland)	73	69	47.5	13.0
	Range 55–73	Range 69–80	Range 17.5–77	Range 13.0–16.8
	Mean 65	Mean 74	Mean 47.3	Mean 14.8

[a] Same as a for Sector 5.
[b] Same as b for Sector 5.
[d] Figures given for S. Korea only.

VII. Sector 7. The Middle East and North Africa

Society	GNP per capita (in dollars)	Per cent of labor force in agriculture	Per cent literate	Marsh's Index of Differentiation
Yemen	50	—	2.5	—
Libya	60	80[a]	13.0	14.8
Iran	108	80	15.0	17.4
Jordan	129	75[a]	17.5	16.1
Morocco	142	71	12.5	18.8
United Arab Repub.	142	64	19.9	23.9
Iraq	156	81	10.0	26.6
Saudi Arabia	170	55[a]	2.5	13.5
Syria	173	70	27.5	18.3
Tunisia	173	68	17.5	25.7
Algeria	178	75	19.0	21.2
Turkey	220	77	39.0	23.9
Lebanon	362	50	47.5	—
	Range 50–362	Range 50–81	Range 2.5–47.5	Range 13.5–26.6
	Mean 159	Mean 70	Mean 18.7	Mean 20.0

[a] Same as a for Sector 5.

VIII. Sector 8. Sub-Saharan Africa*

Society	GNP per capita (in dollars)	Per cent of labor force in agriculture	Per cent literate	Marsh's Index of Differentiation
Togo	50	—	7.5	—
Ethiopia	55	74[a]	2.5	17.3
Sudan	60	74[a]	9.0	17.4
Angola	60	74[a]	2.5	17.1
Uganda	64	76[a]	27.5	18.4
Ruanda	70	—	7.5	—
Mozambique	70	74	1.0	18.3
Nigeria	78	59	10.0	16.2
Kenya	87	47[a]	22.5	31.2
Congo (Leopoldville)	92	84	37.5	19.8
Liberia	100	74[a]	7.5	17.4
Southern Rhodesia	135	60[a]	16.1[b]	31.0
Ghana	172	70	22.5	21.1
Rep. of S. Africa	395	33	42.5	45.3
	Range 50–395	Range 33–76	Range 1–42.5	Range 16.2–45.3
	Mean 106	Mean 66	Mean 15.4	Mean 20.8

* Data available for fewer countries, proportionately, than for other sectors.
[a] Same as a for Sector 5.
[b] Figures for Rhodesia and Nyasaland.

enterprise maintain their autonomy and are of sufficient magnitude to constitute major power centers of the society. The response of government to originative action by corporations or large financial institutions is more reactive and regulative than directive. Production and trade are regarded as spontaneous forces which the state can channel rather than command, restrict by legislation rather than manage, control indirectly through fiscal and tax policies without assuming final authority. There are sector differences among ec-pol societies fully as obvious as the distinctions noted among pol-ec nations. For example, in the more diversified economies so often found in sector 1, the coordinating and regulating of plural economic functions by the state will have more spread and proliferation than is the case in sector 4 (Caribbean societies) where there is an approach to monoculture and excessive dependence on export trade of raw materials with a minimum of processing.

While it is obvious that Communist nations of sectors 2 and 6 belong in the pol-ec category, the placement of other societies is somewhat more difficult, since the compendia of economic and resource data that now abound offer little clue to this dimension, and the political handbooks do not codify their data on this basis. Hence we are thrown back upon certain gross features of national life that give us rough indicators. For the sake of simplicity, we propose that one or more of the following characteristics is a sign of a pol-ec society:

1. A state-run economy in which the economy is often administered by government directive
2. The use of central economic planning for "development" by the government, chiefly visible in the presence of four year plans, five year plans, ten year plans, etc.
3. Governmental apportionment of capital and resources to private sectors and public sectors as a determinant of the direction the economy is to take
4. The widespread acceptance of "socialism" as descriptive of government aims linked with a situation where there has been relatively little capital accumulation or resource development
5. Where the public sector produces up to one-fourth of the GNP
6. Where one-third or more of *paid* employment is in government or government-owned entities.

These are the primary characteristics of pol-ec societies, many of which are interrelated; any single one of these is sufficient to place a society in this category, though the presence of two or more heighten the probability.

If these characteristics have evidential value, it is clear that the majority of the new African states of sector 8 are pol-ec societies, since they display features 1, 5 and 6 of the primary characteristics, i.e., a state-run economy, a public sector producing up to one-fourth of the GNP, and with one-third or more of paid employment in government or government-owned entities (Kamarck, 1967, 35, 54–55, 215). The special emphasis on "African socialism," especially in western African societies, is an added factor giving still more weight to the trend (Hunter, 1962, 288–90). While it is necessary to exempt the Portuguese colonies, Rhodesia, and South Africa from the other pol-ec societies, it seems fair to conclude that the majority of others in the Sub-Saharan section definitely belong in that category.

In the Middle East the outcome is more uncertain. Here an examination of the literature shows that only six out of the thirteen states mentioned above in sector 7 have definitely pol-ec characteristics, and these cluster around factor 2, namely the emphasis on five to ten-year development plans. On this basis the pol-ec societies are Algeria, the United Arab Republic, Libya, Morocco, Tunisia, and Turkey (Legum, 1966, 18–19, 30, 38, 58, 68, 126, and Kamarck, *op. cit.*, 212–13). This is less than a majority of the nations involved, tipping the balance toward the ec-pol category in that sector, with provisional recognition of wide variations in type.

It is much easier to determine the main trend in sector 5 or Non-Communist Asia and Southeast Asia. In this sector the only societies outside the pol-ec category (some of them quite marginal) are Afghanistan, Laos, Malaysia, Thailand, the Philippines, and Japan. All others have primary characteristic 2 (development plans of definite duration with government the directing force),[9] characteristic 4 (socialism as the aim of the political apparatus linked with weak capital or resource development), or both (Sinai, 1964, 181–82; Hunter, 1966, 94–98; Ruppen, 1967, 16–17; Paige, 1967, 21, 29).

On the whole, then, it appears that in addition to the Communist states of Eastern Europe and Asia, the pol-ec societies include a majority of states in sector 5, Non-Communist Asia and Southeast Asia, and a majority of nations in sector 8, Sub-Saharan Africa, together with somewhat less than half the states of sector 7, The Middle East and North Africa. Here it is necessary to utter a warning note. Cursory examination of these results could lead to the premature conclusion that a simple addition of "developing" nations to Communist states is sufficient to identify pol-ec societies. This is not the case, for many if not most of the Iberian societies in sector 3 have an agricultural work force as large proportionately as many in Africa or Asia (see Table 1) but none of the Iberian societies have the primary characteristics of the pol-ec societies. They are definitely ec-pol nations. Much the same can be said for the Caribbean societies which are both "developing" and ec-pol at the same time (excepting Cuba as a special pol-ec variant).

In terms of this broad classification, it seems reasonable to classify sectors 1, 3, and 4 as overwhelmingly occupied by ec-pol societies. This includes the Western European nations with the derivative neo-European complex, the Iberian societies of the eastern and western hemispheres, and the Caribbean societies excepting Cuba. Not surprisingly, these are all capitalist societies, some of which have a mixed economy or welfare state. While the political institutions may have marginal or indirect control of economic processes, market forces have much freer play than they have in the pol-ec societies. In the more highly industrialized nations of sector 1, indirect control of economic forces is exerted chiefly at key points, i.e., "manipulating the macroeconomic variables—increasing the rate of investment by appropriate tax measures, or increasing total gross national expenditure by a budgetary deficit, or shifting the relationship between the domestic cost-price structure and the international ones by changing exchange rates, etc." (Kamarck, *op. cit.*, 216). In no case, however, does this lead to explicit and selective allocation of resources to the private or public sectors as such in times of peace, to long-range development plans in which the government has decisions that override the wishes of the electorate, or action by fiat unaffected by constitutional requirements. All of this is true even in those cases where some nationalization has occurred or where a socialist party is in power for long periods, as in Sweden.

A Combined Typology

To sum up, we may present a composite picture of our two classification schemes, the cultural-historical and the structural, as follows:

TABLE 2. A CLASSIFICATION OF CONTEMPORARY SOCIETIES BY CULTURAL-HISTORICAL SECTORS, AND BY INSTITUTIONAL RELATIONSHIPS OF THE POLITY AND ECONOMY

DIVISION I

Multinational Sectors of the Ec-Pol Type

Sector 1

Western European Nations and the Derivative Neo-European Complex

Sector 3

Iberian Societies of the Eastern and Western Hemispheres

Sector 4

Caribbean Societies (excepting Cuba)

DIVISION II

Multinational Sectors of both Pol-Ec and Ec-Pol Types

Sector 7

The Middle East and North Africa

DIVISION III

Multinational Sectors of the Pol-Ec Type

Sector 2

Eastern Europe—The Communist States

Sector 5

Non-Communist Asia and Southeast Asia

Sector 6

Communist Asia

Sector 8

Sub-Saharan Africa

Why does this typology have relevance for the study of ethnic relations? In the first place, with respect to the sectors, it is postulated that the commonalities of historical and cultural relatedness will display similar intergroup sequences and that policies and practices toward ethnic groups will therefore have more comparable outcomes in any given sector than in other sectors. Secondly, these highly general considerations are given more specification when we add the structural relationships between the polity and the economy. It is hypothesized that in the pol-ec societies, the strict control that government has over economic practices is likely to be matched with overt surveillance and constraint of ethnic groups in direct and deliberate ways; conversely, in ec-pol societies, subordinate ethnics might be expected to have more autonomy, utilizing economic or political means to further their interests without continual intervention by the state. Thus we infer that in both types of society, the attitudes toward ethnic groups will take on the orientation toward the economy. In pol-ec societies where economic action is regarded as an object of mandatory control in the fear that the system may be endangered without it, we may expect a similar stance toward ethnic groups. Ethnic groups and their activities will tend to have high salience. On the other hand, in an ec-pol society, the authorities and the population at large tend to assume that the economy has some sort of self-regulating principle so that economic practices require only occasional regulation or attention from the government—unless and until an emergency arises. The parallel with attitudes toward ethnic groups is plain—they are supposed to find their own way by a set of autonomous adjustments to the society at large, with no political control or direction unless they create a crisis. Under normal conditions the ethnic groups have low salience. In the pol-ec society, the solution of economic problems by legal or administrative action of the government creates a climate in which such actions become normative; hence political supervision or control of ethnic groups tends to be open and unconcealed. In the ec-pol society, control is more often left to the mores or informal custom and infrequently maintained by explicit government action.

Whatever the propositions being tested, or whatever independent and dependent variables may be postulated in the search for generalizations, it may therefore be assumed that the results will vary from sector to sector and from ec-pol societies to pol-ec societies. The purpose of our classification is to provide another important intervening variable. Such contexts of comparability will serve as important guide lines in the analysis to follow.

· NOTES ·

1. Exceptions like Ethiopia or Saudi Arabia are, in a way, not exceptions, since they are often classified as something less than modern.
2. These nine characteristics are partly based on a shorter but suggestive list given by Germani (1964, 399).
3. This theme, for example, almost monopolizes the comparative analysis of Lipset (1963).
4. This corresponds roughly to what Lipset calls "European and English-speaking nations" but excludes the Communist nations of Albania, Bulgaria, Czechoslovakia, Hungary, Poland, Rumania, USSR, and Yugoslavia which he includes in his list. Furthermore, we have added Israel as a derivative European society, regardless of its geographic location.
5. The residual effects of feudalism in Latin America are emphasized at some length in a lively and provocative account by Hartz (1964, 26ff.) who comments on the same phenomenon in French Canada. His account of the colonial "fragments" that develop in terms of the dominant European intellectual currents at the time of settlement is wonderfully suggestive.
6. While the term "tribal" lacks precision because of its unusually wide denotation, it is used here in a nonpejorative sense to indicate social corporate groupings of small or large scale, unified by particularistic bonds like kinship, lineage, language, region, or fealty to a chief. These bonds create an ingroup that shows greater interaction with fellow members than with "outsiders."
7. While this may have been partly true of earlier eras, shared dominance with religious or kinship institutions seems more characteristic of pre-modern societies.
8. Not, however, in the New World, as noted later.
9. Malaysia has development plans but they are not systematic nor comprehensive since they are oriented primarily toward Malays of the rural regions. The government itself is Malay dominated and tries to protect the interests of the Malay elite as much as possible (Myrdal, 1968, 383).

· REFERENCES ·

Apter, David, "Political Religion in the New Nations," in Clifford Geertz (ed.), *Old Societies and New States*. New York: Free Press, 1963.

Germani, Gino, "Social Change and Intergroup Conflicts," in Irving L. Horowitz (ed.), *The New Sociology*. New York: Oxford University Press, 1964.

Hartz, Louis, *The Founding of New Societies*. New York: Harcourt, Brace & World, 1964.

Hourani, Albert, "The Decline of the West in the Middle East," in Richard H. Nolte (ed.), *The Modern Middle East*. New York: Atherton, 1963.

Hunter, Guy, *The New Societies of Tropical Africa*. London: Oxford University Press, 1962.

———, *South-East Asia, Race, Culture and Nation*. New York and London: Oxford University Press, 1966.

Kamarck, Andrew W., *The Economics of African Development*. New York: Praeger, 1967.

Legum, Colin (ed.), *Africa, A Handbook of the Continent*. Rev. ed. New York: Praeger, 1966.

Linz, Juan J., and Amando de Miguel, "Within-Nation Differences and Comparisons: The Eight Spains," in Richard L. Merritt and Stein Rokkan (eds.), *Comparing Nations, The Use of Quantitative Data in Cross-National Research*. New Haven and London: Yale University Press, 1966.

Lipset, Seymour M., *Political Man, The Social Basis of Politics*. New York: Anchor Books, 1963.

Marsh, Robert M., *Comparative Sociology*. New York: Harcourt, Brace & World, 1967.

Myrdal, Gunnar, *Asian Drama, An Inquiry Into the Poverty of Nations*. 3 vols. New York: Pantheon, 1968.

Paige, Glenn D., "1966: Korea Creates the Future," *Asian Survey*, 7:21–30, 1967.

Rupen, Robert A., "The Mongolian People's Republic: The Slow Evolution," *Asian Survey*, 7:16–20, 1967.

Russett, Bruce M., Hayward R. Alker, Jr., Karl W. Deutsch, and Harold D. Lasswell (eds.), *World Handbook of Political and Social Indicators*. New Haven and London: Yale University Press, 1964.

Rustow, Dankwart A., "Politics and Westernization in the Near East," in Richard H. Nolte (ed.), *The Modern Middle East*. New York: Atherton, 1963.

Sinai, I. Robert, *The Challenge of Modernization, The West's Impact on the Non-Western World*. New York, Norton, 1964.

6

🌷

The Socio-Historical
Approach

Many years ago, Georg Simmel employed the simile of visual perspective to illustrate differences in the degree of abstraction employed by observers.

> We obtain different pictures of an object when we see it at a distance of two, or of five, or of ten yards. At each distance, however, the picture is 'correct' in its particular way and only in this way . . . All we can say is that a view gained at any distance whatever has its own justification . . . In a similar way, when we look at human life from a certain distance, we see each individual in his precise differentiation from all others. But if we increase our distance, the single individual disappears, and there emerges instead, the picture of a "society" with its own forms and colors . . . The difference between the two merely consists in the difference between purposes of cognition; and this difference, in turn, corresponds to a difference in distance. (Simmel, 1950, 7, 8)

Simmel's principle, which in this passage is applied to rather extreme differences in abstraction, i.e., the individual and the societal, is a fertile one that can be applied at many intermediate levels as well. Let us call it *the principle of abstraction as a func-*

tion of distance from the data. Close up there is greater specificity of detail, while at greater distances, there are contours and patterns of amplitude or inclusiveness. Choice of distance, as Simmel recognizes, depends on the purpose of investigation.

The aim of these last chapters is to proceed from a panoramic view (at a greater distance) to a more focussed standpoint (at a lesser distance), indicating at each level the mode of attack necessary to advance our knowledge of ethnic relations on a comparative scale. In chapter 6 the view from a greater distance will incorporate the longitudinal dimension, while in chapter 7 the focus will be primarily cross sectional. In this process I shall make use of the analytical tools developed in earlier chapters as pragmatic guides rather than authoritative models. At this stage of our knowledge, tentativeness is the appropriate strategy, with numerous probes in what seem to be the right directions. Anything more pretentious would give us premature closure—conceptual or methodological.

It is therefore fitting to begin, then, at a global distance designated as the sociohistorical level. It is already stated that the present universe of societies includes only those with modern characteristics as outlined in chapter 5. However, it appears that it is impossible to maintain this position consistently if the intergroup sequences are taken seriously. Many of the latter predate the nation-state as now constituted: chattel slavery certainly goes back beyond the fifteenth century, and colonization as the term is employed here is almost as early chronologically. The sequence of annexation, as already noted, cannot be placed arbitrarily this side of the age of nationalism; it extends back indefinitely before that time, and its earlier manifestations have an impact on the later era to which we give major attention. Hence, while modern societies or nation-states are the source of most examples at the sociohistorical level, it is necessary to take account of their predecessors to the extent that they affect our sequences. However we shall not go back beyond the European explorations and voyages of discovery for our time period.

To seek for regularities at the sociohistorical level is to look for broad tendencies, trends, and recurrent sequences of events in such a way that they have a verifiable relationship to "times when and places where." It is to abandon the "harsh insistence that historical data can be dealt with only ideographically" (Becker, 1940, 503).[1]

The purpose of our general theoretical orientation in chapter 1, the sequential patterns introduced in chapter 2, as well as the multinational sectors and structurally differentiated societies of chapter 5 is to furnish the basis for asking significant questions about the changes in ethnic relations that occur in modern societies. For the most part these are questions which are either neglected by conventional histories or touched upon tangentially; here and there will be found historians with generalizing interests and reference will be made to some of them. However, in order to answer the questions that need to be raised here, it will eventually be necessary to have a series of comparative historical studies focussed in such a way as to give answers.

Annexation in Comparative Perspective

In terms of the framework advanced here the sociohistorical level of analysis can be illustrated by considering the sequence of annexation mentioned in chapter 3. On the basis of those categorical distinctions it is possible to advance certain generalizations. *First,* annexation in modern societies is not accompanied by racism.[2] Then in order to present a second generalization, it is elucidative, at this point, to review our discussion of centripetal and centrifugal trends from chapter 2. See again paradigm, p. 192.

A *second* generalization at the sociohistorical level is that the sequence of annexation in modern societies will modally result in condition D. I say modally because an exception is already noted in the Swiss case where, if we go sufficiently far back into history, the dominance of the German element *did* represent condition D, though after the French Revolution, the ruling group changed its ideology shifting the pattern to B where it stands today (the conflict resolved). The Soviet case is somewhat marginal, complicated by the fact that the ruling Party manipulates the variables. In terms of manifest public aims, its initial plan was ostensibly B, while the concealed goal envisaged a movement from D to A. To the extent that the final aim was suspected or recognized by the minorities themselves, it led to a number of open conflicts of which the Basmachi revolt instigated by Muslim tribesmen was only the most salient case (Kolarz, 1952, 174–75). When the annexing authorities suppressed these uprisings by military means, condition D continued, though for how long, only research can reveal. However, these examples do not affect the validity of our second generalization though they suggest that it may *be modified* to read, "the sequence of annexation in modern societies will modally result in condition D during the first stages of interaction."

Then how about later stages of interaction? I suggest that the way this question is approached will depend, in part, on our presuppositions. If conflicts are thought of in terms of their *resolution*, a process of simple reasoning would imply that D would have only two modes of resolution on the basis of the schematic design: either A or B. Logically this would require either a change of ideology on the part of the *superordinates*, in which case the resolution would be B, or the ideology of the *subordinates* would need to change, when the resolution would be A. Keeping attention on the sequence of annexation, the question

FIGURE 6.   CONGRUENT AND INCONGRUENT ORIENTATIONS
TOWARD CENTRIPETAL AND CENTRIFUGAL TRENDS OF SUBORDINATES
AS VIEWED BY THEMSELVES AND SUPERORDINATES

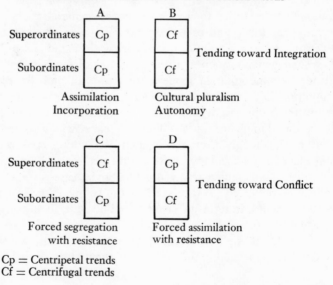

then becomes: which probability is greater, a change in the ideology of superordinates or in that of subordinates? The answer is surely the latter because of the tendency already noted for the superordinates to take their legitimate position for granted. The only authenticated case in which superordinates made the change is Switzerland[3] where the shift to B actually occurred. Does this mean that there are numerous cases where *subordinates* have changed their ideology and accepted solution A? If applied to the annexation sequence, then in the modern world, especially since the rise of nationalism, it is evident, though surprising, that it is almost impossible to find a clear-cut case of movement from D to A, particularly in Europe where perhaps the majority of cases occur. Not only do many minority groups "escape out of the field" by secession and setting up of their own independent states, but the fragments that remain are likely to remain anti-assimilationist and disaffected. Alternative D is still the basic condition even though it appears in latent rather than manifest form.

Another possibility: perhaps the reason why the progression from D to A is so often blocked is the intervening factor of nationalism. Could it be that in the prenationalistic era of Europe, the trend from D to A would be a regular occurrence? One could argue that under such conditions subordinates, lacking the extravagant hopes and intransigent demands of the nationalist period, would be more amenable to accept the viewpoint of their overlords.

A comparison along these lines might yield something definite. But a realistic appraisal brings new difficulties. One of these has already been encountered in chapter 3 where it is noted that annexation is anything but a simple once-and-for-all affair. More often it appears as the last of a successive series of previous annexations extending back hundreds of years. Wars, interregnums, alternating chains of fealty among overlords, the waxing and waning of duchies, domains, kingdoms and empires with their plethora of treaties that changed boundaries every few years: all left their mark and consequences on the national states that followed. Annexations in the modern period must then be considered (in a very large number of cases) as extensions of earlier changes, and even when no overt annexations occur today, the shape and contour of the population elements cannot be understood without the tracing of historical antecedents with the many boundary changes involved. This is especially true in the Balkans.

A second difficulty in comparing nationalistic with prenationalistic societies is this: in order for assimilation or alternative A to become a reality, time is needed for accommodative adjustments, acculturation, compromise, and reconciliation. Where shifts in the ruling regime are frequent, sporadic, arbitrary, and unpredictable, there is no time for a "mold" to set. No sooner are the inhabitants of an area accustomed to one set of masters than they find it imperative to change their ways and adjust to others. Constant interruptions, breaks, and changes in authority figures do not allow the gradual but orderly movement toward acceptance and consent that are characteristic of alternative A. If the prenationalist period has this sort of instability to a far greater degree than the nationalistic period, the former would not only lack comparability, but be unable to furnish true cases of assimilation simply because there was not sufficient time for such a process to occur.[4]

A third difficulty of comparison is of an opposite character. In examining the premodern era, it is surely not implausible to suggest that annexation, which on the surface appears as a violent incorporation of a smaller group by a larger society, may not be *experienced* by the subordinates as a forcible measure at all. In many cases it apparently results from a treaty-making operation in a distant city between two antagonists who have met on the field of battle in far-away regions without disturbing the territory of the annexed group in any way. The newly subordinated, in such cases, could be expected to react mildly or indifferently to the change—much as contemporary employees of an industrial plant that has been purchased by a larger corporation and is "under new management." Such indifferent reactions would be even more likely if the annexed group were isolated peasants having limited communication with centers of power where political decisions affecting their subordinate status were made without their consent or knowledge. To put it another way, ethnicity lacked salience among those local subordinates and was not politicized. Since one of the marks of a modern society, as already mentioned, is the increase of communicative links between city and country (necessary preconditions for politicizing ethnic popular agitation) we would expect a greater probability of undisturbed takeover in premodern than in modern societies and a greater chance for stirring up or inflaming subordinates during the latter period. To the extent that this can be proved and it is shown that the great bulk of the population remained passive in the premodern epoch, alternative A has lost its point and applicability; does not the formulation of condition A assume extensive communication links? Perhaps the changes in communication, literacy, and more extensive participation in pervasive societal roles in the modern period[5] make it essentially noncomparable with an earlier epoch on the dimensions so far utilized. While it is possible to draw broad distinctions between the two periods, one cannot, in all confidence, assert that a paradigm with relevance to modern societies can apply to earlier ones that lack the structural characteristics that may have been taken for granted in setting up the initial scheme.

Returning for a moment to our earlier assumption that a progression from D to either A or B would occur only if conflicts are thought of in terms of their resolution, the question arises: is this assumption valid? Or is it a normative expectation implying that because conflicts *should* be resolved, that they necessarily *will* be? This hidden presupposition could have more than one intellectual source. Not only could it result from an unguarded acceptance of the idea of progress (with which our culture is saturated), but it could arise from an unconscious acceptance of the system analyst's penchant for symmetry and the "holistic optimism" that accompanies it (see p. 36). Both modes of thought could well reinforce each other without full awareness of the investigator. When the premise is examined openly, however, it is soon evident that it must be abandoned since it has neither logical nor empirical validity. This does not entail accepting an opposite assumption, i.e., that such conflicts are *never* resolved, as might be the case if we were dealing with simple categorical exclusions based on Aristotelian logic. Here again we are faced with a dialectical situation in which a total either-or must be replaced by a both-and.

However, social scientists cannot be satisfied with an empty formula of this kind. They must press forward to closer specification.[6] To do this means getting ahead of the previous argument and considering the sequence of voluntary migration as well as the sequence of annexation. For empirically, the best examples of resolution A occur in the sequence of voluntary migration as Lieberson at least suggests in his generalization: "In societies where the indigenous population at their initial contact is subordinate, warfare and nationalism often—though not always—develop later in the cycle of relations. By contrast, relations between migrants and indigenous populations that are subordinate and superordinate, respectively, are generally without long-term conflict" (Lieberson, 1961, 907–08). The first of these types corresponds with our intergroup sequence of colonization, while the second matches the sequence of voluntary migration. Without entering into the ramification of details that furnish the full evidence, a *third* and contingent generalization follows in terms of our paradigm: The probability of progression from D to A is low for cases of annexation, and relatively high for cases of voluntary migration. One reason, of course, is that subordinates and their culture remain "in place" for the alternative of annexation, reinforcing any tendency toward insurgence, while migrants, on the other hand, are uprooted and to a considerable extent, atomized. This weakens their power of resistance and makes them more amenable to the views of superordinates.

It will be noted that Figure 6 does not refer to structural characteristics, and only to a very limited set of cultural elements, i.e., to ideological goals of the subordinates on the one hand, and to superordinate perspectives on what such goals should be for the subordinates. Both of these are normative orientations. The next question is: in the case of annexation (and its complex derivatives) will such orientations be themselves affected by the structural differences in various societies, or are we dealing with uniform results that will occur in any society? Here the other typology of ec-pol and pol-ec societies furnishes a tool for investigation. Questions like these can be submitted to a preliminary test by historical comparisons between annexation and its results in these types of societies with different structural arrangements. A socio-historical study of Western and Eastern European societies during the modern period should furnish some answers.

Remembering the earlier assertion that acceptance of assimilation by both superordinates and subordinates (condition A) is unlikely when preceded by annexation, and that some form of disagreement over the issue is the modal expectation (condition D), it is then a reasonable hypothesis that this disagreement would be more covert in pol-ec societies and more overt in ec-pol societies. This hypothesis implies that the conflict would take a different form but remain unresolved in either case. Manifestations of resistance would take open and perhaps political form in the ec-pol societies, while remaining at the interpersonal or primary-group level in pol-ec societies. Comparisons like these can throw new light on ethnic relations as a whole in terms of their context, on relativistic modes of integration, and also on unsuspected dimensions of the nationality question in Europe. It furnishes a sort of semicontrolled experiment since, in the early years of the twentieth century, most of the Eastern European states now in the pol-ec category entered a nationalistic phase in which they shared constitutional and parliamentary institutions with Western European states so that their political structures were at one time similar (Burks, 1961, 198). On the other hand, the Eastern states experienced a sequence of events that later distinguished them from Western Europe, when the former were incorporated into the Communist bloc, partly by the intermediation of Party activism in the interwar period as well as in World War II, partly by military action of the Soviets more or less coordinated with Party, and guerilla activity within the Eastern countries themselves. Certainly at the end of World War II or shortly afterward, the entire Eastern bloc of countries had a social structure closely analogous to that of the USSR. Did this social structure have a differential effect on ethnic groups of the nationality type in the period from 1945 to the present when compared with effects on nationality groups in Western Europe? A historical study along these lines is needed, for it would fulfill a methodological demand of social science by holding the sequence constant and varying the conditions.

Annexation Reconsidered

A preliminary look at the data reveals that top hierarchical decision on the fate of national minorities in the Eastern countries seems to have been centralized in Moscow. During the interwar period, the centralized Party bureaucracy held out the doctrine

of self-determination to submerged nationality groups as an in-
centive for collaboration—to the Ruthenians, Macedonians, Slovaks, and a number of others (Burks, *op. cit.*, 66, 80–81, 90ff.,
100, 145ff.). After World War II, opportunism on the one hand,
and unilateral decisions on the other, replaced the earlier incen-
tives, fulfilling some hopes and dashing others to the ground.
Ruthenia was annexed from the Czechoslovak Republic to join
its fellow nationals in the Ukrainian Socialist Republic; the Macedonians who were to have had a separate state of their own, were
absorbed into the new Communist Yugoslavia, and when the
latter took an independent course in 1948, breaking the centralized tie with Moscow, the Soviets renounced all responsibility
for anything that happened in Yugoslavia, including the fate of
the Macedonians, while the Yugoslavs poured money and material
into Macedonian territory to pacify the inhabitants who were
given autonomy without independence (Burks, *op. cit.*, 104).
The Slovaks resumed their familiar position of subordination in
Communist Czechoslovakia without much change. In addition
the Soviets made a unilateral decision that some ethnics in Eastern
Europe were unassimilable and dangerous—especially the Germans of whom 14 million were expelled from Poland, Bukovina,
Bessarabia, the Dobrudja, Silesia, and East Prussia, most of these
making their way into a shrunken Germany at the close of the
war (Burks, *op. cit.*, 135). A similar fate befell the Turks, though
the initiative was not from Moscow.

> In 1950–52 the Bulgarian Communists drove out a quarter of a
> million Dobrudjian Turks, or 40 percent of Bulgaria's remain-
> ing Turkish population. Turks were also leaving Communist
> Yugoslavia; in 1954, for example, one-fifth of the 100,000 Tur-
> kish-speaking minority returned to their ancient homeland. The
> limit on the rate of return was the ability of the Turkish econ-
> omy to absorb the returnees. It was clear, however, that in the
> not too distant future there would be no Turks left where
> Communism held sway. (Burks, *op. cit.*, 142)

As noted in chapter 4, the *mode* of assimilation in the Soviet
Union is distinctive; it is an elitist operation in which the Party
establishes a bridgehead within the annexed minority, a coopted
Party elite who serve with their fellow Party members from the
center as economic shock troops whose business is to create a

new collective agriculture or a new industrialism. If and when the expected economic development occurs and the hierarchical power is held firmly, later cultural assimilation, or so it is assumed, will take place. The precise features of this *dirigism* or manipulative elitism have yet to be spelled out, and it constitutes a historical task of the utmost importance to analyze its structural constituents, particularly to determine whether this mechanism is the same in other Eastern European countries as it is in the USSR. The extent and nature of the conflict produced by this policy and the utilization of economic integration as a planned step toward ultimate cultural integration need to be fully explored, especially in comparison with the policies employed by the ec-pol societies of Western Europe. Even though field studies in pol-ec may not be feasible at present, the flood of documents and related secondary researches make it possible to throw additional light on the questions raised here. A related comparison with the mode of annexation occurring in the United States with its Spanish-American population would be most revealing, especially since the structural characteristics in the latter case have operated on unplanned bases with no attempt to set up a definite progression.

It is impossible to delineate this approach to other sequences in other than the briefest terms. In view of space limitations, it is possible to touch on but three additional sequences as subjects for socio-historical investigation: forced migration (slave transfers), colonization, and voluntary migration.

Slavery Sequences and Racism

As for the first, any comparative studies of slavery and its aftermath in the modern world must, so far as this is possible, distinguish the phenomenon from earlier forms. This cannot be done, as some have supposed, by the simple ascription of chattel slavery to the modern period; chattel slavery goes back to some of the earliest civilizations where the basic principle of the status was recognized—in Egypt, Babylonia, Assyria, India, China, Greece, and Rome, as well as in eleventh century England (Davis, 1966, 32, 38). Nor is there a clear break between the transport and extensive use of slaves throughout the Mediterranean during the Renaissance, as compared with the forms that became more dominant in the New World which are more familiar. There is definite continuity between these forms (Davis, *op. cit.*, 42). If there is any watershed at all, it occurred after 1462 when the Portuguese broke the Arab monopoly on the sale of Negroes by establishing direct contact with West African societies, building up their own trade in slaves that extended first to the Iberian peninsula, and then over the Atlantic to the West Indies and the mainland of South America (Davis, *op. cit.*, 44).

What, then, distinguishes slavery in the modern world as an object of socio-historical study? At least four features stand out:

1. It was an integral part and parcel of a colonization process, so that in this particular case there is a unique amalgam of two sequences interacting with each other: forced migration and colonization.
2. It depended on an economic base of a newly established cash-crop economy, furnishing the element that made such an economy productive and lucrative.
3. At least in its heyday, it supplied the financial impetus for commercial dominance in the rivalry of leading European countries, and in Britain the sinews of a burgeoning capitalism.
4. It was a phenomenon of the Western Hemisphere.

While these are its distinguishing marks, our interest in slavery here is chiefly centered on two familiar issues: its impact on Western societies in terms of racism, and its effect on social pluralism.

Regarding the issue of racism, it is important to separate this sharply from another related problem, namely the harshness of the slave regime. It is not fanciful to conceive of a mild racism combined with severe forms of brutality, or, conversely, of a highly exclusionist racism coupled with paternalistic benevolence. The earlier researches of Tannenbaum (1947) and Freyre (1946) have left an abiding impression of Brazilian slavery as a kindly, humane, and even indulgent set of relations between masters and slaves, in stark contrast with a more repressive and harsh regime in the southern United States. Later investigation has not confirmed this view, and there seems to be ample evidence not merely of outright cruelty and barbarity in Brazil, but a rate of mortality among slaves that is practically unmatched. Thus "while Brazil and the United States each entered the nineteenth century with about a million slaves and subsequent importations into Brazil were three times greater than those into the United States, by the Civil War there were nearly four million slaves in the United States and only one and a half million in Brazil." Part of the difference, of course, is due to the much higher rate of manumission in the latter country; other factors were climate, sanitation, and nutrition. Even taking account of all these elements, the differences are striking, however, and as Davis goes on to say, "According to both C. R. Boxer and Celso Furtado, Brazilian sugar planters took a short term view of their labor needs, and accepted the axiom, which spread to the British Caribbean, that it was good economy to work one's slaves to death and then purchase more . . . In 1823, José Bonifacio noted that while Brazil had been importing some 40,000 slaves a year, the increase in the total slave population was hardly perceptible" (Davis, *op. cit.*, 232–33).

So it is important to keep attention centered firmly on racism rather than on its accompanying features of brutality or harsh treatment. When this is done, an examination of the sequence of slavery makes it quite clear that there is an apparent divide between the Iberian nations and those of other Western European countries, or what is noted above in chapter 5 as multinational sectors 3 and 1 respectively. During the period when the slave trade and the institutionalization of slavery were occurring— say from the end of the fifteenth century to the nineteenth century—the maritime powers of the western sector struggling for supremacy: Britain, Holland, and France, set up slave colonies in which separation and avoidance techniques between master and slave were more rigid and unyielding than was the case in the slave colonies of Spanish or Portuguese origin. Socio-historical research on a comparative basis is definitely needed to explain the reasons for this difference.[7] The origins of racism seem to predate slavery which only accounts for its spread and intensiveness. With regard to racism itself, Davis comments:

> that there is evidence of such prejudice in eighteenth century Europe,[8] where slavery could not have been a direct cause. The

fact that Africans had traditionally been associated with Moorish infidelity and with Noah's curse of Canaan may have disposed some Europeans to regard them as fit for bondage. Our
information is still highly fragmentary, but it is possible there
was something in the culture of Western Europe that inclined
white men to look with contempt on the physical and cultural
traits of the African. (Davis, *op. cit.*, 281)

This passage opens up an interesting vista for research. First
and foremost is the issue: is it sufficient to account for the *differences* in racism between the two sectors, or must we go beyond
this to seek out special reasons for heightened racism in the
western European sector considered by itself as Davis suggests?
The former is a much easier task for it can be accomplished by
focussing on the historical experiences of Iberian societies that
were unshared by those farther north, i.e., the Moorish occupation and its accompanying intermixture of racially different
peoples, the incorporation of slaves as an integrated lower stratum
in Spanish and Portuguese kingdoms (Davis, *op. cit.*, 45), and
the meeting of Portuguese and Spanish traders with African
chiefs on a basis of equality when the slave traffic proved ad-
vantageous for both (Davis, *op. cit.*, 282). With the exception of
the last factor which was later shared by Dutch, British and
French traders, these elements were peculiar to the Iberian societies and may furnish initial reasons for the difference. Furthermore the carry-over of feudal or patrimonial relations from the
Iberian peninsula to the American colonies appeared to be the
transplantation of an entire social system (insofar as this was
possible in new surroundings) but with the ethos of feudalism
intact. From the very first, the Iberian colonies took with them
the image of "a hierarchical, diversified, and functionally com-
partmented social order" (Morse, 1964, 124) in which slaves
were an integral and traditional part. They were not an afterthought or a superadded element as they were in British colonies
where slaves brought an element of novelty and unfamiliar problems of adjustment, rendered uneasy and anxious by doubts
implanted from the Enlightenment, and images of an open,
bourgeois society that obviously had little relevance to plantation life.[9] Who was this strange being newly bought and owned,
whose origins and ways were obscure, and whose utility was so
obvious? Certainly not a full-fledged member of society as the

colonist understood society, and to admit such a thought would be to deny the validity of title to property. Hence the slave must be something quite separate, a unique form of life outside the rights and duties of ordinary men. Such an unknown X was a question mark or a blank; it was soon filled in by ad hoc ascriptions attributed to the most salient features of his difference: to color and the traits displayed in the slave relationship.[10] In this way the ideology of racism in North America excluded the Negro from society as another order of being, while the mild racism of Latin America included the Negro as part of the feudal whole. Even as late as the twentieth century, a prominent Ecuadorean could strongly condemn the racial prejudice of the United States for "excluding men of color from the common society" (Hartz, *op. cit.*, 54).

On the basis of these observations, certain inferences about racism resulting from slavery in the New World suggest themselves: (1) we would expect racism to be more extreme in the United States than elsewhere in the Western Hemisphere; (2) manumission would be more restricted in the United States than in other New World regions; (3) race mixture would produce more gradations of status in Latin America, more sharp distinctions in the United States; (4) change in race relations moving in the direction of equality would be more gradual in Latin America, and more fluctuating in the United States, tending more toward accommodative relations in the first case and more conflict or hostility in the latter.

Historical evidence so far appears to support such hypotheses. Concerning the first, a specialist on the history of slavery, David B. Davis asserts that "Well before the Civil War the entire society of the United States became permeated with a deep racial prejudice that far exceeded that of any other nation of the New World" (Davis, *op. cit.*, 286). On the issue of manumission the relative differences between the United States and Brazil are of a sufficient magnitude to verify our inference, though in this case the United States and the British West Indies were more on a par. Brief citations will again suffice:

> The strongest evidence for a radical and fundamental difference regarding manumission is the restrictive legislation of the British West Indies and mainland colonies. From the late seventeenth century to the time of the American Revolution, vir-

tually every British colony enacted laws which in some way limited the master's power to free his slaves . . . By the mid-nineteenth century the American master who wished to free his slaves was forced to rely on legal ingenuity and subterfuge . . . A far more distinctive feature of Latin American slavery was the well-known provision allowing a bondsman to purchase his own freedom . . . (In Cuba) under the system of *coartacion* a slave could make his master agree on a fixed price, which might be set through the arbitration of a local court or official, and the slave might then purchase his liberty in installments . . . The practice of *coartacion* seems to have spread from Cuba to other Spanish colonies . . . In Brazil, even in the early colonial period, it was customary for some masters to free slaves upon payment of the original purchase price . . . It is an incontestable fact that slaves in Latin America had more opportunities for manumission than did those in the British colonies or the United States. (Davis, *op. cit.*, 262–63, 265–67)

The third inference on race mixture, while corroborated by the evidence, is a more complex phenomenon requiring detailed attention. Certainly all forms of slavery in the New World were accompanied by extensive miscegenation,[11] and it is fairly well agreed that miscegenation, in and by itself, is no sign that racism is absent (Davis, *op. cit.*, 274, 282). It is the *results* of intermixture, the variations of color shadings and their correlation with social position that are an index of greater or lesser racism. Parallel with this are the overt or covert forms of concubinage that match the former. Mild racism modally recognizes gradations of color as rough indicators of status differences with an acceptance of concubinage as a fact of life; extreme racism ordinarily polarizes color values (with color of the dominant group as the norm and other colors being deviations from it) with concomitant concealment and condemnation of concubinage. It is significant to observe that historical differences along these lines follow the boundaries of our multinational sectors. As Davis puts the case, "it was more likely for people of racially mixed ancestry to be emancipated and eventually to rise to the status of whites in Latin America than in the British colonies, and that it was similarly more likely in the British West Indies than in the mainland colonies and states" (Davis, *op. cit.*, 280). This corresponds to sector 3 (Iberian societies), sector 4 (Caribbean societies) and sector 1 (Western European nations and the derivative neo-

European complex) remarkably well, even with the few qualifications that might be made.

Such differences reflect demographic as well as structural
influences. While comparative data on the sex ratio are still
somewhat fragmentary, it is clear that the number of white
women in Spanish colonies was uncommonly low in spite of
efforts by the crown to increase them. In the Spanish Indies,
the influx of women from the peninsula was only one-tenth that
of men during the sixteenth century. "Three centuries later,
at the close of the colonial period, Humboldt found only two
hundred and seventeen European women in Mexico City as
against two thousand one hundred and eighteen European men"
(Morse, *op. cit.*, 129). The shortage of white women in the
Caribbean was also noticeable. Davis comments on the acceptance of interracial sex relations as "more common and acceptable
in regions where there were relatively few white women. In
colonial Brazil, the French West Indies, and even Barbados and
Jamaica, planters and administrators met the need for female com-
panionship, as well as for sexual gratification, by living openly
with Negro mistresses who were often accorded many of the
privileges of legitimate wives" (Davis, *op. cit.*, 273). Althoµgh
conclusive reports on the sex ratio in the southern United
States are conspicuously absent, indications point to a more even
balance of the sexes among whites than was the case in Latin
America or the Caribbean.[12] Miscegenation did not have its
roots so much in the scarcity of white women as in the accessibility of Negro women in a slave relation described by Jefferson
as "the most unremitting despotism on the one part, and degrading
submission on the other" (Calhoun, 1918, II, 285). Under these
conditions concubinage, though publicly condemned, was privately fostered to a marked degree. A South Carolina planter is
quoted as saying that "There is not a likely-looking black girl
in the state that is not the concubine of a white man. There is
not an old plantation in which the grandchildren of the owner
are not whipped in the field by the overseer" (Calhoun, *op. cit.*,
II, 296). In a way the process became cumulative as mixed offspring more attractive to whites appeared in greater numbers and
were much sought after. Calhoun declares that "The charms of
concubinage accounted in large measure for the prevalence of
bachelors in the South. A book of Letters from the South and

West (1824) noted that it was very common for rich planters in Virginia to remain bachelors. A work of 1850 referred to the sale of mulatto girls 'in the far South to the abandoned white bachelors who abound in this country' " (Calhoun, *op. cit.*, II, 299).

Thus the more extreme racism that existed in the slave regions of the United States was in contrast with the milder racism of Latin America in two ways: the North American pattern created a greater gulf between whites and non-whites, and this was accompanied by a more clandestine form of miscegenation. In the Iberian hierarchical system of society, it was easier to admit those of intermediate color to an in-between status, and the practice of concubinage was sufficiently traditional to be overt and legitimized. This had its eventual results in giving official standing to intermarriage as well. In the southern United States, however, "there were no gradations between the status of Negro and white; the mulatto did not occupy a half-way position but was seen as essentially a Negro. This bias may well have been the result of moral indignation at racial intermixture, which was more intense where large numbers of white women and a high valuation of marriage made illicit sexual relations less tolerable" (Davis, *op. cit.*, 279).[13]

As for the fourth inference, the fluctuations in American race relations and the violence that accompanied these swings of the pendulum are familiar enough to require only passing comment. The ferocious character of the Civil War was followed by the ostensible peace of Reconstruction which was soon broken, as the gains made by Negroes under protection of Northern bayonets were attacked at first in secret, then openly by the Ku Klux Klan. The compromise of 1877 removed Federal troops and paved the way for the South to reverse the process which they finally did after 1890 with strict segregation laws and modes of disfranchisement. Lynchings increased along with race riots fomented by whites; the NAACP began a counter reaction which had little effect. World War I accelerated the migration process and after the war, Garveyism flourished briefly. In the depression that followed, the Negroes were again catapulted into the depths of economic misery. From the late thirties to the fifties, militancy began to pay off for the Negroes: in legislation, administrative edicts, and court judgments in their favor; all this culminated in the historic desegregation decision of 1954. The momentum, however, continued only briefly and the Negroes soon recognized that laws and judgments were not going to be enforced, and that the affluence of the wider society was not for them. The era of demonstrations followed in the early 1960s to produce still newer legislation. When this too proved to make little difference, the era of riots fomented by Negroes began, spearheaded by Watts and spreading to other cities in other regions. By 1966 the tide began to ebb as the "white backlash" became a force to be reckoned with, bringing a reversal of the upgrade of the sixties. This see-saw phenomenon has been a marked feature of race relations in the United States, unmatched by more gradual changes in Brazil or the Caribbean.

Slavery and the resulting racism have an impact on the centrifugal and centripetal trends of superordinates and subordinates that differs profoundly from the effects of annexation. To review our paradigm once more:

FIGURE 6. CONGRUENT AND INCONGRUENT ORIENTATIONS
TOWARD CENTRIPETAL AND CENTRIFUGAL TRENDS OF SUBORDINATES
AS VIEWED BY THEMSELVES AND SUPERORDINATES

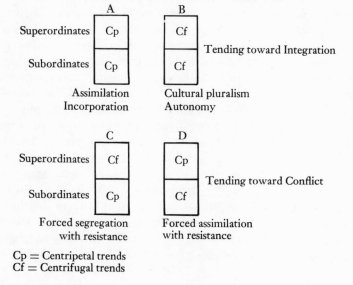

Cp = Centripetal trends
Cf = Centrifugal trends

In simplest terms it might appear that annexation has effect D while slavery has effect C. Yet the applicability of this scheme to the sequence of slavery has relevance only after emancipation. The consequences of race relations in the slave relationship are only fully revealed after societies face the task of integrating former slaves and their descendants into citizens.[14] Here again the differential effects of the multinational sectors are visible. The absolute separation of Negro and white which was an ideological feature of North American slavery becomes translated into forms of segregation with "separate but equal" rationalizations which are really related by continuity to the past; in the Caribbean the separation was only partial and existed chiefly at the elite level where distinctions held firm; in Brazil the hierarchical system carried over its gradations of color as an informal way of categorizing those with equal formal status as citizens.[15] These sector differences make us aware of the fact that our paradigm represents only extreme or pure types, rather than the actual series that are found in the data. While the North American case corresponds most closely with C, the Caribbean example lies somewhere between C and A but closer to C, while the Brazilian situation is also intermediate but closer to A.

The major contrast between C and D is attributable to the racism that characterizes condition C[16] and this reaches its clearest or more distinct form in the United States when we are considering slavery in the New World. It is in the United States, where the subordinate group, torn from its cultural moorings, separated and atomized into a mass of individual units, lacking a center of social identity like language, religion, or kinship, and subject to extreme forms of coercion, that we find the subordinates lacking the unity and cohesiveness of annexed peoples, cut off from the possibility of envisioning the future as one of shared autonomy, or an ideal state where they would have a "land of their own."[17] At the outset, the slaves were an aggregate, not a people. The boundaries and identity of such racial minorities are not determined by the "primordial attachments" within the group but by superordinates who have brought them into being —in this case by forced migration. In its inception, such an aggregate is an artificial entity that becomes defined and regularized in its outlines by coercive actions, customs, and laws of the ruling group. Eventually this external force has internal repercussions in the form of self-awareness as a social reality.[18] Whatever feelings of identity there are develop slowly under the impact of a common fate and arise from common subordination in the present rather than from memories of an ancient past and their renaissance. Consciousness of kind, first uncertain and localized in isolated rural areas, develops into more solid proportions with emancipation, migration, and urbanization, incorporating, as it grows, the Enlightenment ideology of the dominant group relating to free citizenship and human equality. Hence the pressure in the centripetal direction denoted by C, i.e., demand for full participation rather than the limited form indicated by D. Both could conceivably result in A over time, but just as this consummation is prevented in condition D by nationalistic aspirations of the subordinates, it is obstructed in C by the avoidances of racism on the part of superordinates. The probability of progression from C to A will occupy attention after racism receives further attention below.

Slavery Sequences and Pluralism

What are the contributions of the socio-historical approach to the next problem, i.e., the effects of slavery in the New World on social pluralism? First, insofar as it is possible, it is important to disentangle the population elements coming into being as a result of the slavery sequence (intertwined with colonization though it was) with the peoples overrun, and to a large degree displaced by the colonization sequence directly. In at least two West Indian cases, Guyana and Trinidad, sizeable elements were also the product of contract labor transfers. Instead of analyzing the pluralistic *features* of these societies as wholes in view of all the sequences they have experienced, we raise a related but narrower question: how did the introduction of a slave element into Western societies affect the pluralistic structure of these societies?

This is a problem that has received little attention from the historians, though it has caught the attention of anthropologists. However, the early ethnological explorations related to this question were focused chiefly on cultural survivals from the African scene (Herskovits, 1934, 1937, 1941, 1947); they did not analyze the structural impact of slave populations as a part of their task. The problem of analysis is a particularly difficult one because the original formulation of the "social pluralism" concept more or less assumed the crescive characteristics of plural groupings, which meant that they had already formed their own institutions of "kinship, education, religion, property and economy, recreation, and certain sodalities" (M. G. Smith, 1960, 769). Thus the units of observation were tribes and nations with fully developed social systems of their own, or fragments of such units, conquered or migrating, that preserved in microcosm the institutional features of their parental societies. None of these features can be clearly ascribed to the slave masses brought to the Western Hemisphere. It is already evident that such populations lacked such interlocking, autonomously developed, unitary structures. As an atomized aggregate of individuals entering new societies, whatever institutional patterns they developed had to be newly minted as a function of their acculturation to the ways of the masters. If the previous analysis of racism presented above has any validity, one should expect the process of institutional development to be uneven and irregular, with some differentials traceable to the multinational sectors.

On this basis it is plausible to hypothesize that in a society like Brazil where incorporative processes were salient, the Negroes would not develop a full range of institutions peculiarly their own but would tend to take their place and accept corresponding roles in the institutions of Portuguese colonial society. In the West Indies one would expect intermediate features with some autonomous institutions and some shared with the dominant group. Finally, in the United States the prediction would be that Negroes would have more separate institutions than could be found among African descendants in either the Caribbean or Brazil. Two other hypotheses might also seem warranted. *First*, the importance of economic institutions for survival and the crucial importance of the imported slaves for the maintenance of these institutions would insure a solid position in economic life until the major shift from an agricultural to an industrial system came into being. With this change, the economic position of the Negroes, no longer defined by previous norms, would become problematical and institute serious problems of transition. *Second*, the theoretical premises underlying the idea of social pluralism posit a singular, coercive integration of plural societies by overarching political institutions in the hands of a dominant group. If this premise is accepted, one would infer that participation in political processes would be either delayed or obstructed by superordinates—the last and most conclusive link in the process of integration.

The evidence is still too scanty to support these hypotheses in the fullness they require. With regard to the multinational sector differentials, it is fitting to begin with the Brazilian case. Here it would appear that the only separate institutional developments among the Negroes of Brazil were minor in character, a predictable outcome. Bastide asserts that in the early part of the twentieth century, "The Negroes made plenty of institutions for themselves in which they found and fortified their own solidarity; but these were institutions of a recreational type" (Bastide, 1965, 19). The universal spread of Catholicism prevented the rise of separate religious institutions;[19] the kinship patterns of the Negroes were so intertwined with those of the whites that it is difficult to separate them satisfactorily. It is true that the proportion married for both Negro males and females is lower than it is among mulattoes or whites, but this seems to be a function of economic position (Smith, 1963, 471). The most likely conclusion—though not fully proven—is that the proportion of *amasiados* or common-law marriages varies with economic status, being the largest among the darker colored people at the lower end of the scale, somewhat less among the *pardos* or mixed group, and least among the whites. At any rate, sizeable illegitimacy rates exist at all levels of the population and "very little distinction is made between legitimate and illegitimate children" (Smith, *op. cit.*, 460; 463 ff). The important fact is that this is not a *Negro* phenomenon, but simply shows its highest incidence among the darker colored; it does not denote a distinctive family type.

The situation changes in the Caribbean. One way to observe the gross difference is to compare statistics for illegitimacy which show that the percentage illegitimate for all live births is 12.9 in Brazil and 71.6 in Jamaica (Goode, 1966, 487). Though other

Caribbean rates are somewhat lower than those in Jamaica, they are all higher than the level for Brazil (Goode, 1960, 22). Is this a sign of a distinctive family system traceable to slavery? The answer seems to be both yes and no, but with a dialectical twist. In one sense it is quite true that the incidence of consensual unions, easily broken, preceded by frequent pregnancies, resulting in "matrifocal" families, is characteristic of kinship among slave descendants, while these patterns are rare within the European population, more rare, for example, than is the case in Brazil. The institutional gap between superordinates and subordinates is therefore real enough to speak of social pluralism so far as the family is concerned. However, the relationship of this difference to the prior condition of slavery raises further questions. Goode maintains that "illegitimacy rates can be expected to be higher among the lower strata in all societies" and that "to the extent that a given society possesses a high proportion of lower strata families who are concerned little or not at all with their lineage, that society will exhibit a higher total rate of illegitimacy than it would have if the proportion were lower" (Goode, 1960, 27). Accepting Goode's conclusions, it would be necessary to restate the hypotheses above somewhat as follows: the widespread presence of unstable families with high illegitimacy rates is a result of whatever social forces that produce a disproportion of lower status groups unconcerned with the prestige attached to lineage. Slavery and its consequences may be numbered among such forces, but other antecedents may do just as well—for example, an increase in the industrial proletariat for African cities (Goode, 1963, 185).[20] It is also significant that, however widespread such informal unions may be in the Caribbean, "most people do marry eventually and the legal, monogamic union is clearly the ideal" (Goode, 1960, 26).

When comparing the family arrangements in Brazil, the Caribbean, and the United States, one also finds that the familiar stepwise progression is not validated. Taking illegitimacy rates as a rough index of the variations, figures show that the rates are much higher for all political units in the Caribbean (where Negroes constitute majority populations) than they are for Negroes in the United States. While recent figures for the latter are 23.6 per cent (*The Negro Family*, 1965), the rates for West Indian islands fluctuate from a low of 28 per cent in Puerto Rico to 72 per cent in Jamaica, and the majority of cases run over 40 per cent (Goode, 1960, 22). Although there are no comparable statistics in the islands on families with female heads (the proportion in the U.S. is just under 25 per cent) there is a high probability that such families have a higher incidence in the West Indies than on the North American continent. If this is the case, demographic realities would appear to overlie the social and cultural differences between the multinational sectors since the Negro population of most islands is clearly the predominant one, while in the United States it is only 10 per cent of the total. The conclusion seems to follow that structural pluralism as manifested by different family institutions is more clearly present as an aftermath of slavery in the West Indies than in either Brazil or the United States. However, since the data are still scattered and unsatisfactory, it is necessary to pay more attention to historical reconstruction of the social situations following each other in the different colonies in order to reach more solid conclusions.

Returning to a previous hypothesis: that the development of parallel institutions among former slave populations increases in range from Brazil to the West Indies and from there to the United States, when one examines institutions other than kinship, the most direct evidence on the subject is furnished by M. G. Smith's analysis of Jamaican society. He shows in considerable detail that of the three "sections" in Jamaica, the white, the brown, and the black, each has its own distinctive institutional system, whether in religion, education, the economy, legal activities, or the political order (M. G. Smith, 1965, Chap. 7). Although these differences are sometimes designated as diverse alternatives of one institutional system, and at other times as distinctive institutions for each "section,"[21] the main point is clear, namely the degree of enclosure for subordinates is rather high, whether they be brown or black. Of course the same holds for the superordinates, but for a different reason: their institutions are the regnant ones, actually those which set the framework for all others, the latter being dependent. For example, the main economic institutions like banking, insurance, and the export commerce on which the prosperity of the island depends, as well as large sugar or banana estates, are controlled by whites. In the political sphere, the second hypothesis above (participation in political processes will be either delayed or obstructed for the subordinates) is verified. After Emancipation, property qualifications for voting disenfranchised the former slaves; as their restlessness mounted in the 1930s, they were finally granted adult suffrage, but this is partly controlled and nullified in a number of ways. Since the possibilities for economic development and foreign investment are still controlled by the elite, this puts a brake on demands for radical legislation; and the buying of popular leaders is "not unknown in Jamaica" (Smith, *op. cit.*, 172).

Whether the institutional differences that exist in Jamaica are representative of the West Indies as a whole is uncertain and calls for more definitive evidence. Trinidad shows a parallel structure, however. Klass recognizes clear distinctions between white, "colored," and black among the West Indians there, speaking of these as the upper, middle, and lower class (Klass, 1960, 856), a term that Smith repudiates. However Klass does not discuss institutional participation. Braithwaite also refers to the same three classes but adds details on differential participation by color divisions in Trinidad that have marked resemblance to Smith's "sections" in Jamaica. One is led to wonder whether the two designations of class and section may not refer to the same phenomenon. In any case, Braithwaite finds in the lower or black population the familar family institution more maternally dominant with a rough proportion of one-third unions without stability, one-third common-law, and one-third legally married. As for economic participation the males in the lowest division are engaged in manual labor, the women in small-store employment, hard physical labor or domestic service. The blacks are also practically the sole members of revivalist and Seventh Day Adventist sects in the religious sphere. Attendance at school is greatly limited for the blacks; while illiteracy figures for the island are 25 per cent, the proportion is much higher among the lower stratum. In the colored or intermediate division, the family patterns are stable and conventional, religion tends to be Catholic or Anglican, education moves to higher levels, and economic occupations show a large number of professionals, civil servants, and the like. Politically there has been the same gradualism of participation that was noted for Jamaica, with numerous British commissions gravely considering the problem and each recommending slight changes in the direction of representation. Control of the police remains in white hands down to the time Braithwaite writes his account (1953). Finally, he makes it clear that forms of social participation are at least partly linked with ecological factors; this began in the colonial period when special housing in exclusive sections was provided for imported European technicians or administrators, and was continued later; in time there developed a kind of "natural" residential segregation which, though it did not have legal restrictions on the sale of properties, tended to "coincide neatly" with the divisions already mentioned (Braithwaite, 1953).[22]

On the basis of these studies, it is probably justifiable to conclude that the institutional separation of the races has been substantially greater in the West Indies than was the case in Brazil. Is there equal warrant for the judgment that this separation is still greater in the United States? Here I believe the answer is affirmative. While cultural pluralism diminished as the Negroes became "first deculturated, then acculturated to the dominant Western culture" (van den Berghe, 1967, 135), social pluralism persisted through the process of *de jure* and *de facto* segregation to a degree that exceeded its extent in the West Indies where the sheer numbers of the Negro community made this an impractical policy. Thus, in addition to the family patterns already mentioned, there have been, first in the South and later in the North, institutions in the Negro community that paralleled those of white society in nearly all respects: religious, educational, recreational, and even to a limited degree, economic institutions as well (Johnson, 1943; Drake and Cayton, 1945). If it be objected that many of these are variants on a wider institutional theme, the same may be said of Jamaican examples given by Smith to illustrate plural sections. Yet even in Jamaica it is not possible for a Negro to pass through primary, secondary, and collegiate education without any contact with whites, while this happens often in the United States. What Furnivall said of tropical plural societies some twenty years ago seems definitely applicable to the relations between Negroes and whites in the United States today, i.e., "As individuals they meet, but only in the market place, in buying and selling. There is a plural society, with different sections of the community living side by side, but separately, within the same political unit. Even in the economic sphere there is a division of labour along racial lines" (Furnivall, 1948, 304). In the United States, the sequence of slavery has been followed by a more pervasive social pluralism than exists elsewhere in the Western Hemisphere, and one productive of considerable conflict (van den Berghe, *op. cit.*, 134). Our hypothesis about delayed political participation is at least partly confirmed; though Negro franchise was forced upon the South by the victors in the Civil War, the pattern relapsed as the force was removed (however delayed the reaction), and the struggle for franchise is only being partially and painfully rewon today, often in the face of resistance and violence. In the North, a number of effective ways have been found to neutralize Negro political power, from playing off one faction against another to coopting leaders or conducting elections on a city-wide basis (Silberman, 1964, 204–07).

There remains the problem of economic participation during the changeover from agricultural to industrial labor. This problem is minimal in the Caribbean where industry has an insufficient base in natural resources or inadequate inflow of capital for extensive development (Puerto Rico excepted). However, in both the United States and Brazil, industrialization has proceeded rapidly. To what extent has this made the participation of the Negro in economic institutions uncertain and unstable? Van den Berghe's typology of race relations: paternalistic, and competitive, is a good initial guide. The paternalistic type of race relations is characterized by diffuse, intimate, non-competitive, complementary, asymmetrical, and particularistic interaction; the competitive type, on the other hand, displays segmental, impersonal, potentially symmetrical, competitive, and universalistic relationships (van den Berghe, *op. cit.*, 31–33). While he sees the shift from the first to the second type beginning at the close of the Civil War, and only coming to full realization with urbanization and entrance into industrial occupations that came much later, in Brazil he foreshortens the process by beginning long after emancipation and shows how in quite recent years the Negro's movement into industry has rapidly resulted in competitive relations (van den Berghe, *op. cit.*, 70–74, 87–92). To some degree this may oversimplify the process of change in the United States since the institution of farm tenancy made an admirable structural substitute for slavery, embodying the same paternalistic features—a system that maintained itself well into the 1930s and even after. Nevertheless,/van den Berghe's typology furnishes an admirable tool for exploring the place of the Negro in the economic sphere, and it may be supplemented by a somewhat different set of patterns that come into the picture when corporate activities of the unions are considered./The maintenance of particularistic features in such organizations are not only noticeable but striking, and nowhere more so than in exclusionist policies used by them either to keep Negroes out or to control their participation when they are admitted (Simpson and Yinger, 1965, 273–79). A comparative socio-historical account of the integration of slave descendants of the New World into changing economic institutions is still a wide-open field of exploration that so far has produced only slender results. Parenthetically, it is of interest to note that the relevance of van den Berghe's typology has received confirmation in Bastide's account of conditions in Brazil where the shift from paternalistic to competitive relations is clearly marked (Bastide, 1965, 21–22).

So far it has been shown that the socio-historical approach can be productive for studying the sequence of slavery. Limitations of space prohibit equal attention to other sequences, but a few brief remarks on its relevance for research on colonization and voluntary migration may be in order.

Colonization of Limited Settlement and Pluralism

Distinctions between the sequences of colonization having limited, extensive, and massive settlement have already been drawn (see chapter 3). Centering attention on the first of these (limited settlement and postcolonial derivations), it is striking to note that this sequence has appeared chiefly in multinational sector 5 (non-Communist Asia and Southeast Asia) and sector 8 (Sub-Saharan Africa).[23] The postindependence nation-states in these areas have four structural factors that separate them rather sharply from countries in other sectors: (1) a previous history of colonial domination by some European power; (2) a very recent establishment of a new, indigenous, political regime; (3) the status of "developing nations"; (4) a higher degree of social and cultural pluralism than is found in other areas of the world.[24] Leaving aside the first two variables for the moment, and recalling Table 1, pp. 178–81, it will be noted that sectors 5 and 8 belong in the "developing" category on the basis of the statistics furnished there. For countries in these sectors, the GNP per capita is low, the per cent of the labor force in agriculture is high, and on Marsh's index of differentiation, they register low. For non-Communist Asia and Southeast Asia, even with the inclusion of Japan which inflates the result, the mean GNP per capita is only 127, while for Sub-Saharan Africa, again coupled with the deviant high figures for South Africa, we find a mean GNP per capita even lower—106. Concerning the percentage of the labor force in agriculture (where the usual criterion is, *ceteris paribus*, the higher the per cent, the less developed the economy) both sectors are well above the mid-point, non-Communist Asia and Southeast Asia showing a mean per cent of 55, while Sub-Saharan Africa goes still higher to 66. Finally, the Marsh index of differentiation which reaches its apex in sector 1 with a mean figure of 67.6, sinks to a low number of 20.5 for non-Communist Asia and Southeast Asia and a comparable 20.8 for Sub-Saharan Africa.

As for the pluralist dimension, there is now some direct evidence to support the statement that Afro-Asian societies have maximal social and cultural pluralism when compared with other societies. A detailed analysis of 114 nation-states of the world on five available pluralistic indicators[25] combined to form an index, has made it possible to rate various countries on a scoring continuum from 0 to 8. The lower the score, the more homogeneous the population, while the higher the score, the greater the heterogeneity or pluralism (Haug, 1967).[26] Though only one nation rated as high as 8, seventeen were at the zero extreme, nine rated 1, eighteen rated 2, ten rated 3, twelve rated 4, fifteen rated 5, twenty-three rated 6, and nine rated 7. I have taken these ratings for individual nations and classified the countries in the appropriate multinational sectors, summarizing the scores for each sector and dividing by the number of countries to obtain the mean for that multinational sector. The results are as follows:

TABLE 3.   COMPARATIVE PLURALIST SCORES FOR
8 MULTINATIONAL SECTORS

Sector	New Pluralism Score
1. Western European Nations and the Derivative Neo-European Complex	2.0
2. Eastern Europe: The Communist States	2.7
3. Iberian Societies of the Eastern and Western Hemispheres	2.3
4. Caribbean Societies	2.6
5. Non-Communist Asia and Southeast Asia	4.6
6. Communist Asia	2.5
7. The Middle East and North Africa	3.3
8. Sub-Saharan Africa	6.1

From Table 3, not only is it evident that the Afro-Asian regions have the greatest heterogeneity of population, but that the extent of this pluralism is considerably greater in Africa than in the Asian countries.[27] Much if not most of this diversity is indigenous and precolonial. The remainder is brought into being by colonial fiat through the importation of contract laborers and the tolerance or encouragement of immigration, changing the composition of the population and increasing its diversity (Hunter, 1966, 60). This distinction between indigenous and alien groups plays a fateful part in the postindependence relationships.

Even though the plurality of groups predated the colonial period, the organization of such ethnolinguistic groups into territorially defined administrative units unrelated to local realities *was* the work of colonists.[28] The sum total of these units in an area convenient for unified administration was a colony, and this colony was the region that became the ground for a "nation" after independence. Although I have accepted the designation of such nations as "societies," they are actually only societies in the process of formation if societies are defined in their modern manifestations indicated in Chapter 5. And this process apparently requires the antecedent construction of a viable nation-state. As Shils puts it, "The emergence of a social order, the formation of the state, the transformation of tradition, the legitimation of new authority—these are only a few of the most fundamental problems of social science that can be studied in the experience of new states" (Shils, 1963, 9).

The centrality and pervasiveness of politics is a fact of life in the emerging nations where the very basis of unified authority is still problematical and in process of change. Therefore the integration of minorities into new states is part and parcel of the most momentous process of all—establishing the new legitimacy.[29] From a socio-historical standpoint, the main problem to be studied is how the tight, extreme form of social pluralism of the colonial regime is changed into the looser and less rigid pattern that characterizes the postindependence society. This shift from external to internal authority in the system has differential effects on the status and life chances of all, or certainly nearly all, plural groupings within the society. While many related issues call for exploration, the following will serve as examples:

*Needed Socio-Historical Research
on Ethnic Integration in New Nations*

1. Comparative studies of the way that colonial regimes augment pluralism in sector 5 (non-Communist Asia and Southeast Asia) as compared with sector 8 (Sub-Saharan Africa) by contract labor and the admission of immigrants. Not only have the demographic consequences been more massive in the former sector than in the latter (Malaysia and Indonesia as compared with East Africa) but this has been accompanied by differentials in occupational clustering and institutional segmentation of great moment to the integration of plural groups in postindependence societies.
2. Comparative studies of disproportionate utilization of specially selected minorities in the bureaucracy of colonial administrations (as for example India and Ceylon) with the consequences for group status after independence.
3. Comparative studies of the effects of indirect rule on corporate groups who consequentially retained autonomy and traditional (Nigeria, Uganda) or nontraditional (Burma) loyalties in contradiction to the modernizing and/or nationalistic imperatives of ruling groups in the postindependence period.
4. Comparative studies on the ethnic provenience of nationalist elite during the colonial period and the relationship of this to dominant group position after independence. This includes investigation of differential exposure of plural groups to, and

their acceptance of Western education (mission or government schools) as a new source of prestige and power, or the withholding of such education (Congo).

5. Comparative studies of slow vs. rapid relinquishment of colonial domination and their effects on social pluralism. Since examples of both types are found in each sector, this approaches the condition of a controlled experiment (rapid in French Africa and the Congo, slow in Tanzania, Nigeria and Uganda; rapid in Indonesia and Burma, slow in India and Malaysia). The effects on ethnic conflicts after independence are of considerable significance.

6. Comparative studies of linguistic policy (the problem of a common language) as determined by the colonial power setting one pattern, and the consequences of this pattern on the policies of postindependent states. In this respect, sector differences between Africa and Asia are marked, since the latter shows a wider variety of written languages. (Note the differences in literacy between sectors 5 and 8 in Table 1, pp. 178–81.) The press for modernization and the use of a universal language is probably greater in Africa than in Asia where much ambivalence ensues.[30] Militancy for regional languages probably reaches its apogee in India where it has increased its potential for sectional pluralism (Harrison, 1960).

7. Related to #6 above would be comparative studies on the effects of increased communication and horizontal mobility during the colonial period on contacts between ethnic groups, and the consequences of these contacts on intergroup relations after independence. This is an exceptionally difficult problem since dialectical or contradictory results appear; in some cases increased contact makes for greater tolerance and absorption into a nationalist movement, while in others new conflicts have arisen in response to the contact. Special care is needed to specify conditions in each case—the extent of economic competition, political rivalry, linguistic misunderstandings, superordinate goals, and the like.

There are, of course, many other illustrations, but these may be sufficient to indicate the range of questions to be explored. A number of astute suggestions and hypotheses for such an investigation are well summarized in Von der Mehden (1964). Over and beyond these should be continuous attention to the differences between pluralism of the colonial areas and that of the succession states that follow. For this, socio-historical research is a prime requisite, providing a foundation for other investigations discussed in the following chapter. Similar historical explorations are equally needed for examining other sequences as well. For example, the sequence of extensive settlement and its hierocratic consequences have been touched on in chapter 4. A truly comparative account of this would markedly benefit by a socio-historical research matching South Africa, Southern Rhodesia and Algeria, with at least secondary attention to Kenya. As for the sequence of massive settlement resulting in the formation of new states, an entirely different set of questions demand reliable historical answers. The best comparative study of this problem so far seems to have been carried out by Hartz and his colleagues (1964), providing an indispensable foundation for all future work. It is a matter of regret that limitations of space prevent further discussion of these issues here.

Needed Socio-Historical Research on Comparative Types of Voluntary Migration

However because of its major impact on several multinational sectors, the sequence of voluntary migration must be given at least limited attention. First a word about vocabulary. As employed here, the concept of "migration" loses the broad general denotation that it carries for Lieberson (1961) where it refers to any movement of population groups across boundaries. As the term is employed here, migration and colonization both involve such movement, but may be distinguished by a single criterion, i.e., which party to the transaction exerts control in the process? If the control is exercised by the host society, I shall speak of migration; if the control is exercised by the newcomers, it is both simpler and more logical to employ the term "colonization."[31] And, as already shown in chapter 4, voluntary migration is that subtype involving the least coercive control. A second *caveat*: the interest of the present volume is not primarily centered on demographic considerations, the usual discussions of "push" and "pull" in migration, the revised typology of migration movements advanced by Petersen (1958), or the many factors in both the sending and the receiving society making for selective or differential migration;[32] these are certainly adjunct factors overlapping our central problem that have to be taken into account. However the focus of the present inquiry is rather on the formation and perpetuation of ethnic minorities within a receiving society after the migration has taken place. It is the postmigration *effects* which are up for scrutiny.[33]

Here in outline are a number of socio-historical investigations that would greatly enlarge our knowledge of societal pluralities that occur as an aftermath of voluntary migration.

1. A comparative study of what Becker (1940) has called the "marginal trading peoples" in the prenationalist period. While he includes Jewish, Armenian, Parsi, Greek, and Scottish groups, the addition of the Chinese in their overseas migrations would contribute greatly to the relevance of such a research. Instead of focussing on the psycho-social traits of such peoples, as Becker suggests, studies of this kind would gain more depth by centering on the degree of enclosure (institutional separation) in host societies and their effects on integration or conflict in the receiving societies. There appear to be cases here that contradict Lieberson's generalization about lesser conflict in cases of "migrant subordination" as, for example, the instances where Chinese were massacred in the Philippines during the seventeenth century (Hunter, *op. cit.*, 36). This early date makes it impossible to attribute this violence to the colonial situation "where the indigenous populations were subordinate" (Lieberson, *op. cit.*, 907). Parallels with similar massacres or expelling of Jewish populations in Europe might be most instructive.

2. As an offshoot of the above, the differential effects of colonial rule when compounded with permission of voluntary migration could be given comparative assessment by studying Chinese immigrant communities in colonized areas like Malaya, the Dutch East Indies, and the Philippines with a comparable society like Thailand where colonial rule was lacking. This

comparison could well be extended into the postindependence period when authority shifts took place. There seems to be evidence of lesser conflict and greater integration of such immigrant communities in Thailand than elsewhere (Skinner, 1957, 1958).

3. A more extensive socio-historical comparison of immigrant communities in societies of both Asia and Africa in the transition from colonial to independent status. To illustrate: this would include such groups as Indians and Chinese in Burma, Malaya, or Indonesia; or Indians, Arabs, Syrians, and Lebanese in East and West Africa. Such a study would afford several bases of comparison: the differences between multinational sectors, the formation of "horizontal racism," as well as the more complicating racial features associated with the implantation of Middle Eastern groups in African areas.

4. Comparative studies of ethnic settlement in the new countries of sector 1—the United States, Canada, Australia, and New Zealand, with those in sector 3—Brazil, Uruguay, Argentina, and Chile, countries where colonization of massive settlement sucked after it a process of voluminous immigration.[34] To be fully productive, such studies could center on the degrees of pluralistic enclosure experienced by immigrant groups in different sectors, with the aim of explaining these differences.

5. As a special problem related to #4 above, comparative studies of immigrant communities in reciprocal interaction with the larger majorities in each society, with special reference to the rate of migrant replenishment, the waves of "nativist" sentiment, and the cycles of economic rise and decline would afford a chance to establish new generalizations.

6. Concomitant studies in differential rates of integration, the "vanishing" of ethnic minorities as groups, or the preservation of group identities in relation to societal changes, would help to pin-point the crucial variables involved. The use of Gordon's types of assimilation to assess the problem (1964)—or, as we prefer to say, incorporation—would make such a historical comparison more manageable in tracing the process over time.

7. Comparative studies of reciprocal ideological changes in sectors

1 and 3, using Figure 6 as the point of departure. Two possible alternatives using this approach would be:

    a. Where several ethnic groups were present, to determine, if possible, which groups approached the A condition from the outset, as compared with those with a D position, accounting for the differences and tracing the consequences for future integration.

    b. Where several ethnic groups were present and began their sojourn with condition D, to trace the changes toward A or C and the factors associated with the changes over time.[35] Fluctuations in these changes need to be examined as they correlate with massive societal changes like depressions, wars, or other emergencies when there are sometimes shifts in the direction of C (centrifugal trends may well move toward ostracism or expelling of immigrants).

The effects of these ideological changes, including the rise and fall of "ization" movements (Americanization, Brazilianization) on socal pluralism and its erosion or crystallization are of greatest significance.

8. Comparative studies of the differential rate with which ethnic groups in different sectors are incorporated into new societies in relation to the two variables of occupational clustering on the one hand, and occupational opportunities on the other, are of crucial importance. Thus the effects on social pluralism will be vastly different where peasants migrate to dispersed farming areas, cash crop areas, or to manual labor in urban areas; some ethnic groups may have diversified occupational groups moving into mixed areas, others that are disproportionately in trade into urban areas and the like. Since integration is often closely allied with upward mobility, these effects must be assessed over time. This would therefore need to be matched with equal attention to the changing occupational structure of the receiving society.[36]

These are but a few of the socio-historical researches needed for a more solid base in the field of ethnic relations. However, advance cannot wait upon these developments, important though they are. The onward course of research must move on many fronts at once. In the chapter to follow, closer perspectives that give considerably more detailed knowledge in the contemporary scene are examined.

· NOTES ·

1. Kenneth Bock reenforces this position by his following comment about historians: "If they see no generalities or processes in history, we must remember that they are not looking for them. Historians, then, can no more be regarded as qualified to pass judgment on the possibility of finding regularities in historical data than they can be blamed for not seeking regularities. Indeed, it might be said that scholars whose avowed purpose is to concentrate on the individual in history would be the least prepared to estimate the chances for making generalizations" (Bock, 1956, 110).

2. This is not necessarily the case for premodern societies. One of many examples is that of the Tutsi and Hutu peoples in Rwanda and Burundi (van den Berghe, 1967, 12).

3. Though trends in the same direction have occurred in both Belgium and Canada without fully capturing the ideology of dominant groups in either case.

4. Apart from the problem of answering the question, "how much time is enough?" there is a far more crucial issue. For any query about the time necessary for assimilation has the hidden assumption that normal change is slow, gradual, and continuous. Thus, if alternative A is to be explained, all we have to do on this assumption is to posit sufficient time and continuity will do the rest. This is only, however, if we regard continuity as nonproblematical, an assumption that may be quite unwarranted (Moore, 1966, 486). Furthermore, plausible evidence has been furnished to show that the very *idea* of gradual, continuous change rests back on an "unconscious retention of a framework" as old as Comte and Spencer in which there is a "conceptual identification of social process with organic growth process" (Bock, *op. cit.*, 99, 114). No doubt there is continuity between historical events in the sense that tracings of earlier ones can be found in the later, but this does not justify positing *even* succession or *gradualness* without proof.

5. Karl Deutsch speaks of this increased participation in more pervasive roles as "mobilization" and devotes a great deal of space to its analysis (Deutsch, 1965. Chap. 6). As already noted above, the corresponding term in my own analysis is "activation."

6. As Lenski declares, one way of doing this is "the technique of transforming categorical concepts into variable concepts," while another "involves breaking down compound concepts into their constituent elements" (Lenski, 1966, 20). Another mode which we find more useful here is to specify conditions as we shall try to do below.

7. While the contrast is greater for Britain and Holland than it is for France, some differences still remain on a sector basis. Of course the *variation* in these differences should also be explained by such a study, one sometimes traced to a common Catholic ethos, though the connection with racial tolerance is likely to be argued on doctrinal grounds which still leaves a number of wider social questions unanswered.

8. The reference is obviously non-Iberian or Western Europe here.

9. These reflections are indebted to Hartz's researches on colonial "fragments" that will receive attention below.

10. For specific details of the development, cf. Jordan, 1968.

11. Comparative magnitude of miscegenation is not well ascertained, the data being too uncertain. A conservative estimate in the United States is that 70 per cent of American Negroes are partly white or Indian (Herskovits, 1930, 279).

12. Although Negroes tended to outnumber the whites in plantation areas, apparently there were some southern regions where the reverse was true. Calhoun quotes the following passage from an unknown observer who asserted that "In slave states where the colored people are few and the whites numerous, very few slave children claim persons of color for their fathers" (Calhoun, *op. cit.*, II, 295).

13. H. Hoetink's recent volume corroborates a number of these conclusions independently. He stresses the importance of a "somatic norm image" as the basis of racism and attributes the extreme racial distance between groups in the southern United States to the insistence of poor whites on a sharp status separation; such poor whites, he notes, were lacking elsewhere in the Western Hemisphere as an accompaniment of slavery; conversely, he points out that in Latin American societies, the "somatic norm image" that Europeans held of themselves was darker than the one whites had of themselves in the southern United States; as a result, Latins could admit mulattoes as color equals (H. Hoetink, 1967, 120–21, 162–63, 167). This valuable book arrived too late to incorporate a number of its important insights here.

14. The differentials in the process of emancipation furnish a rich and relatively unexplored field for comparative sociohistorical research. There are hints in the literature that emancipation was attended by serious conflict only when slavery was flourishing economically, and not after it showed serious internal weaknesses (Davis, *op. cit.*, 226). There is also the apparent paradox that where racism was weakest, emancipation was delayed the longest, as in Brazil where it did not occur until 1888 (Davis, *op. cit.*, 268).

15. Status gradations took other forms beside color scales. In Cuba, especially, there was a wide span in the occupational hierarchy, and in rural-urban variations quite unmatched elsewhere (Klein, 1967, 144–64).

16. Racism, of course, has many other antecedents besides slavery, as already indicated in Chapter 3.

17. This does not prevent such an ideal of separatism from appearing later, after emancipation, literacy, and increased communication have done

their work, as the Garvey movement and the Black Muslims have shown in the United States, however minor their effects may be. It is significant that such movements have had little influence in Brazil where cultural survivals from the past have been more prominent than is the case in the United States. Rather than attributing these residual tracings to the greater clustering of tribal units in the Middle Passage, Davis suggests that the crucial factor could well be the continual replacement of the slave population which had such high mortality in these regions. "By 1850 most slaves in the United States were removed by many generations from their African origins; this was certainly not the case in Brazil" (Davis, *op. cit.*, 243n).

18. Such an aggregate on the way to becoming more self-defined falls under Bierstedt's category of *societal group*, distinguished from a mere statistical group as follows: societal groups "have like interests but not common interests. They do not, however, in the absence of a social stimulus, enter into social relations with each other" (Robert Bierstedt, 1948, 704). Thus societal groups display forms of self-identification that vary in degree depending on the nature of the external stimuli.

19. The occasional appearance of special cults like the *condomble* and the *macumba* must be acknowledged; these, however, are both minor and local without deep roots in the Negro community which often regards them with disdain (Bastide, *op. cit.*, 23). They may well have resulted from the constant replenishment of the slave population which has been mentioned above.

20. While accepting this conclusion provisionally, I would prefer to stress its tentative character and suggest that sociohistorical studies or those based on aggregate data might well contradict it in the future.

21. A complete separation of institutional orders for the plural sections is not claimed by Smith in his account. To mention only one instance: while there is a single educational system with primary, secondary, and university levels, he asserts that the blacks ordinarily go no farther than the primary grades, the browns tend to move into secondary levels without continuing to the university level, while the whites rather expect to complete all three. This fits each level for appropriate slots in the occupational system. What Smith fails to tell is whether children of all three sections attend the same primary schools, or whether pupils from the upper two sections share the same secondary schools. Some account of residential and ecological patterns would therefore help to complete the picture.

22. A related study by Despres in Guyana shows an even more extreme institutional separation of the African element in that society, though this is, to a considerable degree, a response to a contrasting section of East Indian laborers who attain equal or greater numerical size, and thus are defined as a social threat (Despres, 1967).

23. Sector 7 (the Middle East and North Africa) is something of a marginal case since it has undergone colonialism of both limited and extensive types, as well as a structural substitute for colonialism known as the mandate.

24. A few exceptions to these characterizations must at least be mentioned. Factors (1) and (2) do not apply to Liberia, Ethiopia, Thailand, or Japan; furthermore, Japan is also exempt from factors (3) and (4) so it will not be included in the discussion which follows. The others will come into account as marginal cases that have similar problems of social pluralism uncomplicated by previous colonial policies. South Africa, another unrepresentative case, will be omitted since it follows a different sequence, i.e., colonization of extensive settlement.

25. The five indicators from Banks and Textor (1963) are language, race, religion, sectionalism, and interest articulation by nonassociational groups.

26. I am indebted to Marie Haug for a prepublication copy of this article.

27. To the question, "are these modern nations?" as defined above, the answer must be affirmative in terms of the criteria given in chapter 5. The commitment and aims of the countries involved are the crucial realities that separate them from traditional societies and not some precise cut-off point on a series of indicators.

28. The full force of this transformation is nowhere better presented than by Bohannan in the following passage: "Africa was, before colonial days, full of people on the move. Because of the ways Africans provided for their own subsistence, and because of social, political, and even religious pressures, Africans moved and kept moving. The creation of colonial administration concomitantly created a need to know where everybody was. Moreover, the European background of the administrators told them that people should own their own land, have rights in it against others and against the world, should be citizens of a stable and indeed of a fixed local community. And that meant boundaries . . . One of the most important of all colonial activities was the splitting up of Africa, not just among nations, but among the Africans themselves, by means of legally enforceable boundaries. The whole basis of society was changed from what it had been—groups of people, held together by kingship, kinship, or religion, that occupied and exploited a more or less clearly defined area. It became vast numbers of areas, each occupied by people with citizenship rights in it. The difference may appear small, but the resultant misunderstanding was of staggering proportions" (Bohannan, 1964, 18–19).

29. In terms of Figure 6, we have situation D again, where now the superordinates insist on acceptance of the nationalist ideology and loyalty to a civic whole superseding local, tribal, linguistic, or religious commitments. The subordinates, on the other hand, often reject this and prefer autonomy or secession. The Western observer, whether journalist or social scientist, identifying the views of the rulers with "modernization" and the withdrawal from it as "tradition," often adopts a value bias for the former in spite of himself. This is often masked by the more apparently objective warrant for "national unity" that seems required for societal viability—an imperative overriding all other considerations. Consequently, instead of centering on problems of "discrimination" and "prejudice" which is the stance adopted in the West

where the value bias favors the subordinates, the observer in Afro-Asia tends to put the emphasis on problems of "disunity" or "divisiveness" which subtly transfers the value bias to the superordinates. This can proceed even farther where it conjures up *Realpolitik* justifications for an authority whose legitimacy is assumed as part of the status quo. Such a dialectic of values is constantly operative and its consequences must be kept under tight scrutiny.

30. For a significant account of the major issues involved, cf. Le Page (1964).

31. This will require elimination of a concept like "migrant superordination." As presented here, it must also be remembered that what Lieberson refers to as "migrant superordination" becomes, in our terminology, the first stages of a process that eventually becomes extensive or massive settlement of the colonization sequence. Furthermore, this change in terminology makes the use of such a phrase as "migrant subordinate" quite redundant.

32. For example, T. Lynn Smith explains the much lesser volume of immigration to Brazil in comparison with the greater amount to the United States as due to the different land patterns in Brazil where the system of landed estates prevented the acquisition of small farms to the extent that this was possible in North America where squatters' settlements were finally encouraged and legitimized by the Homestead Act (T. L. Smith, 1963, 119–20).

33. This is why the present mode of classifying subtypes of migration (slave transfers, slave labor transfers, contract labor transfer, reception of displaced persons, and admission of voluntary immigrants) differs from that of Petersen (*op. cit.*) who stresses the exercise of influence over migrants at the point of *departure*, while our interest centers on the point of *entry*.

34. This essentially new form of immigration between countries with developed institutions forms a special case. Its distinctive character has been neatly characterized as follows: "Immigration, considered as Fairchild thought of it a generation ago as a voluntary movement between well-developed countries, is an essentially modern concept, and is the heir to two of the most remarkable phenomena in history—the opening up of a new world to European man through the voyages and discoveries of Portuguese, Spanish and English adventurers, and an upsurge of population which was unique both in its rate of growth and in its extent. And accompanying these developments was the growth of independent nation-states" (Borrie, 1959, 34).

35. There seems to be some evidence that government agencies, as a result of extensive experience with immigrants, are increasingly adopting a normative ("cultural") pluralistic stance in the handling of practical problems (Borrie, *op. cit.*, 91, 93, 95). There is less proof that this attitude becomes widespread in the public majority. Unless racial differences intervene, I therefore hypothesize that the superordinates' preference for assimilation (centripetal tendency) is relatively constant.

Thus most changes would be expected to occur as intermediates between A and D, with B as the rare exception.

36. Recent changes seem to show that with increasing demand for professional, scientific and technical personnel, immigration is no longer a
matter of "ethnic groups" but is coming to be an issue of manpower
requirements that supersede nationality or country of origin. Assimilation at these levels is rapid and extreme mobility makes for international
interchangeability. Likewise, movement now appears to be from developing to "developed" nations which have the greatest demand for such
personnel (Mills, 1966, 33–42; Thomas, 63–72).

· REFERENCES ·

Banks, Arthur S., and Robert B. Textor, *A Cross-Polity Survey*. Cambridge,
Mass.: The M.I.T. Press, 1963.

Bastide, Roger B., "The Development of Race Relations in Brazil," in Guy
Hunter (ed.), *Industrialization and Race Relations*. London and New
York: Oxford University Press, 1965.

Becker, Howard, "Constructive Typology in the Social Sciences," in Harry
Elmer Barnes, Howard Becker, and Frances B. Becker (eds.), *Contemporary Social Theory*. New York: Appleton-Century, 1940.

———, "Historical Sociology," in Harry Elmer Barnes, Howard Becker
and Frances B. Becker (eds.), *Contemporary Social Theory*. New York:
Appleton-Century, 1940.

Bierstedt, Robert, "The Sociology of Majorities," *American Sociological
Review*, 13 (December 1948), 700–10.

Bock, Kenneth E., *The Acceptance of Histories, Toward a Perspective for
Social Science*, University of California Publications in Sociology and
Social Institutions, Vol. 3, No. 1. Berkeley and Los Angeles: University
of California Press, 1956.

Boehm, Max H., "Irredentism," in *Encyclopedia of the Social Sciences*,
VIII. New York: Macmillan, 1937.

Bohannan, Paul, *Africa and Africans*. New York: Natural History Press,
1964.

Braithwaite, Lloyd, "Social Stratification in Trinidad," *Social and Economic
Studies*, 2, Nos. 2 and 3 (October 1963), 15–175.

Burks, Richard V., *The Dynamics of Communism in Eastern Europe*.
Princeton: Princeton University Press, 1961.

Calhoun, Arthur W., *A Social History of the American Family From
Colonial Times to the Present*. 3 vols. Cleveland: Clark, 1917.

Davis, David Brion, *The Problem of Slavery in Western Culture*. Ithaca,
N. Y.: Cornell University Press, 1966.

Despres, Leo, *Cultural Pluralism and Nationalist Politics in British Guiana*.
Chicago, Rand McNally, 1967.

Deutsch, Karl W., *Nationalism and Social Communication*. Rev. ed. Cambridge, Mass.: M.I.T. Press, 1965.

Drake, St. Clair, and H. R. Cayton, *Black Metropolis*. New York: Harcourt,
Brace & World, 1945.

Freyre, Gilberto, *The Masters and the Slaves: A Study in the Development of Brazilian Civilization.* Samuel Putnam (trans.). New York: Knopf, 1946.

Furnivall, J. S., *Colonial Policy and Practice.* Cambridge, Eng.: Cambridge University Press, 1948.

Goode, William J., "Illegitimacy in the Caribbean Social Structure," *American Sociological Review,* 25 (February 1960), 21–30.

———, *World Revolution and Family Patterns.* New York: Free Press, 1963.

———, "Family Disorganization," in Robert K. Merton and Robert A. Nisbet (eds.), *Contemporary Social Problems.* 2nd ed. New York: Harcourt, Brace & World, 1966.

Gordon, Milton M., *Assimilation in American Life.* New York: Oxford University Press, 1964.

Harrison, Selig, *India: The Most Dangerous Decade.* Princeton: Princeton University Press, 1960.

Hartz, *The Founding of New Societies.* New York: Harcourt, Brace & World, 1964.

Herskovits, M. J., *The Anthropometry of the American Negro.* New York: Columbia University Press, 1930.

———, *Life in a Haitian Valley.* New York: Knopf, 1937.

———, *The Myth of the Negro Past.* New York: Harper & Bros., 1941.

———, and F. S. Herskovits, *Rebel Destiny: Among the Bush Negroes of Dutch Guiana.* New York: McGraw-Hill, 1934.

———, *Trinidad Village.* New York: Knopf, 1947.

Hoetink, H., *The Two Variants in Caribbean Race Relations.* New York: Oxford University Press, 1966.

Hunter, Guy, *South-East Asia, Race, Culture and Nation.* New York and London: Oxford University Press, 1966.

Johnson, Charles S., *Patterns of Negro Segregation.* New York: Harper & Row, 1943.

Jordan, Winthrop D., *White Over Black: American Attitudes Toward the Negro 1550–1812.* Chapel Hill, N. C.: University of North Carolina Press, 1968.

Klass, Morton, "East and West Indian: Cultural Complexity in Trinidad," *Annals of the New York Academy of Sciences,* 83, Art. 5 (January 20, 1960), 855–61.

Klein, Herbert S., *Slavery in the Americas: A Comparative Study of Virginia and Cuba.* Chicago: University of Chicago Press, 1967.

Kolarz, Walter, *Russia and Her Colonies.* New York: Praeger, 1952.

Le Page, R. B., *The National Language Question.* London: Oxford University Press, 1964.

Lenski, Gerhard E., *Power and Privilege, A Theory of Social Stratification.* New York: McGraw-Hill, 1966.

Lieberson, Stanley, "A Societal Theory of Race and Ethnic Relations," *American Sociological Review,* 26 (December 1961), 902–10.

Mills, Thomas J., "Scientific Personnel and the Professions," *The Annals of the American Academy of Political and Social Science,* 367 (September 1966), 33–42.

Moore, Barrington, Jr., *Social Origins of Dictatorship and Democracy, Lord and Peasant in the Making of the Modern World.* Boston: Beacon, 1966.

Morse, Richard M., "The Heritage of Latin America," in Louis Hartz, *The Founding of New Societies.* New York: Harcourt, Brace & World, 1964.

The Negro Family, The Case for National Action. Washington, D.C.: Office of Policy Planning and Research, United States Department of Labor, March 1965.

Peterson, William, "A General Typology of Migration," *American Sociological Review,* 23 (June 1958), 256–66.

Shils, Edward, "On the Comparative Study of the New States," in Clifford Geertz (ed.), *Old Societies and New States.* New York: Free Press, 1963.

Silberman, Charles E., *Crisis in Black and White.* New York: Random House, 1964.

Simmel, Georg, *The Sociology of Georg Simmel,* Kurt H. Wolff (trans.). Glencoe, Illinois: Free Press, 1950.

Simpson, G. E., and J. M. Yinger, *Racial and Cultural Minorities.* 3rd ed. New York: Harper & Row, 1965.

Skinner, G. W., "Chinese Assimilation and Thai Politics," *Journal of Asian Studies,* 16 (February 1957), 237–50.

——, *Leadership and Power in the Chinese Community of Thailand.* Ithaca: Cornell University Press, 1958.

Smith, M. G., "Social and Cultural Pluralism," *Annals of the New York Academy of Sciences,* 83, Art. 5 (January 20, 1960), 763–85.

——, *The Plural Society in the British West Indies.* Berkeley and Los Angeles: University of California Press, 1965.

Smith, T. Lynn, *Brazil, People and Institutions.* Rev. ed. Baton Rouge: Louisiana State University Press, 1963.

Tannenbaum, Frank, *Slave and Citizen: The Negro in the Americas.* New York: Knopf, 1947.

Thomas, Brinley, "From the Other Side: A European View," *The Annals of the American Academy of Political and Social Science,* 367 (September 1966), 63–72.

van den Berghe, Pierre L., *Race and Racism, A Comparative Perspective.* New York: Wiley, 1967.

Von der Mehden, Fred R., *Politics of the Developing Nations.* Englewood Cliffs, N. J.: Prentice-Hall, 1964.

Zenkovsky, Serge A., *Pan-Turkism and Islam in Russia.* Cambridge, Mass.: Harvard University Press, 1960.

7

❦

Closer Perspectives:
A Cross-sectional View

Relationships between subordinate ethnic groups and dominant groups, whether the latter be majorities, elites, or paramount among pluralities,[1] while certainly the focus of proposed cross-cultural research, are also, as already noted, a function of societal change on the one hand, and societal structure on the other. In turning from the sweeping, comprehensive prospects of the diachronic approach to the more determinate and distinct outlines of synchronic investigation, the investigator is faced with the apparent paradox that this closer perspective clarifies many elements that may be blurred historically, while obscuring others that are more distinct in process.[2] The inquirer unavoidably confronts the dilemma of all search for truth: it is impossible to know everything from a single perspective. All social scientists are forced, both by the yawning chasm of their ignorance and by the limited range of their concepts, to adopt a course that *alternates between perspectives*. This may be humiliating to those who wager everything on a monocratic solution, though they often escape this embarrassment by strenuous efforts to nullify all evidence from other perspectives. The present procedure will be more modest, attempting only to supplement one viewpoint with the other while seizing any opportunity to bring them into *rapprochement*. Chapter 6 has already made it clear that the socio-historical method can fortify and strengthen its generalizing power by constant attention to structural forms; in the task of cross sectional analysis, it is equally clear that the investigator must remain alert to the dynamic derivations of the elements under scrutiny. So much for prelude.

Elemental Features of Method

In approaching a more narrowly defined set of data in cross sectional analysis, the social scientist encounters problems of method on which the present chapter must touch lightly, though their importance warrants far more space. First of all it is necessary to make explicit an assumption that has remained implicit up to this point, namely, that comparative ethnic relations, as an area of research, is still in its infancy.[3] Furthermore there appear to be modes of investigation that are more relevant to early stages of the scientific quest than to later ones. Kaplan refers to this subject in two ways. In the first place he accepts Hanson's thesis of the two logics, the logic of discovery and the logic of proof, the former "as a study of the reasons for entertaining a hypothesis, in contrast with the logic of proof, which deals with the reasons for accepting a hypothesis" (Kaplan, 1964, 17). While the distinction is not an absolute one since the scientist is not likely to advance a hypothesis in utter disregard of its verifiability, it is nevertheless a real one which makes the logic of discovery a series of probes based on limited inductions that point the way to more rewarding explorations. These are the signs of a nascent stage of scientific development. Kaplan's second observation is equally compelling; "there are two accounts of the reasons which provide understanding, and thereby explanation. I call them the *pattern model* of explanation and the *deductive model*. Very roughly, we know the reason for something either when we can fit it into a known pattern, or else when we can deduce it from other known truths . . . The pattern model may more easily fit explanations in early stages of inquiry, and the deductive model explanations in later stages." Here again the distinction is dialectical rather than dichotomous, for, "From the nature of the whole pattern and some of its parts we can deduce the others; conversely, a deductive relationship might itself be viewed as constitutive of a cognitive pattern" (*Ibid.*, 332).

The reader must surely have observed by this time that the preference in this volume has been for the pattern model. In the formative stage of exploration in which students of ethnic and race relations fortunately or unfortunately find themselves, they are faced with the need for the kind of initial distinctions Weber was once compelled to make in *his* voyage of discovery. As Mc-Kinney has pointed out, during the early period of investigation it is highly useful to set up typologies of "problem relevance" that serve as a bridge between more general theory and empirical observation (McKinney, 1966, 83, 96). The introduction of our ideological paradigm (Figure 6), the multinational sectors, the ec-pol and pol-ec societies, and the ethnic sequences have hopefully made it possible to get a proper amount of firmness in the first grasp of cross-cultural research. These may very well be the scaffolding which can be kicked away when the main outlines of the edifice appear; perhaps the finished product will be a thoroughly deductive system of propositions related to each other by logical interconnection, with all empirical elements fully verified. It would be risky to declare that this edifice is unattainable, for this could very well cut the nerve of the scientific quest which is constantly moving in the direction of deductive, mathematical configurations. My conviction is, however, that such a final consummation will take longer in comparative sociology than in more restricted areas of research, and that much of the initial clarity of deductive systems has been a function of their (often unsuspected) limited range. Cross-cultural verification of such models is notoriously missing except to the most minor degree, partly, of course, because of the enormous expense in time, money, and energy needed to complete the job, and partly (in more cynical vein) because the effort could prove fatal to the symmetry of the original constructs.

Two Forms of Induction and Two Forms of Deduction

On the other hand, a dialectical view of the problem makes it urgent that both typological and deductive approaches be pursued simultaneously since each can enlarge our knowledge in ways that, unsuspectedly, fertilize each other. A brief review of this two-pronged attack may be useful at this point to indicate their mutual relevance. To begin with the first: typologies are in a way simply *one form of induction*, since they furnish classifications suggested by the data on the basis of comprehensive inspection. There is, however, *another way of using induction*. In this latter mode the task proceeds by trying to find generalizations for delimited sets of cases under specified conditions and (in theory at least) replicate these under a much wider set of conditions when, with repeated confirmations, they become statable in general form. Both modes may be pursued together or separately, depending on the circumstances. Since perfect induction with all possible cases examined is rare or impossible, samples are substituted and probabilities assessed. In the very nature of the case, these probabilities fall considerably below 1. Conversely, the *deductive* scientists strike out at once for logically interconnected systems of propositions. Two prominent modes of deductive construction are, *axiomatic reduction* and *pluralistic parallel deduction*. In the former the scientist begins with several related propositions, each of which has received satisfactory confirmation, and by examining their related logical properties, discovers postulates from which they can be inferred. These postulates not only make it possible to deduce each of the original propositions, but when combined engender axioms or theorems by implication, many of which furnish new knowledge. In the second case, that of pluralistic parallel deduction, the scientist begins with theoretical propositions, in certain cases specific inferences from a general theory, in others the central tenet of a limited theory; from each of these propositions, he draws out a series of inferences that become hypotheses for testing.

Whether inductive or deductive, each of these four modes can be conveniently summarized by a set of propositions appropriate to it. To illustrate each mode, we present the following abbreviated outline:

Samples of Typological Inductive Propositions from the Present Volume

1. When the territory of a contemporary nation-state is occupied by peoples of diverse cultures and origins, the integration of such plural groups into the total society will be a composite function of 3 independent and 3 intervening variables.
2. The independent variables are:
    a. Repeatable sequences of interaction that circumscribe the relations between diverse groups from the period of first contact into later phases of the relationship. Each of these sequences carries with it a typical chain of consequences in which one group assumes a superordinate position while one or more of the others plays a subordinate role. (CT)[4] These typical sequences are annexation (CT), migration on a continuum from greater to lesser coercion (CT), colonization and its derivative effects on postindependence states—from lesser to greater demographic preponderance (CT and SA), the emergence of pariahs (SA and CT), and the emergence of indigenous isolates (SA and CT).
    b. The degree of enclosure (institutional separation or segmentation) of the subordinate group or groups from the society-wide network of institutions and associations. While this is derived historically from (a), it is a structural variable that operates autonomously and independently in the present. (SA and CT)
    c. The degree of control over accessibility of scarce resources (economic, political, or prestige factors) in the society by the superordinates, as manifested in the sharing of such resources by subordinates. (CT)
3. The intervening or contextual variables that modify the effects of the independent variables are:
    a. Congruent or incongruent ideologies (centrifugal or centripetal) entertained by superordinates and subordinates

expressing preferred goals for the subordinates (Figure 6). While each of these permutations is clearly linked historically with a particular sequence (independent variable), its effects are contextual and have modifying influences on other independent variables (b and c) that have to be taken into account in contemporary analysis. (SA and CT)

b. Clusters of societies sharing common social organization and cultural features: the eight multinational sectors, each of which may be expected to have its own massive modifying effect on the impact of the independent variables. (SA)

c. A narrower and more selective form of (b) in which only the comparative dominance of political over economic institutions and vice versa is taken into account. This gives a cluster of societies with common structural features that partly coincide with multinational sectors and partly cross-cut them. It is hypothesized that the effects on the integration of plural groups in pol-ec as compared with ec-pol societies will show differentials in modifying the effects of independent variables, and this in ways not fully explainable by the grosser factors of the multinational sectors, making it possible to have greater discriminatory power. (SA and CT)

4. The dependent variables to be explained are the interweaving patterns of integration and conflict between the subordinates and superordinates on the one hand, and between the subordinates and the total society on the other. Such relationships sometimes coincide and sometimes do not. Hence the following three variables will be sufficient to make discrimination between the two possible. The first two variables are correlative and complementary, and the third separable.

a. Objective factors: the participation of subordinates in spheres of institutional and associational activity, including rates of vertical mobility in equal or unequal proportions as compared with the participation of superordinates. (SA and CT)

b. Subjective factors: The extent of satisfaction or dissatisfaction on the part of subordinates with the objective

conditions of (a) as they see them, together with the
ideologies and cultural values that define for them their
place in society including that vis-à-vis the superordinates.
A similar assessment of reactions on the part of dominant
groups. Not only will this involve comparative evaluation
of consensus and dissensus between these views but any
and all indications of a sense of threat in the ideas of
either group about the other. (SA and CT)

c. Overt or covert behavior patterns of greater or lesser
conflict among subordinates or superordinates as this is
directed by one against the other, on some such scale as
LeVine's continuum: physical aggression, public verbal
disputes, covert verbal aggression, breach of expectation,
avoidance, and separation (LeVine, 1961). (CT) On a
more attenuated behavioral level, the patterns of integration could also be assessed by the use of Landecker's four
types: *cultural integration,* which refers to the degree of
consistency among cultural standards; *normative integration* that denotes the degree of conformity to cultural
norms; *communicative integration* where there are greater
or lesser exchanges of meanings between members of
groups; and *functional integration* in which functions
exercised by members of different groups constitute mutual services to a greater or lesser degree (Landecker,
1951). (SA)

This set of typological inductive propositions is stated in the
form of a prospectus for research rather than as a set of conclusions, and hence lacks the definiteness or attestation of the other
inductive mode or the two deductive ones. This is, of course, its
greatest weakness, and one that cannot be overlooked. It is de-
fended here because of the many inductive corroborations it
has received in the all too brief discussions above, and because it
seems appropriate to the exploratory stage of research in which
comparative ethnic relations exist today; in short, inductive typology does not have the premature closure of the other modes. By
selecting a limited number of patterned elements that correspond
with empirical realities at the outset, it escapes total open-ended-
ness while remaining flexible and maneuverable enough to allow

constant revision. Whatever patterns or typologies are postulated are chosen for their fidelity to a large range of data already available from a series of studies, with only the more general theoretic assumption that the relations already perceived could best be derived or explained in the framework of conflict theory in conjunction with system analysis. These two general theories are viewed dialectically as alternatives that have greater or lesser relevance at different points of analysis rather than two sets of dichotomous intellectual systems from which an either-or choice *must* be made for explanatory purposes.

Samples of Inductive Propositions as Established Generalizations from a Single Society or a Subsection of That Society[5]

1. The greater the differentiation of groups and of individual social roles in a society, the greater the probabilities of group conflict. No. 21

2. Intergroup conflict is the more likely the more rapid and far-reaching the social changes to which individuals have to adjust. No. 22

3. When there is an actual threat to the dominance of the in-group, socially legitimated hostilities may appear. No. 23

4. Migration of a visibly different group into a given area increases the likelihood of conflict; the probability of conflict is the greater (a) the larger the ratio of the incoming minority to the resident population, and (b) the more rapid the influx. No. 27

5. Conflict is especially likely in periods of rapid change in levels of living. The probability of conflict is increased insofar as the changes have a differential impact on various groups. No. 28

6. Hostilities and conflicts among ethnic or racial groups are to an appreciable extent interchangeable with "class" conflicts. No. 29

7. Groups which arise out of conflict tend to disintegrate when opposition ceases. No. 31

8. It is a legitimate guess from the scattered evidence at hand that group conflict is not so much a correlate of *differences*

in status as it is of *changes* in status and in the highly visible symbols thereof. No. 33

9. Conflict between persons of different identifiable groups is the more likely when there is no clear definition of the situation, especially with regard to detailed patterns of "appropriate" personal behavior. No. 39

10. A militant reaction from a minority group is most likely when (a) the group's position is rapidly improving, or (b) when it is rapidly deteriorating, especially if this follows a period of improvement. No. 43

11. Group antagonisms seem to be inevitable when two peoples in contact with each other may be distinguished by differentiating characteristics, either inborn or cultural, and are actual or potential competitors. No. 20

It is important to emphasize that the entire compilation from which these propositions are selected is focussed on problems of conflict rather than integration, which explains why the latter get little attention. Perhaps the last two propositions rest on evidence available from more than one society. In the tenth proposition, what confirmation we have is grounded in the study of revolutions taken from a number of countries, and there is internal evidence that proposition 11 rests on observations of more than one society. All of the propositions are stated in general form, though it appears from the references given that supporting data come mainly from American research. An indication of this is the fact that of the 223 titles of books, articles, and monographs used as sources for the propositional inventory, only 3 are devoted wholly to nations outside the United States (Williams, *op. cit.*, 135–45). A later compilation by the same author ten years afterward shows some shift in the cross-national direction where 33 titles out of 210 are devoted to research in nations abroad (Williams, 1957, 455–64).[6] It may be somewhat misleading to refer to the above list of propositions as generalizations since they are explicitly advanced as hypotheses in need of further testing. At the same time, each has the status of a proposition stating invariant relations found to exist on the basis of limited research in a single country.[7] The implication is that replications of the researches on which these propositions rest will strengthen the validity of the as yet tentative generalizations. It is pertinent, therefore, to point out that mechanical replications or their comparable substitutes, if carried out in a number of societies, may well show failure of confirmation because of contextual and typological intervening conditions of the kind already discussed above. While codifications of propositions are of immense value, the process of replicating the research that originally gave rise to them requires an appropriate framework that alerts us to problems of comparability that immediately arise. The inductive typologies advanced above are constructed with this problem in mind.

Samples of Deductive Propositions in the Mode of Axiomatic Reduction[8]

Assume, for example, that the following propositions are given:

1. If national prosperity increases, then the middle classes expand. Economists are fairly well in agreement that the ranks of service occupations, dealers, and brokers, expand during periods of prosperity and in countries with a growing GNP.
2. If the middle classes expand, the consensus of values in the society increases. While disproportionate expansion of lower or upper classes leads to a polarization of values (as Marx argued), a similar expansion of the middle classes promotes the convergence of values in the society.
3. If the middle classes expand, the social mobility increases. The expanding ranks of the middle classes must be filled by persons from other classes, thus promoting mobility.
4. If social mobility increases, the consensus of values in the society increases and vice versa. Social mobility creates families in which fathers, sons and brothers belong to different classes and family loyalties modify class ideologies. This is a reversible proposition: if there is much consensus of values between social strata, then social mobility between them becomes easier.

From this list we may select propositions (1), (2), and (4) as postulates. To restate them with roman numbers:

I. If national prosperity increases, the middle classes expand.
II. If the middle classes expand, the consensus on values increases.

III. If social mobility increases, the consensus on values increases, and vice versa.

The implications of these propositions can now be spelled out in the form of theorems. Postulates II and III combine into the familiar:

3. If the middle classes expand, the social mobility increases thus completing the set of propositions we had at the beginning.

In addition, Postulates I and II render this theorem:

5. If national prosperity increases, the consensus on values increases. Furthermore, if Theorem 3 is combined with Postulate I, we obtain:

6. If national prosperity increases, the social mobility increases. The last two theorems are novel in the sense that they were not included in our original set.

Here again the social scientist begins *in medias res*, with each proposition established by a number of research efforts; the probability seems fairly great that these have occurred in a number of societies. Axiomatic reduction, as this brief example shows, is a method whereby a number of related propositions may be reduced to a smaller number of theorems or axioms that do duty for an entire set. This process requires recognition of interconnection between the denoted events of one proposition and those of another (i.e., the inductive element is not entirely missing), as well as the logical relations between the propositions themselves. However the logical manipulation that reduces the propositions to more comprehensive axioms is a process of synthetic deduction revealing sets or families of particular judgments interrelated with each other and deducible from a more universal proposition. The application of axiomatic reduction to propositional inventories like those of Williams and Westie would, of course, greatly reduce their plurality by showing their logical dependence on a smaller number of axioms. This task, however, awaits the contingent appearance of a social scientist with gifts of logical imagination equalling those of Zetterberg. While that is surely a consummation devoutly to be wished, it is unwise to make the advance of comparative ethnic relations too dependent on such an indeterminate probability. To the extent that others make initial headway on this task, it will both simplify and alter the nature of replication and confirmation.

Samples of Deductive Propositions in the Mode
of Pluralistic Parallel Deduction[9]

1. In general, the larger the number of feasible alternative means for achieving a given goal, the less likely it is that this goal will be incompatible with a second goal, in the sense that this achievement of the former will reduce the probability of attaining the latter, or vice-versa.

   NOTE: To the extent that the possession of resources increases the range of alternative means to a given goal, then the greater the resources the less the likelihood that this goal will be incompatible with others in the above sense.

2. Those goals which permit the least flexibility with respect to choice among alternative means can be expected to have the greatest influence in determining the direction of one's behavior (choice behavior), though not necessarily its intensity or persistence.

   NOTE: This proposition is based on the assumption that individuals will act more or less rationally so as to maximize their chances of attaining all important goals. They are expected to select the most efficient means toward goals that do not permit flexibility, and then to choose means toward other goals (that do permit flexibility) according to their compatibility with the most efficient means toward the first goals.

3. Economic and status factors are most likely to be major determinants of minority discrimination if *both* of the following hold:
   a. there is a relatively small number of means to status and economic goals that are perceived to be efficient; and
   b. discriminatory behavior is perceived to be instrumental, either for large numbers of persons or for influential elites, in achieving status objectives by these most efficient means.
4. In comparing individuals with respect to discriminatory behavior, those persons who are least able to achieve status goals

through means not involving discrimination are most likely to be *motivated* to discriminate. Since these persons may lack the resources to carry out the discrimination, however, it does not follow that actual discrimination will be more pronounced in the case of such individuals.

> NOTE: Given a relatively fixed division of labor or occupational distribution, the decisions of some individuals not to make use of means involving minority discrimination may simply increase the probability that other individuals will be able to avail themselves of these means. For example, the refusal to enter a particular occupation may open up this possibility to someone else.

5. Given a situation in which there is displaced aggression, minorities are likely to be selected as targets for aggression to the degree that such aggression can serve as means to *other* goals. In particular, minorities are especially likely to be selected as targets if:
   a. aggression serves the purpose of reducing competition with the minority or of handicapping potential competitors
   b. aggression serves to facilitate the exploitation of the minority by making it more tractable
   c. the minority is perceived as the actual source of the frustration, or as being in an alliance with the actual source

6. A minority that deviates from important group norms is especially likely to become a target for displaced aggression to the degree that:
   a. the deviance increases the visibility of the minority
   b. the deviance is in itself a frustration to members of the dominant group
   c. the deviance constitutes a threat to sacred traditions
   d. the deviance makes it easier to rationalize aggression, thereby reducing the amount of guilt or self-punishment; and
   e. the deviance leaves the minority unprotected by the larger society and therefore vulnerable to aggression

7. If there are two parties, one dominant, and the other subordinate, the fewer the resources of the subordinate party,

and the fewer its realistic alternatives, the greater is the number of alternatives available to the dominant party in controlling the behavior of the subordinate party.

> NOTE: If economic resources are "closed" (in Nieboer's sense)[10] to the subordinate party, then the dominant party may control it by using either political means (including force) or by controlling the access to the "closed" resources.

8. From the standpoint of the superordinate party it is preferable to control the subordinate party by getting it to accept the dominance relationship as legitimate, rather than to attempt to control it by force. This is particularly true to the degree that:
    a. the application of force increases the risk of overt rebellion; and
    b. the legitimacy of the relationship makes it easier to rationalize one's conduct, avoid guilt feelings, and utilize ideologies to explain away possible incompatibilities with religious or other ethical principles
9. Where resources are closed to the subordinate party, a system of tenancy or contract labor will be preferable (to the dominant party) to one of slavery or serfdom. Slavery and serfdom are therefore more likely to be found in situations in which resources are open, and where labor can be retained only by applying direct force or political controls implying the threat of force.

> NOTE: "Debt bondage" appears to be an intermediate form of exploitation in which political means are used to retain the services of subordinate parties, which remain in perpetual debt to the dominant party.

10. If resources are open and slavery profitable, then it is usually easier to control slaves by force if (i) they are not members of indigenous groups, (ii) have been transported from long distances, and (iii) have diverse cultural backgrounds. This is especially true if:
    a. geographic conditions are such that escape is relatively easy, and where indigenous slaves could not easily be

　　　distinguished from local peasants or other elements of
　　　the population

b. linguistic differences or tribal rivalries inhibit effective
　　slave revolts or other forms of protest

c. it is feasible or necessary to treat slaves harshly, either
　　because the supply is plentiful or because it is economi-
　　cally rational to do so

NOTE: The assumption underlying (c) is that it is easier to ra-
　　　　tionalize the harsh treatment of persons who are essen-
　　　　tially "outsiders." Also, such treatment will be less resented
　　　　by third parties that are indigenous to the area. Assuming
　　　　that slavery constitutes a more extreme form of exploita-
　　　　tion than serfdom, this implies that slavery is more likely
　　　　in the case of imported minorities, whereas serfdom is
　　　　more likely in the case of indigenous peoples.

These ten propositions are the first of a series of ninety-seven
advanced to account for minority relations as a special class of
social phenomena. The source of these propositions is multiple
and diverse, including a considerable number of foreign studies,
though the dominant reliance throughout seems to rest on special
theories constructed to account for limited classes of events. For
example, in the ten propositions above, the author draws on
psychological theories of choice behavior, the psychological
theory of frustration-aggression, and Nieboer's theory about the
socioeconomic conditions that facilitate slavery. From these special
theories, Blalock deduces these and other singular propositions
grouped around thematic or situational areas of major significance
like "Frontier Contact Situations," "Middleman Minorities,"
"Power and Discrimination," "Minority Percentage and Discrimination," etc. Thus his pluralism assumes a double form: (1) the
deductions are made from a plurality of special theories; and (2)
the deductions are organized around multiple themes. Discrepancies which might be expected to develop from such a multiform
approach are largely resolved by a set of common assumptions
about causal relations[11] which apparently stem from a unity of
outlook in general theory not fully articulated. However, Blalock's
obvious preference for explanations that could be derived from
conflict theory rather than from system analysis gives a coherence
and internal consistency to his whole set of propositions that are

noteworthy.[12] It is not overstating the case to say that his theoretical propositions constitute the clearest and most impelling articulation of power and conflict analysis yet applied to minority relations, focussed as they are on carefully circumscribed zones of special relevance.

Having reviewed two inductive and two deductive ways of proceeding, it is now useful to summarize them in such a way that quick comparisons can be made. Table 4, pp. 250–51, facilitates this.

A quick glance at Table 4 reveals that inductive typology is in no sense a substitute for these other methods, but rather constitutes a supplement to them. In one sense it is misleading to dignify it as a method; it is rather a scheme, a framework, or a program of investigation sufficiently comprehensive to embrace the findings, propositions, and methods of the other modes, though not, we insist, at face value. For the replications implied by the inductive propositional inventory, the plausible theorems of axiomatic induction, and the limited universals of pluralistic parallel deduction, it raises the issue of contextual comparability that cannot be lightly dismissed. Committed to no single general theory, nor to any monopolistic method of research, it appropriates freely from each the most fitting intellectual tools for advancing our knowledge. This is not eclecticism, though it may be only one step removed from it. Eclecticism borrows on an ad hoc basis without regard for consistency or any guiding framework. Inductive typology, as set forth in these pages, is specifically constructed for the task of comparative research in ethnic relations, with types and patterns that follow the contours and shapes of historic and structural realities on a world-wide scale. As indicated in Table 4, inductive typology is conservative in the search for generalizations, assuming at the outset that they are more likely *within* patterns and types than *between* them. To those who claim to have found the latter, it interposes contextual skepticism and thrusts the burden of proof on the claimants. Conversely, however, inductive typology makes no claim to be the sole avenue to scientific truth. While it approaches the data from above, so to speak, in its initial concern with sequences, structures, and sectors while working its way down to middle

TABLE 4. SELECTED INDUCTIVE AND DEDUCTIVE MODES OF OPERATION AS VIEWED FROM SEVERAL PARAMETERS

Parameters	Inductive Typological Mode (the present volume)	Inductive Propositional Inventory (Robin M. Williams, tr.)	Deductive Approach in Mode of Axiomatic Reduction (Hans L. Zetterberg)	Deductive Approach in Mode of Pluralistic Parallel Deduction (Hubert M. Blalock, Jr.)
Range of generalization	Limited within patterns of types	Limited mainly to a single society	Presumptive universal	Presumptive universal
Focus	On broad ranges of data	On restricted ranges of data	On restricted ranges of data	On restricted ranges of data
Direction of analysis	From parts to wholes and wholes to parts	From parts to wholes	From parts to wholes	From parts to wholes
Certainty	Limited verification. General low level of validity. Presumptively higher with continuous application of scheme.	Islands of certainty in a single society.	Islands of certainty cross-cutting an unspecified number of societies.	Islands of certainty cross-cutting an unspecified number of societies.

Point of departure. Core of central attention	Societal pluralities, cultural and structural	Pluralities in the United States, predominantly "racial" in type	Uncertain	Pluralities in the United States, predominantly "racial" in type
Relation to theory	Alternating links to conflict theory and system analysis assuming a dialectical relation between them.	Uncertain, varying with the particular research utilized	Uncertain	Deductions from special theories presumptively unified in line with conflict theory
Methodological stance	Open, flexible	Relative closure	Closure	Closure

and lower ranges, it discovers the same interconnections and invariances found by pluralistic parallel deduction on the way up. Thus what is described above as the typical characteristics of Brazilian race relations, is also outlined in detail by Blalock in his propositions about "continuum conditions" numbered 85 to 87 (Blalock, *op. cit.*, 219). This convergence, like others that appear from time to time, give assurance that the different modes of attack do not produce contradictory results but arrive at the same conclusions, requiring no more than semantic adjustments to make them identical. Consequences like these should discourage theoretical or methodological imperialism with which we are too often surfeited. Further discussion of inductive typology in these closing pages must, therefore, not be interpreted as an attempt to displace other equally valid operations.

From Micro to Macrostudies

One dilemma, and perhaps the major one facing comparative research is that, at the very moment when social scientists need methods and conceptualizations that enable them to deal with larger wholes like total societies, their most effective research tools are, all too often, the very ones fitted for miniscule units of single societies. Sociology appears best equipped today, as one quip has it, to learn more and more about less and less. Specialization, in more detailed and intricate forms of research, has created a widespread bias for "manageable units" which, by definition, are limited and micro in nature.[13] Examples are plentiful in sociological journals from which I take the following at random: "Argot, Symbolic Deviance and Subcultural Delinquency," "Occupational Determinants of Geographic Mobility Among Professional Workers," "Ethnicity and Extended Familism in an Upper-Middle-Class Suburb." In spite of the clear gains from studies like these, this sort of microanalysis has, in Deutsch's words, "consisted of attempts to isolate very small classes of special aspects of social life, to define them as sharply and reproducibly as possible, so that the definition will enable any number of observers to pick out pretty much the same events, and then to generalize only about those limited classes under sharply defined contingencies" (Deutsch, 1966, 29). For any one engaged in macrosociological or comparative thought, Deutsch's image conjures up the frightening thought that the Ph.D. dissertation may have subtly become the paradigm for research design in our generation.

I would not be misunderstood. Social scientists everywhere not only recognize but freely accept the demands of strict validity and reliability that microstudies are in a position to control. Until these demands are met for the total corpus of the social sciences, they will be to that extent incomplete and unsatisfactory. If we wait, however, until every step of the way has been cleared by microstudies, a millenium would hardly suffice. To fill the vast gap in between, what seems to be developing in comparative studies is a composite method that combines the use of documentation, aggregate data, secondary analysis, and reliance on strategic individual researches at the field level. The compound results of these efforts have advanced our knowledge of total society functioning which microanalysis by itself can not attain. And the information received from such large-scale explorations has strong evidential value, more and more refined by constant application of validity and reliability criteria. Some of these studies are carried out in the absence of direct field research by the investigator,[14] others are supplemented by more extensive field experience.

Examples of the first type are Lipset's *Political Man* (1963), and *The First New Nation* (1963).[15] In the former, the author explores the correlates of democracy with economic development, forms of legitimacy, working class organization, electoral processes, political party participation, and the like. In the latter, Lipset compares the social and political development of new nations, using the United States as the central case; in this essentially sociohistorical study he explores these developments in light of the different value systems in each nation; these value systems are distinguished and differentiated by means of Parsons' pattern-variables with the addition of an elitist-egalitarian configuration.

As for the second type, i.e., the use of the composite method combined with field research carried on by the scientist himself, the most pertinent case for our purpose is the four-nation study of race relations recently completed by van den Berghe—*Race and Racism,* 1967—a work to which the present volume is substantially indebted. In this work, the author shows that in all four societies, Mexico, the United States, Brazil, and South Africa, the paternalistic pattern of race relations has been eroded, sometimes taking the competitive form, sometimes transmuted into class differences. The differentials between extreme and mild racism are traced to the convergent or divergent effects of variables like cultural decapitation, miscegenation, religious differences, and structural variations. While the trajectory of race relations in each society is clearly outlined, the author also relates this to larger issues of social organization, and in the end, presents us with a profile of national differences highly useful for further analysis (cf. van den Berghe, *op. cit.*, chap. VI).

An important factor in the success of *Race and Racism* in its dissection of four national cultures is the consistent application of the "plural society" model; the societies under scrutiny varied along gradations of the model, each traceable to a special set of historical circumstances. It is the aim of inductive typology to extend and elaborate this type of analysis in several ways; three of these are immediately relevant to van den Berghe's own approach. One mode of procedure is to conceptualize the degrees of separateness or segmentation in a more or less plural society on a continuum from complete insulation to total integration, recognizing each extreme as an ideal limit only approximated in real life. This independent variable I have called the "degree of enclosure." A second way is to specify or give determinancy to the notion of "historical circumstances" by placing historical events within repeatable sequences which have similar consequences in different societies. Depending on the problem to be investigated, these sequences can be viewed either as independent or intervening variables. In the third place, the present volume has narrowed the wide range of cultural relativism to a few intermediate forms in the multinational sectors where societal influences are assumed to have a relative uniqueness within each sector. In a comparative study the sector differentials constitute another intervening variable that must be taken into account in the shaping of events.

By the use of these typological variables it is possible to arrive at the same sort of conclusions reached by van den Berghe and give rise to other inferences as well. Thus while our analysis coincides with his on the correlation of more extreme racism with greater structural pluralism, inductive typology also enables us to say that the variations in racism are a function of particular sequences when engaged in by superordinates from particular multinational sectors. In comparing Brazil with South Africa, for example, we find that both have experienced the sequence of colonization with extensive settlement. In addition, Brazil compounded colonization with slavery. On both these counts we might expect Brazil to have not only greater pluralism but more extreme racism. Yet it had the least. By applying sector analysis to ferret out the differentials, we note that the settlement of Brazil was from Sector 3 (Iberian societies) while that of South Africa was from Sector 1 (Western European nations). This allows us to say that in this case we are justified in adopting the proposition: the variability in the extent of racism owes more to the differential national provenance of the superordinates than to the sequences in which it is found.[16]

A Leading Hypothesis

To get the most intelligence from a single proposition of the highest generality, the following procedure is a helpful one: making use of two independent variables from the general scheme of inductive typology, suppose that a leading hypothesis is set up for preliminary exploration; where will it lead? For example: "the higher the degree of enclosure of the ethnic group coupled with the higher the degree of control over the group's scarce rewards by the superordinates, the greater the conflict. Conversely, the lower the degree of enclosure coupled with the lower degree of control over scarce rewards, the greater the integration." Leaving aside for the moment all questions of definition or operationalizing such categories, what results are forthcoming? An antecedent glance at some of the major sequences raises an initial question: does this proposition have equal validity for ethnic groups emerging from the sequence of annexation, migration subforms like slavery, slave labor movements, contract labor migrants, displaced persons or voluntary migrants, the different peoples in the wake of colonization of limited, extensive, or massive settlement? At this level we find that the general proposition does not hold. There are ethnic groups with relatively high degrees of enclosure that have a low degree of conflict with superordinates; they are found less often in the sequence of annexation (though the addition of northern territories to Thailand in the nineteenth century was not followed by rebellion); in the case of migration, high degrees of enclosure show low levels of conflict mostly in the sequence of voluntary migration where the newcomers establish agricultural communities outside the mainstream of the society (Mennonites, Hutterites). In the case of colonization and its aftermath, a whole series of tribes and ethnolinguistic groups practicing hunting and/or self-subsistent agriculture remain segmentally enclosed even to the present day without coming into direct conflict with superordinate groups; in general the policy of "live and let live" is accepted on both sides. This is especially true for the aftermath of colonization of limited settlement in Africa and Asia.[17] Yet the other factor, i.e., control of scarce rewards by superordinates can well be missing in such cases when subordinate ethnic groups are economically autonomous, politically acephalous, or subject to leaders in kinship networks if not informally designated. Such groups are in society but not of it from the standpoint of the ruling portions of the population.

As for colonization with extensive settlement, similar phenomena appear in the postindependence period—many ethnic groups remain in isolated enclaves without coming into conflict with superordinates—at least in recent times. There are indications, however, that the extended settlement of the dominant group has had its repercussions in the *past*, though subservience today is mingled with ambivalent reactions to assimilation and incorporation. Such, for example, is the situation for the Aymara Indians of Peru who rebelled against the Spanish-mestizo rulers in the last quarter of the eighteenth century but came to accept a dependent condition where deference and obsequious servitude was rewarded and legitimized as normative (Hickman, 1963, 12–13). The Aymara of Peru are not, however, as self-subsistent as the interior tribes of Africa or the hill peoples of Thailand and Burma. In the Peruvian case there are definitely "two poles of

Peruvian life," one in coastal towns and cities occupied by the ruling mestizo, the other in the interior, chiefly mountainous areas where the great bulk of the Indian population lives (Mishkin, 1946–48, II 413). But at the same time, the Aymara, in addition to their agricultural pursuits, are entering the money economy as draft laborers, as miners, supplementing earnings in cottage industries, hat making, and working their way into the lower ranks of officialdom. Uneven educational opportunities beckon and as some attain literacy they also gain voting rights, and small numbers enter new occupations (for them at least) to become airplane pilots, priests, doctors and lawyers (Hickman, *ibid.*); those who attain such positions in the wider society then enter the category of mestizos themselves.

Repeating the exploratory hypothesis once again: "the higher the degree of enclosure of the ethnic group coupled with the higher the degree of control over the group's scarce rewards by the superordinates, the greater the conflict; conversely the lower the degree of enclosure coupled with the lower degree of control over scarce rewards, the greater the integration," it is necessary to insist that this proposition requires further specification when applied to the sequence, *emergence of indigenous isolates.* In this sequence the hypothesis is confirmed only (1) when the isolates reach a certain threshold of activation in the system, and (2) in a specified multinational context (see pp. 177ff.). In this instance, as with other hypotheses to be explored in comparative ethnic relations, the investigator can proceed either separately or concurrently in one of four ways:

1. Hold the types of society constant and vary the ethnic sequences.
2. Hold the ethnic sequences constant and vary the type of society.
3. Hold both the type of society and the ethnic sequence constant.
4. Vary both the type of society and the ethnic sequence.

The brief discussion above has utilized the second of these approaches to illustrate the relevance of inductive typology for the solution of a specific problem. In actual research the specification must, of course, be sharpened more critically. The "threshold of activation" must be made measurable in such a way that it is applicable to the actual societies selected for research. Parenthetically, it is a plausible inference that societies with higher degrees of urbanization and industrialization will have more highly activated ethnic groups; hence it would be worthwhile to see whether there is a linear relationship between activation and increasing differentiation of the society on Marsh's index (see p. 178). Likewise measures are needed to operationalize "degree of enclosure." On this point, foundations for such a measurement have been laid by Despres (1967) in his analysis of African Creole and East Indian social structures in British Guiana at the local level and at the national level.[18] Since his research was carried on in a society with a relatively low degree of differentiation (thus where the distinctions between local and national are quite sharp) the task remains to find measures of associational and institutional participation that can be used equally well for societies at many different levels. In terms of our sequential analysis, too, British Guiana is relatively unique, experiencing both the sequence of slavery and of contract labor, with the bulk of the population derived from the two sequences. Any measure constructed for use in British Guiana would therefore require considerable modification in order to have wider application.

Returning again to the four typological approaches, it is appropriate now to indicate briefly the utility of each type (except for the second which has already been illustrated above in brief detail). The advantage of the first alternative (holding the types of society constant while varying the ethnic sequences) is that it can furnish clues to the relative weight of the two variables in determining forms of conflict or integration. An example would be the study of Indian-Caucasian relations (sequence of massive colonization) and resident-immigrant relations (sequence of voluntary migration) in Canada and the United States. Such comparisons would help determine the relative importance of societal and sequential variables. The third alternative (holding both the type of society and the ethnic sequence constant) can be illustrated by a study of mestizo-Indian relationships in Bolivia and Chile, or resident-immigrant relationships in the United States and Australia. This is a crucial comparison because, on the basis of typological unity, one should expect similarities or uniformities to predominate. The greater the number of discovered differences (ecological, demographic, occupational, structural, cultural) that appear when the types are equalized in this manner, the clearer will be their significance for modifying and refining the original scheme. This sort of comparison is well suited to test Popper's demand for falsification (Popper, 1959). Finally, instead of heightening the similarities to find the difference, a fourth alternative is to magnify the differences to seek out similarities by varying both societal and sequential types simultaneously. At first glance, this destroys comparability at a single blow when, let us say, the investigator compares a contract labor group like East Indians in Trinidad with an annexed group like Kazakhs in Russia, or, to take another example, compares a group of voluntary migrants like Caribbean Negroes in Britain with emergent pariahs like the ex-untouchables of India. However far-fetched such cases may appear, their exploration will have residual value, for if they reveal, in spite of their differences, verifiable interactive relations that are similar, we have come close to the common character of all ethnic relations. If these are unexpected or unpredicted features, they will, in turn, require a reformulation of basic theory. A variation on this fourth method would be to compare societies that have obvious phenomenal ethnic features that make them alike, but differ in their sequential patterns and societal types, as for example examining the bifurcated societies having, in each case, two major ethnic divisions. These break down into two subtypes already noted by Geertz (Note 1, pp. 275–76): the bi-polar, in which the two groups are of an approximately equal size— Lebanon with Muslims and Christians; Belgium with Flemings and Walloons. Or the other form of bifurcation is the clear division into majority and minority like Ceylon with Singhalese and Tamils, or Canada with English and French-speaking populations. If comparative studies were made with only this sort of similarity but with other differences in sequence and societal structure still present, it might turn out that the common demographic contours in such cases had verifiable similar consequences that were clearly marked. In such a case, this would enable us to incorporate supplementary propositions about demographic variables that would at least have validity for bifurcated societies, whatever their classification in other respects.

Two other important questions deserve passing comment in our rapid review. One is the position of ethnic groups in stratification systems, and the other (closely related) problem is the comparative rigidity of racial lines with increasing complexity of social systems. Inductive typology, while giving no definitive answers, at least points in the direction where more solid conclusions can be substantiated.

✱⁹ *Ethnic Stratification*

Total omission of the stratification issue so far in our discussion has probably appeared gratuitous to more than one reader. This, especially, in view of the fact that the most imposing substantive contribution to comparative ethnic relations in recent years, Shibutani and Kwan's *Ethnic Stratification* (1965), has conceptualized the entire field as a study of stratification. Their approach has comprehensive validity so long as we are confined to the "conventional wisdom" of most sociological treatises on the subject where the well-worn paths are familiar and surprises are ruled out by gentle consensus on the boundaries of "ranking systems." However, the focus on plural societies which I have insistently emphasized throughout these pages points to a structural set of relationships not quite identical with the usual "hierarchies" of conventional stratification theory but independent, both analytically and empirically. The central variable, "degree of enclosure" does not imply anything whatever about the "relative social status" of any enclosed ethnic group. High degrees of enclosure may accompany low, intermediate, or high social status and the two principles are independent, even though they indubitably reinforce each other under special conditions. In these latter conditions they appear reducible to status factors only because that is the familiar mode of interpretation.

After analyzing the factor of pluralism in 114 countries on the basis of Banks and Textor's categories, as quoted above, Marie Haug sums up her conclusions as follows:

> These findings lend striking support to the notion that pluralism
> is a factor which cannot be ignored in social system analysis.

While it is possible that a scale could be devised differentiating various degrees of stratification within societies, there is no indication that it would produce similar results. The implication is that pluralism is not simply another form of social stratification which can be subsumed under that variable, but constitutes a special condition of diversity which varies widely in degrees across societies. As such it must be considered as a factor in the development of any universally applicable system theory. (Haug, 1967, pp. 303–04.)

✓ It must be freely admitted that even though pluralism and status stratification are independent variables, there is no society in which rankings of higher and lower are not made. It does not follow, however, that this entitles us to categorize all diversities on the hierarchical model as Shibutani and Kwan appear to do. In this case, as in so many others we have examined, the two variables bear a dialectical relationship to each other—complementary rather than dichotomous. Indeed it is often the case that increased activation of ethnics in developing societies decreases their enclosure in the pluralistic structure, while increasing their participation in a society-wide hierarchy. This is neatly shown by Benedict's diagram of the changes occurring in Mauritius as follows:

FIGURE 9.   CHANGES OCCURRING IN MAURITIUS

1. *Traditional*

MANAGERS	EUROPEANS
WHITE COLLAR	CREOLES
TRADE	CHINESE
LABOR	INDIANS

2. *Transitional*

MANAGERS

WHITE COLLAR

TRADE

LABOR

EUROPEANS CREOLES CHINESE INDIANS

Taken from Burton Benedict, "Stratification in Plural Societies," *American Anthropologist,* 64 (1962), 1241.

As Benedict remarks, "Economically and occupationally Mauritius appears to be changing from a society which is ethnically stratified with each ethnic section confined to a single set of occupations to a society which is economically stratified with each ethnic section pursuing a whole range of occupations. This is an emerging structure. More top positions are still to be found among Europeans; more lower positions are still to be found among Hindus; retail trade is still largely the province of the Chinese. It will be noted that this transformation does not necessarily abolish the plurality of the society. The distinction between ethnic sections may remain, and this means that there will be several upper classes, not a single one embracing all sections. Nevertheless, the possibility exists for the rapprochement of communities on class lines rather than on purely ethnic, religious, or linguistic ones" (Benedict, 1962, 1240–41).

The section of Benedict's diagram marked "Traditional" is presented in the framework of traditional stratification theory and hence partly obscures the vertical forms of cleavage that separate ethnics from each other in family, education, religion, and politics as well as the economic sphere (the latter assuming first place in the analysis). The disjunction between ethnic pluralism and occupational (society-wide) class structure is more clearly visible in the "Transitional" diagram.

In Mauritius, social and cultural pluralism tend to vary together or reinforce each other. The dissociation of ethnic groups from each other is, to a very large extent, a function of marked cultural differences derived from separate traditions, each cohesively binding its members together over against others. However in societies where social and cultural pluralism vary independently (as in the United States for the Negro minority) we find a parallel disjunction in the stratification picture. Although the cultural differences between Negroes and whites are minimal, the structural separation is highly pronounced by reason of formal or informal segregation imposed by whites. Warner (1936, 235) has called this the caste line and portrayed it as follows:

FIGURE 10. THE CASTE LINE

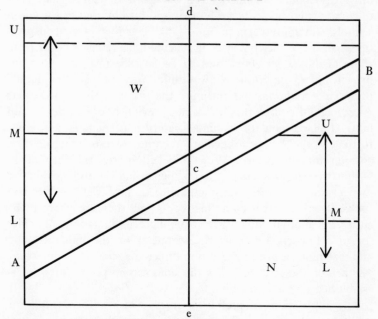

Taken from W. Lloyd Warner, "American Class and Caste," *American Journal of Sociology*, 42 (September 1936), 235.

What Warner speaks of as the caste line (AB) separating Negroes from whites is actually the boundary of a pluralistic structure different in kind and mode from the status patterns represented by the dotted horizontal lines. The independent significance of this pluralistic enclosure can be judged from the fact that the horizontal lines take on a separate meaning when they appear below the line AB. Thus while the ethnic sectors in Benedict's diagram simultaneously refer to both social and cultural pluralism, the corresponding ethnic sector in Warner's diagram (marked N) designates social pluralism without corresponding cultural pluralism.

If we think in terms of social rewards for subordinate ethnic groups, these two systems operate differently. In Mauritius the Creole, Chinese or Indian who wishes for the time being to be upwardly mobile on the societal occupational ladder, may take on a new language, educate himself and his children in European schools, and apply for a position ranking higher in general prestige than his former one had. If accepted, his rewards come from those in the ladder above him. If he fails, he may still have approval and favor from fellow ethnics for "keeping the faith," preserving tradition, and retaining the ways of their forefathers (provided, of course, that he has not previously cut all ties behind him). This cushion for wounded vanity is predictable and comforting. In the American scene there is no corresponding cultural cushion for the Negro. When blocked in the mobility climb within the larger society, his compensating rewards within his own group are not the satisfactions of immemorial loyalties and faiths. If any rewards come his way at all, they are likely to be either the anodyne of theatrical middle class imitations of white society (Frazier, 1957) or the stimulant of the militants who mobilize him for group aggression directed against the oppressors. Neither of these rewards has the consolatory power of a long-established cultural tradition.

The implications of pluralistic analysis as a necessary foil for traditional stratification theories appears most clearly when "race" complicates the picture. While both Mauritius and the United States display what is here called extreme or vertical racism, a pluralistic assessment adds still another dimension. In the United States race relations have a stark, unrelieved quality because social pluralism is modified, little if at all, by cultural pluralism. In Mauritius, on the other hand (as in South Africa and Southern Rhodesia as well) race relations are mitigated by the fact that social pluralism goes hand in hand with cultural pluralism, with the latter reinforcing group cohesion.[19] One is tempted to hypothesize that the North American type of race relations is harder to bear than the form appearing in Africa or Mauritius, that the former may result in more sporadic and unpredictable violence, while the latter is more congruent with a slow, solidary and concerted effort to attain mobility goals on a group basis. The riots of Watts, Cleveland, Newark, and Detroit lend some plausibility to the first part of the hypothesis; the second remains buried in the future of South Africa.

The Color Line—How Solid?

Turning now to the second question, one may ask, what changes in the rigidity of racial lines occur with the increasing complexity of social systems, particularly those of urbanization and industrialization? By an a priori application of system analysis, it is plausible to argue that the emergence of a new industrial system with its patterns of universalism, achievement and efficiency, the allocation of both material and human resources for maximal productivity, and the primacy of rationalized technology are all in conflict with an essentially preindustrial system of production utilizing a subordinate racial labor force recruited by slavery or colonization. The sheer efficacy of the new economic system has led to its triumph, to an order that shows remarkable likeness in country after country, and to a set of international markets that sustain it. Wherever the inevitable march of the system continues, it would seem to replace particularism with universalism, ascription with achievement, and diffuseness with specificity. Competition and social mobility become the social channels for allocating workers; manual, entreprenurial and managerial skills become the sole criteria for recruitment and advancement. In such a system there is no longer any place for traditional impediments like paternalism, nepotism, racialism, or other particularistic anachronisms. Merit becomes the touchstone. The inherent tendencies of the system are eventually supposed to sweep away all "artificial" restrictions, and racism will therefore disappear with the rest.

This statement of the argument is doubtless overdrawn, even *a reductio ad absurdum*, perhaps. Proponents of the view will hardly assert it so boldly or without reserve. Yet many hints in the literature express more than ordinary hope in the efficacy of the industrial system both to challenge and transform existing racial lines, accomplishing the task indirectly as a by-product of its own internal development. To this essentially optimistic view, Blumer has recently advanced a totally opposite thesis, backed by imposing evidence. Not only does he contend that industrial relations empirically conform to the racial patterns of any given society, but breaks in the color line are more affected by political action than by the internal working of industrial systems themselves. His position is clear and forthright:

> As far as I can determine, available evidence everywhere sustains the thesis that when introduced into a racially ordered society industrialisation conforms to the alignment and code of the racial order. Where the racial order is clear-cut and firm, the industrial apparatus will develop a corresponding racial scheme; where, contrariwise, the racial order is vague and weak, racial alignments in industry will be ambiguous and changeable. (Blumer, 1965, 245)   .

In those cases where racial ordering undergoes change in the direction of greater equality, Blumer declares, "The evidence seems to me to lead overwhelmingly to the conclusion that such changes do not arise from inner considerations of industrial efficiency. Instead they arise from outside pressures, chiefly political pressures" (Blumer, *op. cit.*, 247).

Blumer's evidence for his first conclusion comes from studies of Southern industry in the United States where the participation of Negroes has remained at lower levels consonant with the pattern of the traditional racial order, even when plants are brought in from the North. To a lesser degree, similar alignments appear outside the South where supervisory or management positions for Negroes are rare or where control of credit by whites impedes Negro entrepreneurial activity. Likewise in South Africa, the racial patterns of the preindustrial era are carried over into the industrial system with Africans not only restricted to lower levels, but in recent years excluded from trade unions and the right to strike. However, in Brazil where race lines are traditionally not so sharp, the industrial system reflects the variability of race position existing in the society at large.

In support of his thesis on the importance of political action, Blumer shows that it has been legislative, judicial, or administrative measures that have had the most decisive effect on changing racial patterns in American industry, even though this has led to no more than minor modifications. And while political pressures in the United States have weakened racial alignments, in South Africa they have been "sharpening and intensifying" them by continual extension of apartheid.[20] In many of the newly in-

dependent states where industry is managed initially by expatri-
ates, the political pressures are such that nationals are brought
into managerial levels, sit on boards, and have ultimate expectation
of replacing outsiders. It is not the inherent logic of the industrial
system that brings this about but the political realities of the
situation.

These conclusions seem inescapable[21] and they lend considerable support to the tentative thesis advanced above that more
weight can be given to the impact of multinational sectors and
their configurations than to other variables. Further investigation
of Blumer's propositions can be incorporated into studies of the
degree of enclosure experienced by racial subordinates in associational and institutional networks other than the industrial. Differentials can be compared across multinational sectors where one
may expect specific forms of integration to vary by sector. It is
significant that, with the rise of urbanization and industrialization, the *mode* of integration seems to incorporate vertical mobility as a normative expectation. As Blumer suggests, the weight of
political decisions may be disproportionate in affecting the outcome. This point is underlined by David Apter's contention that
a major aim of every political process in the modern world is
"to expand mobility opportunities" (Apter, 1958, 221).

Comparative Mobility

There is no question that studies of differential mobility for
ethnic groups on a comparative basis is a central issue, and very
likely *the* crowning question in our whole analysis. Unfortunately
it is the very area in which we have the least reliable data (with
the possible exception of corresponding evidence on degrees of
enclosure). Comparative studies of mobility in different societies,
most of which rely on aggregate data and surveys, are usually
confined to a limited number of nations (in sector 1—Western
Europe and the Neo-European Complex—as a rule) where "social bookkeeping" over time provides a relatively adequate base
for such assessments, supplemented by sample surveys oriented
to census statistics. Even in such areas, the almost exclusive emphasis on intergenerational mobility measured by the two indi-

cators of manual vs. non-manual occupations is highly selective and leaves out many important features we need to know (Lipset and Bendix, 1960). "Changes in the distribution of citizenship rights or in social acceptance are not likely to be in the forefront . . . Thus the definition of social mobility and the indicators employed to measure it provide only a limited slice of the phenomena commonly regarded as social mobility by other social scientists" (Fox and Miller, 1966, 217). An even greater deficiency appears in the study of mobility among ethnic groups since statistics on occupational distribution for such groups are rare, impressionistic, or lacking altogether. To compound the difficulties, not only do sets of occupational categories form quite different patterns in developing nations from the ones to be found in highly industrialized societies but the criteria for prestige and advancement will tend to differ too.[22] It is difficult, therefore, to pursue the study of mobility on a cross-national basis without extensive field investigation which, in the early stages at least, will consist of carefully sampled survey researches. Problems of strict comparability in occupational structures for all nations are insoluble in the present state of our knowledge. However the chance of finding common elements is greatly increased by the more modest effort of seeking them first in each multinational sector. Establishment of even limited uniformities at this level would furnish clues for more extended generalizations, whether of the contingency type, the specification type, or the universal type.[23]

In notably plural societies such as the one studied by Benedict (quoted above) and probably in others of the same sector (8), a field study could well distinguish at the outset between ascriptive occupations and mobile occupations (those identified with mobility opportunities or aspirations). The extent to which the former are traditional with subordinate ethnic groups, and the latter are customary for superordinates, ethnic-free, or losing their ethnic character need assessment. Differential access to the mobile occupations for each of the plural groups, while it is not measurable directly, can be inferred by sample surveys of adult males by ethnic group and occupation at community levels of increasing size. Further interview samples from each plural division are needed to give social perceptions of access to mobile occupations; of typical channels of mobility (education, wealth, political activity, cooptation); restrictions on mobility (traditional cultural preferences, discrimination, legal or structural factors); the changes of mobility rates in different ethnic groups observable over time and how they are viewed in relation to "own" group; group belief systems or ideologies—centrifugal or centripetal, superiority themes, protest themes; estimation of self-and-other roles regarding group position, etc.[24] This type of exploration would help to determine both degrees of ethnic enclosure and rates of mobility, the latter having a much broader range than present-day studies can give us.

Intersocietal Linkages

Macrosociological analysis cannot, of course, be based on the assumption that one can study any single society as isolated or autonomous, with all its changes completely self-generated. The multinational sectors outlined in chapter 5 should, of course, dispel any such idea. Yet the historical-cultural interconnections within each sector are but one of many types of confluence to be kept in sight quite steadily. The most prominent intersocietal links and perhaps the most clearly demonstrated are those of an economic nature. Thus Gunnar Myrdal points out that the accelerated pace of scientific and technical advance in agricultural productivity and the manufacture of synthetic substitutes in the West has drastically reduced the demand for Asia's raw material exports on which her economic health depends. In parallel fashion, progress in Western medical science has enabled Asian countries to cut their death rate so radically that a population explosion has resulted—making the task of development that much harder. Hence technological gains in the West often actually depress economic development in the East (Myrdal, 1968, I, 698–99).

Such cross-national chains of dependence and interdependence occur in many spheres of social life, so it is imperative to approach modern societies not only as sets of internal processes, but as collectivities adapting to external forces as well. For the student of ethnic and race relations there are three types of intersocietal linkages that create recurrent problems for research. In every case they are potential fulcrums of division that can be manipulated from outside a society while having strong repercussions within; it is therefore fitting to call them the "links that divide." They are:

1. Irredentism
2. Power bloc rivalries (communist vs. capitalist, etc.)
3. International extensions of religious influence for political purposes

Irredentism is defined as "any movement which aims to unite politically with its co-national mother state a region under foreign rule" (Boehm, 1932, VIII, 325). Ordinarily this refers to a situation where ethnics residing in a nation-state which they do not rule, share the language, customs, and sense of nationality with fellow ethnics who rule a neighboring state. The latter, on the well-known nationalist assumption that a nation should be ethnically homogeneous, regards its "fellow nationals" as unfortunate subjects of a "foreign" power to be redeemed and united with their colleagues by political or military means. While they are subjugated they are unredeemed (irredents) but this is an inherently unstable position which history is bound to correct. It is therefore a duty to promote national aspirations and loyalty among the unredeemed, stirring them to rebel against their rulers so that they can unite with fellow nationals in a fully redeemed nation.

Irredentism has run its classical course in European history where, since the rise of nationalism, the term nation has been practically synonymous with ethnic homogeneity as an ideal, however far it may be from realization. Such an ideal made it possible for those speaking the Polish language to share a sense of nationality though ruled by three different states (Prussia, Austria, and Russia) from 1795 to 1918, and to maintain a subterranean thrust toward independence which could only be released with the balance-of-power shift resulting from World War I (Znaniecki, 1952, 33). This was admittedly an exceptional case since, at the time, there *was* no mother state. But recent European history abounds with other examples—Italians under Austrian rule, Austrians under Italian rule, Germans under Czech rule, Bulgarians under Rumanian rule, Magyars under Czech rule, and so on. This is not, of course, a purely European phenomenon for it appears among the Kurds in Turkey and Syria, the Malays in southern Thailand, the Somalis in east Africa, etc. On the premise that irredentism is more likely in the first flush of nationalism, it is worth exploring whether the phenomenon will appear more frequently in Africa and Asia than in regions of older nations where nationalism has more maturity and less élan.

A second type of situation in which extranational forces may intervene is the notorious tug of war between communist and capitalist power blocs for commitment of neutralist or "third world" nations to one side or the other. This rivalry runs the gamut from military or insurgency operations to ideological infiltration. It has led one leader of a new nation to declare that even "peaceful co-existence between the two blocs provokes and feeds violence in the colonial countries" (Fanon, 1963, 62–63). The nature of the contest cannot be viewed simplistically. While it may appear that the communists stand to gain from internal disorders in all new nations, actual practice is far more circumspect and sophisticated—certainly for the Russian as distinct from the Chinese version. The demands of foreign policy limit both tactics and strategy at local levels; in India, in the need to keep a firm alliance with Congress Party leaders, Soviet diplomats resolutely looked the other way when the Congress crushed a Communist revolt in Kerala and when Indian Communists were jailed in major cities of the subcontinent. A similar situation obtained in Egypt. Along parallel lines, the Soviets have accepted "national democracy" in Africa as a sort of temporary substitute or transitional stage to a socialist revolution, and have been careful not to alienate nationalist leaders with obvious popular control of the masses, preferring rather to push for provisional goals like anti-Americanism by playing the neocolonial theme to widen freedom of action in the future. By overstepping this cautious policy in Guinea, the Soviets suffered a setback which reinforced the efficacy of a more global policy. In Latin America the attempt to enter popular fronts has not been notably successful and the push from Cuban revolutionaries has led to more militant activities chiefly in the universities which do have some outreach into the peasantry. However, in Latin America as a whole, the attraction for the peasant-oriented Mao doctrines is becoming more widespread (For an extended discussion, cf. Cyril E. Black and Thomas P. Thornton, 1964, esp. part III).

As for the relationship of the communists to ethnic minorities in the emergent nations, a tenable hypothesis is that where such minorities have already made a bid for power in the country, and the American sphere of influence is not of strategic importance, the communists will not exploit this internal division for their own purposes. On the other hand, where a minority has held a previously quiescent position but the nation as a whole is compliant to American interests, the communists will seek to mobilize the discontent of the minority to serve the dual purpose of embarrassing the local government and weakening the American position in the land. An example of the former type appears in Iraq where the Kurds openly espoused their own brand of nationalism and secessionism; however, for the USSR to support this divisive movement would have alienated Iraqi society as a whole and turned the Iraqis irrevocably against the Soviets. Therefore the Russians turned a deaf ear to Kurdish demands (Manfred Halpern in Black and Thornton, *op. cit.*, 310). Conversely in Thailand which has been allied with American policy, tribes of Laotian stock in the northeast and the Shan in the northwest have been isolated from the central Thais for some time; currently they appear to be trained for insurgency operations against the Thai state for larger strategic anti-American purposes, some of which are related to the Vietnam conflict (Harrison Salisbury in *New York Times*, June 26, 1966). These two examples may, of course, reflect the differences in foreign policy of the Russian as distinct from the Chinese version and might furnish an alternative hypothesis.

It would be one-sided to approach this question purely from the communist angle. United States support for the military in South America appears to be based on the notion that local armies are the strongest bulwark against communism and thus will represent United States needs in the area. "Simply put, the present turn to counterinsurgency as a style of politics marks a return to military solutions for economic problems, rather than economic solutions for military problems" (Horowitz, 1966, 285). Likewise the operations of the CIA in preparing anti-Castro

Cubans to make a military landing on the Bay of Pigs, their backing of one Laotian leader against another, and their attempted overthrow of Sukarno of Indonesia are now part of the record (Schlesinger, Jr., 1965, 223–97, 325–27, 532). It is significant that "The CIA had its own political desks and military staffs; it had in effect its own foreign service, its own air force, even, on occasion, its own combat forces" (Schlesinger, *op. cit.*, 427). There seems to be little evidence that such forces have been used directly to support any minority group militancy toward a ruling regime, so far.

Regarding other techniques, it is worth commenting that foreign aid to developing countries by the United States, however mixed with humanitarian motives, has included generous grants for the local military, has been presented to Congress and the public as a mode of combating communism abroad, has been specifically used to shore up weak political structures to preserve their "independence," and has often included explicit provisions for promoting private American investment abroad (Schlesinger, *op. cit.*, 594–600). Eventually, economic aid by both the United States and the USSR has proved to be another form of rivalry for commitment in the cold war, with each side scoring "points" against the other in a propaganda contest. This tug of war keeps internal divisions of nation-states alive, with important repercussions for both domestic and foreign policy of the new nations.

A third type of manipulation across national borders can be illustrated by the religious solidarities that span several countries, or, in some cases, even continents. Thus the attempt of the Vatican to send a plenipotentiary to Poland on the occasion of a national anniversary in 1966 met with countermeasures by the Communist government, at the same time widening the breach between the regime and its Catholic adherents ("Double Anniversary," *Newsweek*, July 11, 1966). In the Indian province of Kerala in 1960, when the political rivalry between Communist and Congress Parties became overheated, Catholic Christians, though in a minority, became the most militant supporters of the Congress, apparently with the blessing, if not the actual intervention of the hierarchy from outside (Author's interview data, 1960).

Similar use of religious loyalties to promote political ends has been characteristic of Islam in the Mediterranean world. Thus a

Syrian leader makes it quite clear that citizenship in the Arab regions will be a function of religious affiliation in the following pronouncement:

> We, the Syrians, advocates of Arab unity, consider ourselves to be a part of the Arab nation and consider our Syrian father-land to be part of the greater Arab fatherland. Our republic today is a member of the Arab League and will tomorrow, by the grace of God, be part of a single Arab state. According to the lowest estimate the Arabs number seventy million of whom sixty-eight are Muslims and two are Christians, and all the states of the Arab League (except for Lebanon which has a special position) either specify that the religion of the state is Islam in their constitutions, as is the case with Egypt, Iraq and Jordan; or else their existence is implicitly based on that fact, as is the case with Saudi Arabia and Yemen. Thus the establishment of Islam as the state religion will be a strong factor for unity be-tween ourselves and our Arab brethren and a formal symbol of the *rapprochement* between the states of the Arab League. (Sheikh Mustafa as-Sibai in al-Monar, quoted by G. E. von Grunebaum in Richard N. Frye [ed.], 1957, 21)

Likewise Cairo has made religion a tool of foreign policy by setting up an Islamic Congress that stresses the key role of Al Azhar University as the major center of Muslim learning, des-patching its teachers to centers like Nigeria and Somaliland (Vati-kiotis, 1961, 191). Scholarships for the university draw students from Muslim lands throughout Africa and Asia, even as far away as the Philippines ("Filipino Muslims," 1964). Pakistan, as a Muslim state, has attracted both military and political leader-ship away from the Muslim minority in India (Smith, 1957, 276). In Southeast Asia, Buddhism appears in a new political guise, now supporting, now opposing communist aspirations in several coun-tries (Benz, 1965).

Other illustrations abound, but the above will suffice to show that the assessment of societal forces in any nation-state cannot consider the social system as hermetically sealed, but must take account of it *both* as a semiautonomous center, and as a field of intersecting forces from without, particularly when the latter influence internal divisions that have direct or indirect repercus-sions on intergroup relations. The influence of this variable needs careful examination for realistic appraisal in every case, and it is susceptible to power-conflict interpretation as well as to system analysis (Etzioni and Dubow, 1967, 153–58).

A Final Note

The inductive typologies advanced in this volume offer a chance to enlarge and systematize the study of comparative ethnic relations and, at this stage, are exploratory, calling for searching criticism and evaluation. They are instruments of what Kaplan (1964, 17) calls the logic of discovery rather than the logic of proof. In other words, they advance reasons for *entertaining* hypotheses rather than reasons for *accepting* them. And at the outset of the journey, this is a crying need. At the same time, the whole thrust of exposition in the present work is toward the broader vistas that encompass whole societies in which ethnic and racial subcommunities are in process of ever-changing adjustment. At the macrosociological level, this all too brief exposition aims to show that (1) intergroup research on a comparative basis can contribute to our general sociological knowledge about the ways societies cope with major problems of integration and conflict, and (2) that the germinal ideas of polarity and dialectical relations in Simmel's sketch of a general theory can be the tentative basis for flexible exploration of intergroup relations in shifting situational contexts. I can only hope that the translation of his lively and imaginative insights into the focussed and mundane forms of investigation demanded in our day may not wholly dim the excitement and the promise of new discoveries still over the horizon.

· NOTES ·

1. Some notice must be given to those immediately observable pluralities discernible at the common sense level. Here the gross differences stand out at the first approach to the data as in Geertz's classification of plural groupings in the "new states." Five patterns emerge: (1) the majority-minority pattern where the dominant group has a clear numerical majority with the subordinates a demographic minority (Ceylon

with Singhalese and Tamils); (2) a central-peripheral pattern with a dominant group geographically or politically central set over against a number of fairly large peripheral groups (Indonesia with Javanese versus other island peoples, or Burma with Burmese versus Shans, Karens, etc. in the north); (3) a bi-polar pattern of two nearly evenly matched groups of major size (Malaysia with Malays and Chinese, or Lebanon with Muslims and Christians); (4) the gradated type with a number of large groups and others diminishing in size to those of smaller and smaller magnitude (India, the Philippines, Nigeria, and Kenya); and (5) multiple ethnic fragmentation (the Congo, and perhaps a number of African states). These distinctions are based on obvious, immediate, spatial, or demographic considerations at the opposite pole from M. G. Smith's analytical and structural categories. Let us call them *inspectional* and *structural* pluralism respectively, the former being an inductive taxonomy at a low level of abstraction, the latter an analytical set of distinctions at a high level of abstraction. Perhaps Geertz's inspectional pluralism has more utility for conflict theory, while Smith's structural pluralism has at least some affinity with systems analysis. Both, however, take their place in the dialectic of investigation and Geertz's typology can be held in reserve as an important tool of research for future productiveness (Geertz, 1963, 117–18).

2. A paradox as old as Zeno (sixth century B.C.).
3. The same, of course, can be asserted of comparative sociology as a whole (Marsh, 1967, 20).
4. The symbols CT and SA used throughout, indicate that the proposition in question is more closely related by inference to conflict theory (CT) or system analysis (SA) as theories of higher generality. If both symbols appear together, the one given first has the greater (but not the exclusive) explanatory power.
5. These examples are selected from the propositional inventory in Robin M. Williams, Jr., *The Reduction of Intergroup Tensions* (New York: Social Science Research Council, 1947). Numbers following each proposition refer to the numeration given in Williams' book. Used by permission.
6. This trend toward a more extensive use of foreign sources for summarization purposes is sharply reversed in a third survey by Westie who mentions 101 titles as his primary sources, only 11 of which refer to studies conducted wholly outside the United States (Westie, 1964).
7. A more recent contribution of the same author presents another series of such propositions embedded in the context of separate research operations rather than in codified form (Williams, 1964).
8. Quoted from Zetterberg, 1963, 33–34.
9. Quoted from Blalock, 1967, 204 ff.
10. The reference is to H. J. Nieboer, *Slavery as an Industrial System* (The Hague, Martinus Nijhoff, 1910).
11. Cf. the author's earlier work, i.e., Blalock, 1964.
12. For example, Blalock's starting point is clearly with individuals rather

than with systems or societies (cf. especially, Blalock, 1967, 21–26). It is especially interesting to note that Blalock defends this preference on methodological rather than strictly theoretical grounds. However, since the two approaches are not in watertight compartments, we are again forced to recognize a dialectical relation here as elsewhere.

13. This in spite of the fact that a few macrosociological contributions in the last decade have made their way against the current, receiving lengthy attention from Sorokin (1966, 177) in an attempt to right the balance.

14. Though, needless to say, each one makes extensive use of the field researches *already* completed.

15. It is undeniable that *Political Man* includes at least a modicum of Lipset's own field research on trade union democracy, but the book as a whole is best categorized as a *tour de force* of secondary analysis.

16. This proposition is stated at a rather broad, comprehensive level, but it can be given greater specificity of detail by means of Hartz's hypothesis (Hartz, 1964) that in colonization, the stage of development reached by the parent society will be reflected in the sort of society established by the colonizers in their new frontier society. Colonizers leaving a home society in Stage 1 will create institutions and adopt ideologies in their new environment that are congruent with Stage 1. Those who leave at Stage 2 when different currents of thought and different social structures appear will produce new forms congruent with Stage 2. This hypothesis is worth exploring for the sequence of voluntary migration as well, though it has received little attention in that context.

17. For the nature and incidence of such groups in Southeast Asia, cf. LeBar et al., 1964 (these are not listed by countries of residence). For a simpler enumeration of such groups in Africa, nation by nation, cf. Junod, 1963.

18. Since Despres found a high degree of enclosure or separation between the two groups at both local and national levels, their almost sole common participation at the national political level precipitated violent conflict. This substantiates the first condition of our exploratory hypothesis but not the second, since neither of these groups had more than limited control over the other's scarce rewards. The relationship was therefore one of intense competition and rivalry.

19. The South African authorities are exploiting this feature *a l'outrance* in the Bantustan programs.

20. Further confirmation of Blumer's conclusions comes from more recent African developments. South Africa pursues her apartheid policy under fire from sub-Saharan nations in the Organization of African Unity. Recent independence for Lesotho, Botswana, and Swaziland, has created an association of these three states all dependent on South Africa for their economic existence. "All three have a customs union with South Africa which collects import duties for them. They use South Africa's currency, the Rand, and they form an inseparable part of the South African network of communications and power. South African ad-

visers are scattered throughout their administrative departments, and South African finance is moving in on development plans" (Mostert, 1967). Over half of Lesotho's labor force works in South Africa. (*Ibid.*) If these three nations join the Organization of African Unity, their indebtedness to South Africa can so well influence their interests that they can be a bloc helping to neutralize the hostility of other African states to South Africa and thus strengthen the latter's hand to continue the apartheid policy.

21. Blumer also casts doubt on the assertion that race relations become typically competitive in the transitional period since there is the greatest variability in this respect (Blumer, *op. cit.*, 236–37).

22. It is true that consensus on prestige ranking of occupations in industrial societies is remarkable, as Inkeles and Rossi have shown (1956). Corresponding studies in Brazil and the Philippines, while purporting to show congruent rankings, are only partly successful. In Brazil, the subjects employed to do the grading were University students from a relatively upper stratum and hence not representative (Hutchinson, 1957). In the Philippines the broader based sample of judges was counterbalanced by the fact that only about half the occupations ranked corresponded with the lists employed for industrial societies (Tiryakian, 1958).

23. For these three types as well as the replication type cf. March, 1967, 41 ff.

24. Here such questions are relevant as, "What kind of education should our kind of people receive? Their kind of people?" "What kind of jobs should our men prepare for? Their men?" "What kind of government posts should our men have? Their men?" These and other types of data useful for field research are suggested briefly in Appendix 2.

· REFERENCES ·

Allport, Gordon W., *The Nature of Prejudice*. Cambridge, Mass.: Addison-Wesley, 1954.

Apter, David, "A Comparative Method for the Study of Politics," *American Journal of Sociology*, 64 (November 1958), 221–37.

Benedict, Burton, "Stratification in Plural Societies," *American Anthropologist*, 64 (1962), 1235–46.

Benz, Ernst, *Buddhism or Communism, Which Holds the Future of Asia?* Richard and Clara Winston (trans.). New York: Doubleday, 1965.

Black, Cyril E., and Thomas P. Thornton (eds.), *Communism and Revolution, The Strategic Use of Political Violence*. Princeton, N.J.: Princeton University Press, 1964.

Blalock, Hubert M., *Causal Inferences in Non-Experimental Research*. Chapel Hill, N.C.: University of North Carolina Press, 1964.

——, *Toward a Theory of Minority Group Relations*. New York: Wiley, 1967.

Blumer, Herbert, "Industrialisation and Race Relations," in Guy Hunter (ed.), *Industrialisation and Race Relations, A Symposium.* London and New York: Oxford University Press, 1965.

Despres, Leo A., *Cultural Pluralism and Nationalist Politics in British Guiana.* Chicago: Rand McNally, 1967.

Deutsch, Karl W., "The Theoretical Basis of Data Programs," in Richard L. Merritt and Stein Rokkan (eds.), *Comparing Nations, The Use of Quantitative Data in Cross-National Research.* New Haven and London: Yale University Press, 1966.

"Double Anniversary, Communist-Catholic Clash," *Newsweek,* 68 (July 11, 1966), 42.

Etzioni, Amitai, and Frederic L. DuBow, "Some Workpoints for a Macro-sociology," in Samuel Z. Klausner (ed.), *The Study of Total Societies.* New York: Anchor Books, 1967.

Fanon, Frantz, *The Wretched of the Earth.* New York: Grove, 1963.

"Filipino Muslims," *Hibbert Journal,* 63 (Autumn 1964), 39–41.

Fox, Thomas, and S. M. Miller, "Occupational Stratification and Mobility," in Richard L. Merritt and Stein Rokkan (eds.), *Comparing Nations, The Use of Quantitative Data in Cross-National Research.* New Haven and London: Yale University Press, 1966.

Frazier, E. Franklin, *Black Bourgeoisie.* New York: Free Press, 1957.

Geertz, Clifford, "The Integrative Revolution," in Clifford Geertz (ed.), *Old Societies and New States.* New York: Free Press, 1963.

Germani, Gino, "Social Change and Intergroup Conflicts," in Irving L. Horowitz (ed.), *The New Sociology.* New York: Oxford University Press, 1964.

Hartz, Louis, *The Founding of New Societies.* New York: Harcourt, Brace & World, 1964.

Haug, Marie R., "Social and Cultural Pluralism as a Concept in Social System Analysis," *American Journal of Sociology,* 73 (November 1967), 294–304.

Hickman, John Marshall, *The Aymara of Chicera, Peru: Persistence and Change in a Bicultural Context.* PhD. Thesis, Cornell University, 1963. Used by permission.

Horowitz, Irving L., *Three Worlds of Development, The Theory and Practice of International Stratification,* New York: Oxford University Press, 1966.

Hunter, Guy, *South-East Asia, Race, Culture and Nation.* New York and London: Oxford University Press, 1966.

Hutchinson, Bertram, "The Social Grading of Occupations in Brazil," *British Journal of Sociology,* 8 (July 1957), 176–89.

Inkeles, Alex, and Peter Rossi, "National Comparisons of Occupational Prestige," *American Journal of Sociology,* 61 (January 1956), 329–39.

Junod, Violane I., *The Handbook of Africa.* New York: New York University Press, 1963.

Kaplan, Abraham, *The Conduct of Inquiry, Methodology for Behavioral Science.* San Francisco: Chandler, 1964.

Landecker, Werner S., "Types of Integration and their Measurement." *American Journal of Sociology,* 56 (January 1951), 323–40.

LeBar, Frank M., Gerald C. Hickey, and John Musgrave (eds.), *Ethnic Groups of Mainland Southeast Asia.* New Haven: Human Relations Area Files Press, 1964.

LeVine, Robert A., "Anthropology and the Study of Conflict: an Introduction," *Journal of Conflict Resolution,* 5 (March 1961), 3–15.

Lipset, Seymour M., *The First New Nation, The United States in Historical and Comparative Perspective.* New York: Basic Books, 1963.

———, *Political Man, The Social Bases of Politics.* New York: Anchor Books, 1963.

———, and Reinhard Bendix, *Social Mobility in Industrial Society.* Berkeley and Los Angeles: University of California Press, 1960.

McKinney, John C., *Constructive Typology and Social Theory.* New York: Appleton-Century-Crofts, 1966.

Marsh, Robert M., *Comparative Sociology, A Codification of Cross-Societal Analysis.* New York: Harcourt, Brace & World, 1967.

Mishkin, Bernard, "The Contemporary Quechus," in Julian H. Steward (ed.), *The Handbook of South American Indians,* II. Washington D.C.: Bureau of American Ethnology, Bulletin 143, 1946–1948.

Mostert, Noel, "Africa: New Nations and New Alignments," *Reporter,* 36, 13 (June 29, 1967), 27–30.

Myrdal, Gunnar, *Asian Drama, An Inquiry into the Poverty of Nations.* 3 vols. New York: Pantheon, 1968.

Popper, Karl, *The Logic of Scientific Discovery.* New York: Basic Books, 1959.

Salisbury, Harrison, "Unrest in the Hills Besets South Asia," *New York Times,* June 26, 1966.

Schlesinger, A. M., Jr., *A Thousand Days.* Boston: Houghton Mifflin, 1965.

Shibutani, Tamotsu, and Kian M. Kwan, *Ethnic Stratification, A Comparative Approach.* New York: Macmillan, 1965.

Simpson, George E., and J. Milton Yinger, *Racial and Cultural Minorities.* 3rd ed. New York: Harper & Row, 1965.

Smith, Wilfred C., *Islam in Modern History.* Princeton, N.J.: Princeton University Press, 1957.

Sorokin, Pitirim A., *Sociological Theories of Today.* New York: Harper & Row, 1966.

Spicer, Edward H. (ed.), *Human Problems in Technological Change.* New York: Russell Sage Foundation, 1952.

Tiryakian, Edward A., "The Prestige Evaluation of Occupations in an Underdeveloped Country: The Philippines," *American Journal of Sociology,* 63 (January 1958), 390–99.

Trager, Frank M., *Burma, Kingdom to Republic, A Historical and Political Analysis.* New York: Praeger, 1966.

Vander Zanden, James W., *American Minority Relations, The Sociology of Race and Ethnic Groups.* 2nd ed. New York: Ronald Press, 1966.

van den Berghe, Pierre L., *Race and Racism,* New York: Wiley, 1967.

Vatikiotis, P. J., *The Egyptian Army in Politics.* Bloomington, Ind.: Indiana University Press, 1961.

von Grunebaum, G. E., "Problems of Muslim Nationalism," in Richard N. Frye (ed.), *Islam and the West.* 's-Gravenhage, Holland: Mouton, 1957.

Warner, W. Lloyd, "American Class and Caste," *American Journal of Sociology,* 42 (September 1936), 234–37.

Westie, Frank R., "Race and Ethnic Relations," in R. E. L. Faris (ed.), *Handbook of Modern Sociology.* Chicago: Rand McNally, 1964.

Williams, Robin M., Jr., *The Reduction of Intergroup Tensions.* New York: Social Science Research Council, 1947.

————, "Racial and Cultural Relations," in Joseph B. Gittler (ed.), *Review of Sociology*. New York: Wiley, 1957.

————, *Strangers Next Door*. Englewood Cliffs, N.J.: Prentice-Hall, 1964.

Zetterberg, Hans L., *On Theory and Verification in Sociology*. Rev. ed. New York: Bedminster Press, 1963.

Znaniecki, Florian, *Modern Nationalities*. Urbana, Ill.: University of Illinois Press, 1952.

Appendix 1

*Colloquy
with Colleagues*

Although the topical content of the preceding chapters is focussed on a particular subfield of investigation, i.e., ethnic and race relations, my aim is to present this as a major concern of sociology as a whole, for *all* sociologists, and to draw specialized themes into the main stream of universal issues in the social sciences. In the main body of the work, therefore, the target audience has been extensive and far-reaching—at least wide enough to attract some hitherto uncommitted neophytes and advanced students into an exciting area of exploration. Such is the hope, at any rate.

However, such an approach, like any other, has the defects of its virtues. The more I reflect on what I have been forced to leave out, in the earnest effort to be inclusive, the more ironical the outcome appears. By placing such ostensibly defensible limits on the exposition, I have unintentionally built up—as a by-product—a gradual accumulation of residual comments that ought to be shared with fellow specialists, a few things that can be said *en famille*, as it were. And since, in the production of books the Appendix has become the traditional repository for all left-overs, there can surely be no harm in assigning the present miscellany to my own confederates, i.e., to those who have committed themselves to a life-interest in the study of ethnic and race relations, with special attention to those among them who are contemplating field research in the future.

Deliberate Omissions

There are a number of topics that have been purposely excluded throughout this book. One is an explicit focus on issues of ethnic identity which have perennial interest for so many writers. To a certain degree I have given this *implicit* recognition in the discussion of centripetal and centrifugal tendencies where, however, I have kept the main focus on interactive relationships. There is no reason why this implicit feature cannot become explicit in the solution of a particular research problem so long as one keeps central the consequences of identity feelings and attitudes for reciprocal action.

For a somewhat different reason, I have given no attention to detailed ethnographic or descriptive monographs devoted to ethnic communities or subsocieties, in spite of the immense contributions such studies have made and will continue to make for research on a comparative basis. Maximum benefits from such investigations, however, are likely to come when they are fitted into a cross-national framework after they have been completed, or can be incorporated into such a framework in projected future research. Without this wider relevance, they can too easily degenerate into isolated fragments of mostly exotic significance.

A number of other concerns have contributed fractional data for ethnic relations—the list grows long: family patterns, biological race differences, intelligence testing, comparative crime rates, civil liberties, intermarriage, marginality, ecological distribution, and countless others. These scattered remnants give the neophyte (or even the seasoned specialist) an impression of unrelieved variety in which each inquirer pursues a path of his own, unrelated to central issues. By eliminating such problems, I have endeavored to keep attention fixed on themes that, in my opinion, are most important for basic research.

While questions of policy are implicit throughout—and there is no intention either to downgrade them or the "action research" that often fortifies them—I am convinced that in the long run, the strategy rather than the tactics of policy will profit immeasurably from basic comparative analysis. This, of course, is a value assumption, a faith if you will, but one that many social scientists apparently share. How widespread this assumption is in the world at large is quite another question. In an era where ethnic relations have precipitated so many emergencies, so many dramatic incidents, and so many crackling brushfires all over the world, the voice of basic research is pretty well drowned out by cries for quick solutions, many of them sounding like new reprisals. In such an atmosphere, support for basic research is highly problematical, even among agencies and foundations that ostensibly espouse it. The launching of these modest proposals is premised on the belief that even this first step can begin a cumulative process that will prove itself as secular changes gradually bring us a more favorable climate.

Research Design

The use of multinational designs in comparative research has gradually increased in the last few years. Close examination of these studies will repay the effort, both to reveal how others solve the large-scale problems arising, and to observe pitfalls to be avoided in the future. Notable examples are Almond and Verba's study of civic culture (1963), Buchanan and Cantril's research into common ideas about foreign peoples (1953), explorations by the Organization for Comparative Social Research in seven countries of Western Europe (Rokkan, 1955), the Whiting investigation of comparative childrearing methods (1963), or Campbell and LeVine's outline of research on ethnocentrism (1961). In reviewing these and other similar designs, however, it is well to note that each of them more or less stands alone as a self-contained study of a limited problem; there is little if any provision for making any single research a stepping stone to future investigation. What seems to be emerging is a further demand for multinational designs *in succession* so that research becomes a continuous process. Only when such designs are planned so that each multinational research builds on the results of the previous one will it be possible to reap the full benefit of large-scale effort. Hence the importance of institutions or research centers that survive well beyond the lifetime of individuals or teams engaged in singular efforts, however rewarding.

Such ideal plans must, of course, be envisaged as final goals, though at the same time it remains necessary to be critical and realistic about absolute counsels of perfection. Field conditions have shattered too many over-neat formulations, and provisions must be made for this. The dilemma between rigidity of method and flexibility of operation cannot be escaped. If the investigator in the field is put in a straitjacket without a chance to exploit new and unsuspected opportunities, he may dutifully carry out his assignment knowing full well that the resulting data are faulty or meaningless. On the other hand, complete freedom to explore at will can bring results that have little relevance for the original problem to be solved. Complex, rigid designs, as Hyman so well remarks, "are not suited to overseas exploration since they require a great deal of prior knowledge and precise formulation . . . We may well be able to plan some useful arrangements suitable for looser problems, feasible for the beginner[1] who has to work under difficult conditions, that may nevertheless reduce considerably the ambiguity of his findings" (Hyman, 1964, 160). Probably Ward's suggestion is a reasonable one when he contends that research plans passing the scrutiny of awards committees should be held lightly and be freely modified since "no one really knows in advance what is and what is not a feasible research project in a developing society" (Ward, 1964, 52). Similar flexibility in theory construction is called for as the spotlight moves from one situation to another. It is for this reason that elaborate chains of inference from either systems analysis or power-conflict theory have been avoided in our general presentation. They constitute two main arsenals, but neither is a commanding general.

Data Collection

Perhaps a few words about data-collecting bodies or agencies may not be out of place. To begin with, the rapid growth of area centers in the last decade certainly presents the student of comparative ethnic research with a richer and more reliable source of data than would have been thought possible a generation ago. Prior acquaintance with the research collected and catalogued in these centers is becoming a prerequisite for field investigation in almost any overseas country.[2] At the same time some caution is needed. At the outset it is well to keep in mind the distinction between an *area* specialist and a *problem* specialist. The former has his chief commitment to a particular region and the extension of knowledge about the peoples and institutions of the area, whether it be Southeast Asia, Oceania, Sub-Saharan Africa, or Latin America. The latter focuses on a problem or field of investigation that will display different cultural and institutional embodiments as he moves from one area to another. If the problem specialist immerses himself too intensively or uncritically in the relatively unique features of a single region in response to the specialized interests of the "old area hands" who form an attractive ingroup, he may find that his center of interest shifts to theirs as he becomes drawn into a kind of area-vortex. This is not in any way to deny the legitimacy and, indeed, the necessity for area specialization. It is only to suggest that there is an equal necessity for problem specialists who can keep their area interests instrumental to their main task.[3]

Similar unanticipated limitations can narrow the horizon of the problem specialist even in the absence of an area center. Weiner remarks that in a surprising number of cases, the social scientist preparing to work in a particular country, will, as a graduate student, avoid courses and seminars in American institutions and also the opportunity to work on domestic research projects in favor of more intensive studies of the society where he plans to do field research, supplemented, perhaps, by additional study in international relations. The upshot of this one-sided preparation is that "the young social scientist who leaves for his first overseas field research is likely to have less field research training than his colleagues undertaking a research project in the United States" (Weiner, 1964, 106).

The proliferation of sample surveys throughout the world has produced data collections with far more information than anyone has yet exploited for secondary analysis. Both the Roper Public Opinion Research Center at Williams College and the Survey

Research Center at the University of California in Berkeley have acquisitions particularly valuable for such purposes, the latter presenting more materials from developing nations and somewhat more selective on theoretical or methodological grounds.[4] Archives of overseas research in the political field including more than restricted survey materials are also especially rich in data. The Inter-University Consortium for Political Research utilizing the facilities of the Survey Research Center of the University of Michigan now has fifty participating universities, and the Yale Political Data Program is another notable repository which not only engaged in extensive data processing but has published its *World Handbook of Political and Social Indicators* (Russett, 1964). Documentary research facilities for the developing areas are quite extensive and cannot be enumerated here; they are admirably summarized by Coleman (1964, 189–234). Several interdisciplinary research institutes at major universities have a wealth of information that is cross-national in character: The Institute of Communications Research at the University of Illinois, the Center for International Studies at the Massachusetts Institute of Technology, the Institute for Social Research at the University of North Carolina, the Stanford University Studies in International Conflict and Integration, and the International Population and Urban Research Program at the University of California are perhaps the most striking examples. Organization of retrieval systems like the General Inquirer and SYNTOL are now fairly well established, promising increased access to information unavailable at local levels (Scheuch and Stone, F. G. Levy, 1966). Action to make survey and other data accessible to social scientists of all nations has already been initiated by the International Social Science Council, the International Committee on Social Science Documentation, and UNESCO (Rokkan, 1966).

It is important that social scientists engaged in research on comparative ethnic relations do not allow themselves to be relegated to a passive role in the use of such data collections. Particularly in the case of retrieval systems, they have a responsibility to see that categories significant for their work be incorporated in the indexing of cross-national data.

Ideological Hang-Ups

Perhaps most fateful of all, field research in the area of comparative ethnic relations is a highly sensitive subject, no matter where
it is investigated. In addition to the usual obstacles that face the
fitting of designs to national conditions (which are formidable
enough in their own right), there is an internal recalcitrance to
having "outsiders" wash the dirty linen of a country in public
so that it lies open to international inspection. This is true both
for the "powers that be" in each society, and for the members of
ethnic or minority groups who may have an equally vested interest in secrecy and an equally firm conviction that no outsiders
can truly understand the full meaning of what takes place in their
home locality. Kipling's lines express these sentiments quite accurately:

> The Stranger within my gate
> He may be true or kind
> But he does not talk my talk—
> I cannot feel his mind.
> I see the face and the eyes and the mouth,
> But not the soul behind.
>
> The men of my own stock
> They may do ill or well,
> But they tell the lies I am wonted to,
> They are used to the lies I tell;
> And we do not need interpreters
> When we go to buy and sell.[5]

If the resistance to research is not a concerted one (where both
those in upper and lower positions join forces in a sabotage
effort), the situation may become even more complicated if one
side cooperates and the other holds back—for perfectly under-
standable reasons. In either case the investigator is on the horns
of a painful dilemma. In order to do his work, he needs sponsorship, and the natural place to begin is with officials in the administration. Without their sanction he may be unable even to
begin his work. However if it appears that he is in any way iden-

tified with the government, members of some ethnic groups may refuse cooperation to one who can do them damage by revealing confidential information to officials. But suppose that the researcher finally convinces them that he is not in league with the administration and that he is sympathetic to their "cause," he then lays himself open to suspicion of being "anti-government" as the authorities become aware of his activities—and they usually do in time. He then runs the risk of being ejected entirely because, in the eyes of officials, he has violated an implied obligation to them, even though this has not been fully specified. In other situations he may come across activity in the ethnic group that is technically illegal. When he does not report this to authorities, they may create serious difficulties since they regard such reporting as his duty; if accounts of such activity appear in his publications, he can well be under fire from the administration for not revealing it earlier, and from his informants who now experience reprisals for deeds that would have remained unknown except for published research. To remain an objective observer—in the eyes of others, let alone oneself—is particularly difficult in this area of research, and especially where neutrality violates the personal code of the investigator.[6] Even if we insist that objectivity and neutrality are not identical (and the distinction must be made) this does not solve the problem of daily decision in the process of research. Not only must the investigator have unusual tact and skill in handling such problems—which, after all, others have solved previously in various ways—but fidelity to his own discipline demands that he leave the field open rather than closed to future research.

Sponsoring Agencies for Research

For these and related reasons, the task of research in comparative ethnic relations cannot be left to UNESCO or any other United Nations agency in spite of plausible reasons for thinking so. Member states, feeling themselves threatened by "premature exposure" of their internal problems could not only halt an investigation already in progress but prevent it from taking place in the beginning. The latter course seems more likely in view of McGranahan's[7] comment:

The United Nations is an organization of states or governments and does not deal directly with populations, except at the
request of governments. As a rule, governments are not interested in having United Nations social scientists undertake opinion polls or attitude studies or content analyses within their
territories, particularly in relation to matters of a political or
semipolitical nature . . . (although) they do welcome international intervention in their economic and social development.
(McGranahan, 1966, 526)

Only an organization detached from official obligations can pursue
a fully scientific course in such a sensitive field, and even then, its
network of arrangements requires the greatest care to prevent
them from smothering research with special provisos.

For the investigator from the United States there is an even
deeper crisis. Not only is the American image abroad increasingly
damaged, necessitating elaborate apologetics even for an innocuous
role, but "The fact that so much international research sponsored
from the United States has emphasized Cold War issues has also
helped to establish abroad the notion that surveys are simply a
tool of intelligence" (Hyman, *op. cit.*, 151). The backlash from
Project Camelot in Chile (Horowitz, 1965) has had repercussions
throughout Latin America as a whole, throwing suspicion on
research sponsored in the United States even when under private
auspices. Revelations in early 1967 of CIA sponsorship for many
seemingly innocent organizations and activities overseas has spread
similar suspicions to authorities in other areas until claims for
disinterested research meet with mounting incredulity. In turn,
this is leading the community of American social scientists to
raise troublesome questions about support for their research,
much of which has come in the past from federal agencies. As
these questions press in upon them, some are recognizing for
the first time that government support brings an implied obligation to sustain government policy in exchange. Others are beginning to reveal (privately rather than publicly) that they have
been visited by intelligence agents in the field with the positive
expectation that researchers will "tell all."[8] It is not even unknown for social scientists to report unintended commitments in
the signing of contracts to divulge confidential information from
their research to official agencies.[9] For any one attempting field
work in such a sensitive area as comparative ethnic relations,

these are facts particularly hard to live down. It is certainly no easier to be regarded as a spy than to be thought a subversive. In today's international climate, both can occur simultaneously.

In order to forestall such objections—and they can be predicted with some certainty—the study of comparative ethnic relations on a world-wide scale may have to cut itself off from an American base and become (as it should be in any case) an association of social scientists from many countries pursuing common aims in collaboration. The most likely link is with the International Social Science Council which has no commitments except to the advance of social science and cooperation in the growth of knowledge. Support for such ongoing research would necessarily be limited to private sources and foundations which might restrict operations for a time until outstanding publications had a cumulative effect. If a center is needed, it should be established at a neutral location like Geneva, Switzerland, where skepticism about national bias would prove insignificant. Collaboration of European colleagues already engaged in the field would bring about cross-fertilization of projects and methods as yet untapped. One thinks of the Centre International des Relations entre Groupes Ethniques[10] in Paris which has already initiated a number of researches, and the community of social scientists in Muenchen under the leadership of Emerich Francis with its central European studies as examples of the genre. The growing interest in problems of national pluralism, both among social scientists and the public at large makes this consummation not an impossible dream but a conceivably possible reality.

· NOTES ·

1. Judging from a number of Hyman's examples, these more flexible designs are by no means confined to beginners.
2. The linguistic equipment furnished by these area centers is not the least of their services and is now taken for granted as part of the preparatory stage for training.
3. Having said this, one must also freely acknowledge that to some degree, at least, "area specialization is a *necessity*, not a choice" and that a scholar who is labelled an area specialist is "more comparatively minded than the huge majority of his colleagues who are in fact narrow North Americanists. The North Americanists are in fact so narrow and pro-

vincial that they don't realize they are . . . the most inveterate of area specialists. Homo Yankee Suburbiansis is equated to Homo Sapiens" (Pierre van den Berghe, personal communication).

4. A notable analysis of these and other data centers with guiding principles for their critical use is given by Converse (1966).

5. "The Stranger," 1933 ed. of Rudyard Kipling's Verse, p. 535.

6. These and other value impingements on field research are sagaciously treated in Barnes (1963) to which the above discussion is greatly indebted.

7. Donald V. McGranahan is Director of the Survey, Research, and Development Branch, United Nations Bureau of Social Affairs.

8. Confidential statements to the author by field workers and those with access to government agencies.

9. Confidential statements to the author by field workers and those with access to government agencies.

10. This center, under the direction of Otto Klineberg, has devoted itself primarily to social-psychological research on attitudes, identity problems, and similar themes. These can well be integrated with and contribute to a wider range of structural problems.

· REFERENCES ·

Almond, Gabriel, and Sidney Verba, *The Civic Culture*. Princeton, N.J.: Princeton University Press, 1963.

Barnes, J. A., "Some Ethical Problems in Modern Fieldwork," *British Journal of Sociology*, 14, No. 2 (June 1963), 118–34.

Buchanan, William, and Hadley Cantril, *How Nations See Each Other*. Urbana, Ill.: University of Illinois Press, 1953.

Campbell, Donald T., and Robert A. LeVine, "A Proposal for Cooperative Cross-Cultural Research on Ethnocentrism," *Journal of Conflict Resolution*, 5 (March 1961), 82–108.

Coleman, James S., *et al.*, "Appendices" (on documentation for developing areas) in Robert E. Ward (ed.), *Studying Politics Abroad*. Boston: Little, Brown, 1964.

Converse, Philip E., "The Availability and Quality of Sample Survey Data in Archives Within the United States," in Richard L. Merritt and Stein Rokkan (eds.), *Comparing Nations, The Use of Quantitative Data in Cross-National Research*. New Haven and London: Yale University Press, 1966.

Horowitz, Irving Louis, "The Life and Death of Project Camelot," *Transaction*, 3, 1 (November/December 1965), 3–7 and 44–47.

Hyman, Herbert H., "Research Design," in Robert E. Ward (ed.), *Studying Politics Abroad*. Boston: Little, Brown, 1964.

Kipling, Rudyard, *Rudyard Kipling's Verse*. London: Hodder & Stoughton, 1933.

Levy, Francis G., "An Outline of Two Systems: SYNTOL and the General Inquirer," in Richard L. Merritt and Stein Rokkan (eds.), *Comparing*

Nations, The Use of Quantitative Data in Cross-National Research. New Haven and London: Yale University Press, 1966.

McGranahan, Donald V., "Comparative Social Research in the United Nations," in Richard L. Merritt and Stein Rokkan (eds.), *Comparing Nations, The Use of Quantitative Data in Cross-National Research.* New Haven and London: Yale University Press, 1966.

Rokkan, Stein, "An Experiment in Cross-National Research Cooperation," and "Party Preference and Opinion Patterns in Western Europe," *International Social Science Bulletin,* 7 (1955), 645–46 and 575–96.

———, "International Action to Advance Comparative Research: The Role of UNESCO," in Richard L. Merritt and Stein Rokkan (eds.), *Comparing Nations, The Use of Quantitative Data in Cross-National Research.* New Haven and London: Yale University Press, 1966.

Russett, Bruce M., *et al., World Handbook of Political and Social Indicators.* New Haven and London: Yale University Press, 1964.

Scheuch, Erwin K., and Philip J. Stone, "Retrieval Systems for Data Archives: The General Inquirer," in Richard L. Merritt and Stein Rokkan (eds.), *Comparing Nations, The Use of Quantitative Data in Cross-National Research.* New Haven and London: Yale University Press, 1966.

Ward, Robert E., "Common Problems in Field Research," in Robert E. Ward (ed.), *Studying Politics Abroad, Field Research in the Developing Areas.* Boston: Little, Brown, 1964.

Weiner, Myron, "Political Interviewing," in Robert E. Ward (ed.), *Studying Politics Abroad, Field Research in the Developing Areas.* Boston: Little, Brown, 1964.

Whiting, Beatrice (ed.), *Six Cultures.* New York: Wiley, 1963.

Appendix 2

❦

Types of Data Collection
Required for Testing
Major Propositions

I. Demographic and Economic Variables
for Population Groups

1. Size, age composition, birth rates, death rates, family size, rates of increase.
2. Occupational distribution of population groups: agricultural, mercantile, commercial, industrial wage workers, managerial, entrepreneurial.
3. Income levels for occupational segments and relation to national levels.
4. Urban-rural differentials of population groups and occupational segments of such groups.
5. Location of economic elites—managerial? Entrepreneurial? From what population groups?
6. Cultural definitions of spending, saving, investment, and occupational preferences in different population groups.

II. Educational Variables for Different Population Groups

1. Literacy rates for population groups; comparison with national figures.
2. Types of public and private schools at primary, secondary, and upper levels, including trade, agricultural, and technical schools.
3. Attendance in each type of school by members of each population group.
4. Estimation of typical routes from education to occupation for those with each type of schooling.
5. Cultural definition of educational preferences by members of different population groups: agreement or disagreement on membership of "educational elites."

III. Kinship Organization for Different Population Groups

1. Differentials in family structure in various population groups: consanguine-conjugal variations, endogamous-exogamous rules, forms of inheritance, etc.
2. Differential effects of plural family structures on occupational selection.
3. Differential effects of plural family structures on school attendance, types of schooling, or length of schooling.
4. Kinship hierarchies and elite families in traditional forms for each population group.
5. Effects of plural family structures and attendant values on urbanization, occupational achievement, and vertical mobility.

IV. Political and Military Dimensions in Relation to Different Population Groups

1. How many people from each population group are in governmental positions: in administrative, military, civil service, legislative, and judiciary posts?

2. Estimate the loci for authoritative decisions in governmental structure. What appear to be the elite decision-making units and where is their location in the government (administration, military, legislature, or cliques within these sectors)? How does this vary with regard to types of issues?

3. Assess representation from each population group in the political elites. Does this change over time?

4. What is the relation of charismatic figures to elites? Their derivation from what population groups? Dependence on such groups for support?

5. Estimate differential demands on government for types of decision with respect to issues, and with respect to representation on the part of different population groups. Are conflicts plural or do they polarize into major cleavages?

6. Assess the role of political parties as channels for effective demand for decisions on issues and channels of access to governmental positions. Participation of different population groups through voting, access to party machinery, and leadership positions.

7. Estimate typical routes of mobility through the party to governmental positions (of both elites and nonelites) from different population groups.

8. What is the relation of 6 to previous economic, educational, and kinship patterns?

V. Associational and Communication Networks

1. Mapping of voluntary associations and differential participation in them from the population groups. Are such associations primarily ethnic or interethnic? What are the forms of each? How do members of elites as noted in I, II, III, and IV participate?

2. How do associational groups function as independent centers for formulation of opinion and political demands? How are they related to political parties?

3. Newspaper circulation and its relation to differential literacy patterns with estimate of differential impact on population groups, voluntary associations, etc.

4. Estimation of control over newspaper content and where this control is exercised: i.e., within governmental elite, economic elite, or other, and how this relates to the elite provenance from any one of the population groups. Linguistic variations may be important here.

5. Examination of radio stations, programs of broadcasting, the dispersal and distribution of radio sets, and listening habits in various population groups.

6. Estimation of control over radio broadcasting content, by whom exercised, patterns of selectivity in programming, possible targets of communication, and the like, with respect to various population groups. Linguistic variations. Place of the elite in control.

7. Spread of influence of radio communication over different segments of the population and its impact on public opinion with respect to political and other issues.

8. General political implications of communications processes revealed in examination of newspaper and radio output.

VI. Stratification Patterns in Reference to Different Population Groups

1. Differential ranking *within* each population group on various parameters like economic, prestige, and political factors, and comparison with the positions of elite already determined in I, II, III, and IV.

2. Differential ranking *between* population groups (ranking of groups as a whole) on the same parameters. The relation of this ranking to the elite positions mentioned above.

3. Estimation of those who do the major ranking for the entire society. To what extent is this a fairly general consensus, and to what extent is it imposed by dominant groups or coalitions of groups?

4. Assessment of major forms of dominance and subordination among and between population groups as a whole. Possible overlapping with elite systems already determined. Forms of permeability or impermeability.

5. Differential singling out of population groups as salient minori-

ties by stigmatization and/or forms of discrimination such as:
Segregation
Social distance systems
Restrictions on occupation or occupational mobility
Restrictions on education, quota systems, etc.
Restrictions on political participation, citizenship, migration
Language restrictions barring access to occupational or governmental positions
Withdrawal of police protection and encouragement of mass action against subordinates
Use of channels of communication to spread rumors, accusations, etc.

VII. Belief Systems in Dominant and Subordinate Groups

1. Assessment of belief systems in dominant groups through quota sampling interviews with respect to:
Group superiority themes, racism, cultural or historical eminence, etc.
National unity themes related to justification for group dominance
Social distance themes vs. assimilation themes
Legitimizing policies of imposed authority
2. Assessment of belief systems in subordinate groups (using similar methods) with respect to:
Reactive themes of protest
Views of legitimacy of power wielded by dominants
Themes of goals connected with resistance to superimposed authority
Ideological goals connected with resistance to superimposed authority
3. Estimation of group ideologies colored by extra-societal norms, values and ideas: communist, socialist, cooperative, "labor movement," "development" schemes. Influence of such ideologies in both dominant and subordinate groups, and their relation to political demands ascertained in IV.

4. Assessment of ideological conflicts and their potential for collective behavior outbreaks.
5. Estimation of self-and-other assigned roles in the interaction between dominant and subordinate groups through extension of interviews above, with such items as:

> "What kind of education should our kind of people receive? Their kind of people?"
>
> "What kind of occupations should our men prepare for? Their men?"
>
> "What kind of government posts should our men have? Their men?"
>
> "What rights should our kind of people have? Their kind of people?"

These items correspond in type with the intervening variable of the intergroup arena as conceptualized in the memorandum.

VIII. Social Actions and Interactions in Dominant and Subordinate Groups

1. Taking Dohrenwend and Smith's spheres of activity[1]—political, economic, military, kinship, religious, educational, medical, social-recreational—find some way of estimating the nature of intergroup contacts in each sphere between dominants and subordinates. Then instigate the following inquires:
2. What are the typical modes of behavior and interaction in each sphere, noting crystallized roles of dominance, deference, impersonality, withdrawal, correctness of etiquette, etc.
3. What seem to be the overt forms vs. covert attitudes involved in these interactions? This raises questions of role, status, and self-definition on the part of participants in such interaction spheres.
4. Estimation of the types of relationships that appear with greater or lesser frequency in the various spheres. Examples: sharing of associational (including political party) memberships, friendship patterns, intermarriage, clique formations, and the like.
5. Interpret the relationship between such interaction patterns and the belief systems outlined in VII.

· NOTE ·

1. Dohrenwend, G. P., and R. J. Smith, "Toward a Theory of Acculturation," *Southwestern Journal of Anthropology*, 18 (Spring, 1962), 30–39.

Appendix 3

Selected
Bibliography

Adams, Ruth (ed.), *Contemporary China*. New York: Vintage, 1966.

Ahmad, Aziz, *Studies in Islamic Culture*. Oxford: Clarendon Press, 1964.

Alford, Robert R., *Party and Society, The Anglo-American Democracies*. Chicago: Rand McNally, 1963.

Allardt, Erik, and Yrjo Littunen (eds.), *Cleavages, Ideologies, and Party Systems. Transactions of the Westermack Society*, Vol. X. Helsinki: Academic Bookstore, 1964.

Almond, Gabriel A., and James S. Coleman (eds.), *The Politics of the Developing Areas*. Princeton, N.J.: Princeton University Press, 1960.

Anand, V. K., *Nagaland in Transition*. New Delhi: Associated Publishing House, 1967.

"The New Immigration," special issue of *Annals of the American Academy of Political and Social Science*, Vol. 367 (September 1966).

"Social and Cultural Pluralism in the Caribbean," special issue of *Annals of the New York Academy of Sciences*, Vol. 83, Art. 5. New York: Published by the Academy, 1960.

Apter, David E., *The Gold Coast in Transition*. Princeton, N.J.: Princeton University Press, 1955.

———, *The Politics of Modernization*. Chicago: University of Chicago Press, 1965.

Arra, Hassan, *The Kurds, An Historical and Political Study.* London: Oxford University Press, 1966.

Bacon, Elizabeth E., *Central Asians Under Russian Rule, A Study in Cultural Change.* Ithaca: Cornell University Press, 1966.

Baklanoff, Eric N., *New Perspectives of Brazil.* Tennessee: Parthenon Press, 1966.

Banton, Michael, *White and Coloured, The Behavior of British People Towards Coloured Immigrants.* London: Jonathan Cape, 1959.

———, *Race Relations.* London: Tavistock, 1967.

Baptista, Elsie W., *The East Indians.* Catholic Community of Bombay, Salsette and Bassein, Bandra (Bombay 50): The Bombay East Indian Association, 1967.

Barnabas, A. P., and Subhash C. Mehta, *Caste in Changing India.* New Delhi: Indian Institute of Public Administration, 1965.

Barringer, Herbert R., *et al.* (eds.), *Social Change in Developing Areas, A Reinterpretation of Evolutionary Theory.* Cambridge, Mass.: Schenkman, 1965.

Baudet, H., *Paradise on Earth.* New Haven: Yale University Press, 1965.

Belshaw, Cyril S., *Under the loi Tree, Society and Economic Growth in Rural Fiji.* Berkeley: University of California Press, 1964.

Bendix, Reinhard, *Nation-Building and Citizenship, Studies of Our Changing Social Order.* New York: Wiley, 1964.

——— (ed.), *State and Society: A Reader in Comparative Political Sociology.* Boston: Little, Brown, 1968.

Benedict, Burton, *Mauritius: Problems of a Plural Society.* London: Pall Mall, 1965.

Bennigsen, Alexandre, and Chantal LeMercier-Quelquejay, *Islam in the Soviet Union.* London: Pall Mall, 1967.

Bequiraj, Mehmet, *Peasantry in Revolution.* Ithaca: Cornell University Center for International Studies, 1966.

Berger, Morroe, *The Arab World Today.* New York: Doubleday, 1962.

Beteille, Andre, *Caste, Class and Power, Changing Patterns of Stratification in a Tanjore Village.* Berkeley: University of California Press, 1965.

Blalock, H. M., Jr., *Toward a Theory of Minority-Group Relations.* New York: Wiley, 1967.

Blishen, Bernard R., *et al.* (eds.), *Canadian Society, Sociological Perspectives.* New York: Free Press, 1961.

Bock, Kenneth E., *The Acceptance of Histories.* Berkeley and Los Angeles: University of California Press, 1966.

Bone, Robert C., Jr., *Contemporary Southeast Asia*. New York: Random House, 1962.

Bopegamage, A., and P. V. Veeraraghaven, *Status Images in Changing India*. Delhi, Bombay, Manaktalas: Unesco Research Centre, 1967.

Borrie, W. D., *The Cultural Integration of Immigrants*. Paris: UNESCO, 1959.

Boxer, C. R., *Race Relations in the Portuguese Colonial Empire, 1415-1825*. Oxford: Clarendon, 1963.

Brass, Paul R., *Factional Politics in an Indian State; The Congress Party in Uttar Pradesh*. Berkeley: University of California Press, 1965.

Burgin, Trevor, and Patricia Edson, *Spring Grove: The Education of Immigrant Children*. London: Oxford University Press, 1967.

Burks, R. V., *The Dynamics of Communism in Eastern Europe*. Princeton, N.J.: Princeton University Press, 1961.

Cahnman, Werner J., and Alvin Boskoff (eds.), *Sociology and History, Theory and Research*. New York: Free Press, 1964.

Carstens, Peter, *The Social Structure of a Cape Coloured Reserve*. New York: Oxford University Press, 1967.

Carter, Gwendolyn (ed.), *Five African States: Responses to Diversity*. London: Pall Mall, 1964.

—— (ed.), *National Unity and Regionalism in Eight African States*. Ithaca: Cornell University Press, 1966.

Chand, Tara, *The Influence of Islam on Indian Culture*. Allahabad: University Press, 1952.

Chaudhuri, Nirad C., *The Continent of Circe, An Essay on the Peoples of India*. New York: Oxford University Press, 1966.

Choi, Dharom P. (ed.), *Portrait of a Minority: Asians in East Africa*. New York: Oxford University Press, 1966.

Clebert, Jean-Paul, *The Gypsies*. London: Vista, 1963.

Clegg, Edward, *Race and Politics: Partnership in the Federation of Rhodesia and Nyasaland*. London: Oxford University Press, 1960.

Clough, Shepard B., *A History of the Flemish Movement in Belgium, A Study in Nationalism*. New York: Smith, 1930.

Cole, Fay-Cooper, *The Peoples of Malaysia*. New York: Van Nostrand, 1945.

Coleman, James S., and Carl C. Rosberg (eds.), *Political Parties and National Integration in Tropical Africa*. Berkeley: University of California Press, 1964.

Conquest, R., *The Soviet Deportation of Nationalities*. London: Macmillan, 1960.

Coulthard, G. R., *Race and Colour in Caribbean Literature*. London: Oxford University Press, 1962.

Crozier, Brian, *The Morning After, A Study of Independence*. New York: Oxford University Press, 1963.

Das, A. K., *Trends of Occupation Pattern Through Generations in Rural Areas of West Bengal*. Calcutta: Scheduled Castes and Tribes Welfare Department, Government of West Bengal, 1968.

Davies, A. F., and S. Encel (eds.), *Australian Society, A Sociological Introduction*. New York: Atherton, 1965.

Davis, David Brion, *The Problem of Slavery in Western Culture*. Ithaca: Cornell University Press, 1966.

Davison, R. B., *Commonwealth Immigrants*. London: Oxford University Press, 1964.

Delf, George, *Asians in East Africa*. London: Oxford University Press, 1962.

de Reuck, Anthony, and Julie Knight (eds.), *Caste and Race: Comparative Approaches*. London: Churchill, 1967.

Desai, Rashmi, *Indian Immigrants in Britain*. London: Oxford University Press, 1964.

Desai, Sapur Faredun, *A Community at the Cross-Road*. Bombay: New Book Co., 1948.

Despres, Leo, *Cultural Pluralism and Nationalist Politics in British Guiana*. Chicago: Rand McNally, 1967.

De Vos, George, and Hiroshi Wagatsuma, *Japan's Invisible Race*. Berkeley and Los Angeles: University of California Press, 1966.

Diamond, Stanley, and Fred Burke, *The Transformation of East Africa*. New York: Basic Books, 1967.

Dickie-Clark, H. F., *The Marginal Situation*. London: Routledge & Kegan Paul, 1966.

Dodds, Norman N., *Gypsies, Didikois, and other Travelers*. London: Johnson, 1966.

Domnitz, Myer, *Immigration and Integration: Experiences of the Anglo-Jewish Community*. London: Council of Christians and Jews, 1967.

Drysdale, John, *The Somali Dispute*. London: Pall Mall, 1964.

Easton, Stewart C., *The Rise and Fall of Western Colonialism*. New York: Praeger, 1964.

Ethnic and Cultural Pluralism in Intertropical Communities. Bruxelles: International Institute of Differing Civilizations, 1957.

Fanon, Frantz, *Studies in a Dying Colonialism*. New York: Monthly Review Press, 1965.

———, *The Wretched of the Earth*. Constance Farrington (trans.), New York: Grove, 1963.

Farmer, B. H., *Ceylon: A Divided Nation*. London: Oxford University Press, 1963.

Finkle, Jason L., and Richard W. Gable (eds.), *Political Development and Social Change*. New York: Wiley, 1966.

Fitzherbert, Katrin, *West Indian Children in London*. London: Bell, 1967.

Fong, Ng Bickleen, *The Chinese in New Zealand*. Hong Kong: Hong Kong University Press, 1959.

Foot, Paul, *Immigration and Race in British Politics*. Harmondsworth, Eng.: Penguin, 1965.

Frazier, E. Franklin, *Race and Culture Contacts in the Modern World*. New York: Knopf, 1957.

Furnivall, J. S., *Colonial Policy and Practice*. Cambridge, Eng.: Cambridge University Press, 1948.

Gaikwad, V. R., *The Anglo-Indians*. Bombay: Asia Publishing House, 1967.

Geertz, Clifford (ed.), *Old Societies and New States*. New York: Free Press, 1963.

Ghai, Dharam P. (ed.), *Portrait of a Minority; Asians in East Africa*. New York: Oxford University Press, 1966.

Ghurye, G. S., *Social Tensions in India*. Bombay: Popular Prakashan, 1968.

Gillion, K. L., *Fiji's Indian Immigrants*. Melbourne: Oxford University Press, 1962.

Glass, Ruth, *Newcomers: The West Indians in London*. London: Allen & Unwin, 1960.

Gluckman, Max (ed.), *Closed Systems and Open Minds: The Limits of Naivety in Social Anthropology*. Chicago: Aldine, 1964.

Goldberg, Ben Zion, *The Jewish Problem in the Soviet Union*. New York: Crown, 1961.

Goldhagen, Erich, *Ethnic Minorities in the Soviet Union*. New York: Praeger, 1968.

Gross, Feliks, *World Politics and Tension Areas*. New York: New York University Press, 1966.

Gupta, Sisir, *Kashmir: A Study in India-Pakistan Relations*. London: Asia Publishing House, 1966.

Halpern, Manfred, *The Politics of Social Change in the Middle East and North Africa*. Princeton, N.J.: Princeton University Press, 1967. (paperback ed.)

Handbook on Scheduled Castes and Scheduled Tribes. New Delhi: Government of India, Office of the Commissioner for Scheduled Castes and Scheduled Tribes, 1968.

Harre, John, *Maori and Pakeha: A Study of Mixed Marriages in New Zealand*. London: Pall Mall, 1966.

Harris, Marvin, *Patterns of Race in the Americas*. New York: Walker, 1964.

Hartz, Louis, *The Founding of New Societies*. New York: Harcourt, Brace & World, 1964.

Hawkes, Nicholas, *Immigrant Children in British Schools*. London: Pall Mall, 1966.

Hayward, Victor, E. W. (ed.), *The Church as Christian Community: Three Studies of North Indian Churches*. London: Lutterworth Press, 1966.

Heard, Kenneth, *Political Systems in Multi-Racial Societies*. Johannesburg: South African Institute of Race Relations, 1961.

Hernton, Calvin C., *Sex and Racism in America*. New York: Doubleday, 1965.

Hoetink, H., *The Two Variants in Caribbean Race Relations*. New York: Oxford University Press, 1966.

Hollingworth, Lawrence W., *The Asians of East Africa*. London: Macmillan, 1966.

Hopper, Janice (ed. and trans.), *Indians of Brazil in the Twentieth Century*. Washington, D.C.: Institute for Cross-Cultural Research, 1967.

Horowitz, Irving L., *Three Worlds of Development*. New York: Oxford University Press, 1966.

Hottinger, Arnold, *The Arabs*. Berkeley: University of California Press, 1963.

Hourani, A. H., *Minorities in the Arab World*. London and New York: Oxford University Press, 1947.

Hunter, Guy, *Southeast Asia, Race, Culture and Nation*. New York: Oxford University Press, 1966.

—— (ed.), *The New Societies of Tropical Africa*. London and New York: Oxford University Press, 1962.

—— (ed.), *Industrialization and Race Relations*. London and New York: Oxford University Press, 1965.

Husain, S. Abid, *The Destiny of Indian Muslims*. London: Asia Publishing House, 1966.

Huxley, Elspeth, *Back Street New Worlds: A Look at Immigrants in Britain*. London: Chatto and Windus, 1964.

Indonesian Sociological Studies: Selected Writings of B. Schrieke, Part One. The Hague: van Hoeve, 1966.

Isaacs, Harold R., *India's Ex-Untouchables*. New York: John Day, 1964.

——, *American Jews in Israel*. New York: John Day, 1967.

Isherwood, H. B., *Racial Integration*. London: Britons, 1966.

Jackson, John Archer, *The Irish in Britain*. London: Routledge & Kegan Paul; and Cleveland: The Press of Western Reserve University, 1963.

Janowitz, Morris, *The Military in the Political Development of New Nations, An Essay in Comparative Analysis*. Chicago: University of Chicago Press, 1964.

Janowsky, Oscar I., *Nationalities and National Minorities with Special Reference to East-Central Europe*. New York: Macmillan, 1945.

Jesman, Czeslaw, *The Ethiopian Paradox*. London: Oxford University Press, 1963.

Johnston, Ruth, *Immigrant Assimilation: A Study of Polish People in Western Australia*. Perth: Peterson Brohenska, 1965.

Jones, L. W., *The Population of Borneo: A Study of the Peoples of Sarawak, Sabah, and Brunei*. London: Athlone, 1966.

Jordan, Winthrop D., *White Over Black: American Attitudes Toward the Negro, 1550–1812*. Chapel Hill, N.C.: University of North Carolina Press, 1968.

Ju-K'ang T'ien, *The Chinese of Sarawak*. London: Athlone Press, London School of Economics Monographs on Social Anthropology, No. 12, 1950.

Junghann, Otto, *National Minorities in Europe*. New York: Covici-Friede, 1932.

Junod, Violaine I. (ed.), *The Handbook of Africa*. New York: New York University Press, 1963.

Karandikar, M. A., *Islam in India's Transition to Modernity*. Bombay: Orient Longmans, 1968.

Katrak, Sohrab, K. H., *Who Are The Parsees?* Karachi: Pakistan Herald Press, 1965.

Keur, J., and D. Keur, *Windward Children*. Assen, Holland: Van Gorcum, 1960.

Kitchen, Helen, *A Handbook of African Affairs*. New York: Praeger, 1964.

Klausner, Samuel Z. (ed.), *The Study of Total Societies*. New York: Doubleday, 1967.

Klein, Herbert S., *Slavery in the Americas: A Comparative Study of Virginia and Cuba*. Chicago: University of Chicago Press, 1967.

Kolarz, Walter, *Russia and Her Colonies*. New York: Praeger, 1952.

Kraus, Michael, *Immigration, The American Mosaic: From Pilgrims to Modern Refugees*. New York: Van Nostrand, 1966.

Kung, S. W., *Chinese in American Life*. Seattle: University of Washington Press, 1962.

Kunstadter, Peter, *Southeast Asian Tribes, Minorities and Nations*,

Volumes I & II. Princeton, N.J.: Princeton University Press, 1967.

Kuper, Hilda, *Indian People in Natal.* Natal: The University Press, 1960.

Kuper, Leo, *An African Bourgeoisie.* New Haven: Yale University Press, 1967. (paperback ed.)

Ladas, Stephen P., *The Exchange of Minorities: Bulgaria, Greece and Turkey,* New York: Macmillan, 1932.

Lambert, Jacques, *Latin America: Social Structure and Political Institutions.* Berkeley: University of California Press, 1967.

Leach, E. R. (ed.), *Aspects of Caste in South India, Ceylon and Northeast Pakistan.* Cambridge, Eng.: Cambridge University Press, 1960.

LeBar, Frank M., *et al., Ethnic Groups of Mainland Southeast Asia.* New Haven: Human Relations Area Files Press, 1964.

Legum, Colin, *Africa, A Handbook to the Continent.* Rev. ed. New York: Praeger, 1966.

Lemarchand, Rene, *Political Awakening in the Congo: The Politics of Fragmentation.* Berkeley: University of California Press, 1964.

Levy, Marion J., Jr., *Modernization and the Structure of Societies,* 2 vols. Princeton, N.J.: Princeton University Press, 1966.

Lewis, I. M., *Modern History of Somaliland.* New York: Praeger, 1965.

———— (ed.), *Islam in Tropical Africa.* London: Oxford University Press, 1966.

Lewis, W. Arthur, *Politics in West Africa.* London: Allen & Unwin, 1965.

Lijphart, Arend, *The Trauma of Decolonization, The Dutch and West Guinea.* New Haven and London: Yale University Press, 1966.

Lind, Andrew W. (ed.), *Race Relations in World Perspective.* Honolulu: University of Hawaii Press, 1955.

Little, Kenneth, *West African Urbanization: A Study of Voluntary Organizations in Social Change.* Cambridge, England: Cambridge University Press, 1965.

Longrigg, Stephen H., *The Middle East, A Social Geography.* Chicago: Aldine, 1963.

Lystad, Robert A. (ed.), *The African World, A Survey of Social Research,* New York: Praeger, 1965.

Mahajani, Urha, *The Role of Indian Minorities in Burma and Malaya.* New York: Institute of Pacific Relations, 1960.

Mair, Lucy, *New Nations.* Chicago: University of Chicago Press, 1963.

————, *The New Africa.* London: Watts, New Thinkers Library, 1967.

Majumdar, D. N., *Caste and Communication in an Indian Village.* Bombay: Asia Publishing House, 1962.

———, *Races and Cultures of India.* Bombay: Asia Publishing House, 1958.

Mankekar, D. R., *On The Slippery Slope in Nagaland.* Bombay: Manaktalas, 1967.

Mannoni, O., *Prospero and Caliban.* New York: Praeger, 1956.

Mansur, Fatima, *Process of Independence.* London: Routledge & Kegan Paul, 1962.

Marsh, Robert M., *Comparative Sociology.* New York: Harcourt, Brace & World, 1967.

Mason, Philip, *Prospero's Magic, Some Thoughts on Class and Race.* London: Oxford University Press, 1962.

——— (ed.), *India and Ceylon: Unity and Diversity.* London: Oxford University Press, 1967.

Matras, Judah, *Social Change in Israel.* Chicago: Aldine, 1965.

Mayer, Adrian C., *Indians in Fiji.* London: Oxford University Press, 1963.

McCord, William, *The Springtime of Freedom: The Evolution of Developing Societies.* New York: Oxford University Press, 1965.

Merritt, Richard L., and Stein Rokkan (eds.), *Comparing Nations.* New Haven: Yale University Press, 1966.

Metge, Joan, *A New Maori Migration: Rural and Urban Relations in Northern New Zealand.* London: Athlone, 1964.

Mitchell, Sir Harold, *Caribbean Patterns—A Political and Economic Study of the Contemporary Caribbean.* Edinburgh and London: Chambers, 1967.

Mitchell, Richard Hanks, *The Korean Minority in Japan, 1910–1963.* Berkeley: University of California Press, 1967.

Montague, Joel B., Jr., *Class and Nationality.* New Haven: College and University Press, 1966.

Moore, Barrington, Jr., *Social Origins of Dictatorship and Democracy, Lord and Peasant in the Making of the Modern World.* Boston: Beacon, 1966.

Mujeeb, M., *The Indian Muslims.* London: George Allen and Unwin, 1967.

Myrdal, Gunnar, *Asian Drama: An Inquiry into the Poverty of Nations.* 3 vols. New York: Pantheon Books, 1968.

Nair, Kusum, *Blossoms in the Dust.* London: Gerald Duckworth, 1961.

Nash, Manning, *The Golden Road to Modernity: Village Life in Contemporary Burma.* New York: Wiley, 1965.

Ness, Gayl D., *Bureaucracy and Rural Development in Malaysia.* Berkeley: University of California Press, 1967.

Nogueira, O., *Plantation Systems of the New World.* Washington, D.C.: Pan American Union, 1959.

Orans, Martin, *The Santal: A Tribe in Search of a Great Tradition.* Detroit: Wayne State University Press, 1965.

Palmier, L. H., *Indonesia.* New York: Walker, 1965.

Panikkar, K. M., *The Foundations of New India.* London: George Allen & Unwin, 1963.

Patterson, Orlando, *The Sociology of Slavery: An Analysis of the Origins, Development and Structure of Negro Slave Society in Jamaica.* London: MacGibbon & Kee, 1967.

Patterson, Sheila, *Dark Strangers.* London: Tavistock, 1963.

Pentzopoulos, Dimitri, *The Balkan Exchange of Minorities and its Impact Upon Greece.* Paris and The Hague: Mouton, 1962.

Pienar, S., and Anthony Sampson, *South Africa: Two Views of Separate Development.* London: Oxford University Press, 1960.

Pierson, Donald, *Negroes in Brazil.* New ed. Carbondale, Ill.: Southern Illinois University Press, 1967.

Porter, Arthur T., *Creoledom: A Study of the Development of Creole Society.* London: Oxford University Press, 1963.

Porter, John, *The Vertical Mosaic, An Analysis of Social Class and Power in Canada.* Toronto: University of Toronto Press, 1965.

Price, Charles A., *Southern Europeans in Australia.* Melbourne: Oxford University Press, 1963.

Purcell, Victor, *The Chinese in Southeast Asia.* London: Oxford University Press, 1965. (2nd ed.)

————, *Malaysia.* New York: Walker, 1965.

Pye, Lucian W., and Sidney Verba (eds.), *Political Culture and Political Development.* Princeton, N.J.: Princeton University Press, 1965.

Qureshi, I. H., *The Muslim Community of the Indo-Pakistan Subcontinent.* The Hague: Mouton, 1962.

Raghavan, M. D., *India in Ceylonese History, Society and Culture.* New York: Asia Publishing House, 1964.

Ravenholt, Albert, *The Philippines, A Young Republic on the Move.* New York: Van Nostrand, 1962.

Rex, John, and Robert Moore, *Race, Community and Conflict: A Study of Sparkbrook.* London: Oxford University Press, 1967.

Rodrigues, Jose Honorio, *Brazil and Africa.* Berkeley: University of California Press, 1965.

Rogers, C. A., and Charles Frantz, *Racial Themes in Southern Rhodesia.* New Haven: Yale University Press, 1962.

Rose, Saul (ed.), *Politics in Southern Asia*. London: Macmillan, 1963.

Rosenthal, E. I. J., *Islam in the Modern National State*. Cambridge, Eng.: Cambridge University Press, 1965.

Rotberg, Robert I., *The Rise of Nationalism in Central Africa*. Cambridge, Mass.: Harvard University Press, 1966.

Royal Commission on Bilingualism and Biculturalism, *Preliminary Report*. Ottawa: Queen's Printer, 1965.

Rubin, Vera (ed.), *Caribbean Studies: A Symposium*. Jamaica: Institute of Social and Economic Research, 1957.

Rudolph, Lloyd I. and Susanne Rudolph, *The Modernity of Tradition*. Chicago: University of Chicago Press, 1967.

Russell, Peter (ed.), *Nationalism in Canada*. Toronto: McGraw-Hill Company of Canada, 1966.

Russett, Bruce M., *et al.*, *World Handbook of Political and Social Indicators*. New Haven and London: Yale University Press, 1964.

Sachs, Emil Solomon, *The Anatomy of Apartheid*. London: Collets, 1965.

Salontos, Theodore, *The Greeks in the United States*. Cambridge, Mass.: Harvard University Press, 1964.

Sampson, Anthony, *Common Sense about Africa*. London: Gollancz, 1960.

Sangave, Vilas Adinath, *Jaina Community, A Social Survey*. Bombay: Popular Book Depot, 1959.

Schwartz, Barton M. (ed.), *Caste in Overseas Indian Communities*. San Francisco: Chandler, 1967.

Schwartz, Mildred A., *Public Opinion and Canadian Identity*. Berkeley: University of California Press, 1967.

Segal, Ronald, *The Race War*. New York: Viking, 1966.

Selzer, Michael, *The Outcastes of Israel: Communal Tensions in the Jewish State*. Jerusalem: Council of the Sephardic Community, 1965.

Shibutani, Tamotsu, and Kian M. Kwan, *Ethnic Stratification*. New York: Macmillan, 1965.

Shils, Edward, *Political Development in the New States*. The Hague: Mouton, 1966.

Shuval, Judith T., *Immigrants on the Threshold*. New York: Atherton, 1963.

Sikhism and Indian Society, Transactions of the Indian Institute of Advanced Study. Vol. 4. Simla: Rashtrapati Nivas, 1967.

Sinai, Robert, *The Challenge of Modernization: The West's Impact on the Non-Western World*. New York: Norton, 1964.

Singer, Marshall R., *The Emerging Elite, A Study of Political Leadership in Ceylon*. Cambridge, Mass.: M.I.T. Press, 1964.

Singer, Milton and Bernard S. Cohn, (eds.), *Structure and Change in Indian Society*. Chicago: Aldine Publishing Co., 1968.

Singh, Amar Kumar, *Indian Students in Britain: A Survey of Their Adjustment and Attitudes*. London: Asia Publishing House, 1963.

Singh, Khushwant, *A History of the Sikhs*. 2 vols. Princeton, N.J.: Princeton University Press, 1966.

Singh, Patwant, *India and the Future of Asia*. New York: Knopf, 1966.

Sinha, V. K., (ed.), *Secularism in India*. Bombay: Lalvani Publishing House, 1969.

Skinner, G. W., *Leadership and Power in the Chinese Community of Thailand*. Ithaca: Cornell University Press, 1958.

—— (ed.), *Local, Ethnic and National Loyalties in Village Indonesia, A Symposium*. New Haven: Yale University, 1959. (Cultural Report Series, Southeast Asia Studies.)

Smelser, Neil J., and Seymour M. Lipset (eds.), *Social Structure and Mobility in Economic Development*. Chicago: Aldine, 1966.

Smith, Donald Eugene, *India as a Secular State*. Princeton, N.J.: Princeton University Press, 1963.

Smith, M. G., *The Plural Society in the British West Indies*. Berkeley and Los Angeles: University of California Press, 1965.

Smith, T. Lynn, *Brazil, People and Institutions*. Rev. ed. Baton Rouge: Louisiana State University Press, 1963.

Smith, William Cantwell, *Islam in Modern History*. Princeton, N. J.: Princeton University Press, 1957.

——, *Modern Islam in India*. London: Gollancz, 1946.

Snyder, Frank G., *One Party Government in Mali: Transition Toward Control*. New Haven: Yale University Press, 1965.

Sorrenson, M. P. K., *Maori and European since 1870—A Study in Adaptation and Adjustment*. London: Heinemann Educational Books, 1967.

Srinivas, M. N., *Caste in Modern India and Other Essays*. Bombay: Asia Publishing House, 1962.

——, *Social Change in Modern India*. Berkeley: University of California Press, 1966.

Strauz-Hupe, Robert, and Harry W. Hazard (eds.), *The Idea of Colonialism*. New York: Praeger, 1958.

Steward, J. H. (ed.), *The People of Puerto Rico*. Urbana, Ill.: University of Illinois Press, 1956.

Taft, Ronald, *From Stranger to Citizen: A Survey of Studies of Immigrant Assimilation in Western Australia*. London: Tavistock, 1965.

Teller, Judd L., *The Kremlin, The Jews and the Middle East*. New York: Yoseloff, 1957.

Thomas, M. M. and R. W. Taylor, (eds.), *Tribal Awakening, A Group Study*. Bangalore: Christian Institute for the Study of Religion and Society, 1965.

Thompson, Virginia, and Richard Adloff, *Minority Problems in Southeast Asia*. Stanford: Stanford University Press, 1941.

Trimingham, J. Spencer, *Islam in East Africa*. London: Oxford University Press, 1964.

Unnithan, T. K. N., (ed.), *Towards a Sociology of Culture in India*. New Delhi: Prentice-Hall of India, 1965.

van den Berghe, Pierre L., *South Africa, A Study in Conflict*. Middletown, Conn.: Wesleyan University Press, 1965.

———— (ed.), *Africa, Social Problems of Change and Conflict*. Middletown, Conn.: Wesleyan University Press, 1965.

————, *Race and Racism*. New York: Wiley, 1967.

Van Lier, R. A. J., *The Development and the Nature of Society in the West Indies*. Amsterdam: Koninklijk Institut v.d. Tropen, 1950.

Vidyarthi, L. P., (ed.), *Leadership in India*. Bombay: Asia Publishing House, 1967.

Von der Mehden, Fred, *Politics of the Developing Nations*. Englewood Cliffs, N.J.: Prentice-Hall, 1964.

Wagley, Charles, and Marvin Harris, *Minorities in the New World*. New York: Columbia University Press, 1958.

Wagner, Edward, *The Korean Minority in Japan, 1904–1950*. New York: Institute of Pacific Relations, 1950.

Wallerstein, Immanuel, *The Road to Independence: Ghana and the Ivory Coast*. Paris: Mouton, 1965.

———— (ed.), *Social Change, The Colonial Situation*. New York: Wiley, 1966.

Weiner, Myron, (ed.), *State Politics in India*. Princeton, N. J.: Princeton University Press, 1968.

————, *The Politics of Scarcity*. Bombay: Asia Publishing House, 1963.

Weingrod, Alex, *Israel: Group Relations in a New Society*. London: Oxford University Press, 1965.

Wheeler, Geoffrey, *Racial Problems in Soviet Muslim Asia*. New York: Oxford University Press, 1962.

Whitten, Norman E., *Class, Kinship and Power in an Ecuadorian Town: The Negroes of San Lorenzo*. Stanford: Stanford University Press, 1965.

Wickberg, Edgar, *The Chinese in Philippine Life*. New Haven: Yale University Press, 1965.

Wiesel, Elie, *The Jews of Silence: A Personal Report on Soviet Jewry.* New York: Holt, Rinehart & Winston, 1966.

Williams, Lea E., *The Future of the Overseas Chinese in Southeast Asia.* New York: McGraw-Hill, 1966.

Winiata, Maharaia, *The Changing Role of the Leader in Maori Society.* London: Hurst, 1967.

Wood, Susan, *Kenya, The Tensions of Progress.* London: Oxford University Press, 1960.

Worsley, Peter, *The Third World, A Vital New Force in International Affairs.* Chicago: University of Chicago Press, 1964.

Yarwood, A. T., *Asian Migration to Australia; the Background to Exclusion, 1896–1923.* London: Oxford University Press, 1964.

Zenkovsky, Serge A., *Pan-Turkism and Islam in Russia.* Cambridge, Mass.: Harvard University Press, 1960.

Zinkin, Tanya, *Challenges in India.* London: Chatto & Windus, 1966.

————, *India.* New York: Walker, 1965.

Zubrzycki, Jerzy, *Settlers of the Latrobe Valley: A Sociological Study of Immigrants in the Brown Coal Industry in Australia.* Canberra: Australian National University Press, 1965.

Index

About the Author

R. A. Schermerhorn, Professor of Sociology at Case Western Reserve University, is on leave for the 1968–1970 academic years to teach at the Indian Institute of Technology in Kanpur, India. A specialist in race and ethnic relations, Professor Schermerhorn has written several books in the field, including *These Our People: Minorities in American Culture* (1949) and *Society and Power* (1961). He was Fulbright Visiting Professor of Sociology at Lucknow University, India (1959–1960), and has also taught widely in the United States.

MA

I